International Relations
Theory and Conflicts in World Society

International Relations Theory and Conflicts in World Society

P. N. Chaturvedi

KUNAL BOOKS

New Delhi-110002, India

KUNAL BOOKS
4596/1A, First Floor,
11, Daryaganj, New Delhi-110002
Phones: 9811043697, 011-30125412
E-mail: *Kunalbooks@gmail.com*

International Relations: Theory and Conflicts in World Society

First Published 2010

ISBN - 978-81-910085-0-0

Published in **India** by Prem Singh Bisht for Kunal Books, and printed at **Deepak Offset Press**, Delhi.

PREFACE

International relations is study of the relations among states and other political and economic units in the international system. Particular areas of study within the field of international relations include diplomacy and diplomatic history, international law, international organisations, international finance and economics, and communications, among others. In addition, increased attention has been paid in recent years to developing a more scientific understanding of the international system as a whole.

The history of international relations is often traced back to the Peace of Westphalia of 1648, where the modern state system was developed. Prior to this, the European medieval organisation of political authority was based on a vaguely hierarchical religious order. Westphalia instituted the legal concept of sovereignty, which essentially meant that rulers, or the legitimate sovereigns, had no internal equals within a defined territory and no external superiors as the ultimate authority within the territory's sovereign borders.

International relations represents the study of foreign affairs and global issues among states within the international system, including the roles of states, inter-governmental organisations (IGOs), non-governmental organisations (NGOs), international non-governmental organisations (INGOs), and multinational corporations (MNCs). It is both an academic and public policy field, and can be either positive or normative as it both seeks to analyze as well as formulate the foreign policy of particular states. It is often considered a branch of political sciencc (especially after 1988 UNESCO nomenclature), but an important sector of academia prefer to treat it as an interdisciplinary field of study.

International society is a moving complex of overlapping and nested structures and situations of conflict, power balancing, balances of powers, and structures of expectations. The keynote is change, alteration, transformation, and the mechanism and manifestation of this is conflict behavior. As do all societies, international society has two faces. One is of conflict, change, a struggle and dialectic of power. The other is equilibrium, societal norms and structures which at any one point in time appear to describe society. Indeed, without a process or conflict view of international society, the normal state of affairs is stability, of functions maintaining the system and adjusting individuals to it. Indeed, within this snapshot view international conflict appears deviant, an aberration of the system. Consensus and equilibrium rather than conflict would be the defining characteristics of the society.

In international relations, many structures of expectations are formalized, involving written agreements, contracts, or treaties defining the rights and obligations of cosigners. Some structures of expectations (like the UN Charter) formalize law norms, which define the membership in the structure, the rights and obligations of members, and authoritative roles (positions). Authoritative roles are those that within the structure of expectations carry the right to give certain commands for their incumbents and the obligation to obey for the other members. They carry the right to punish disobedience. In the development of law norms and authoritative roles evolves the sociological group. In international society the state is one such group and an international organisation is another.

Contents

1

Jews and Arabs in Israel

Israelis live very much in the shadow of the Israeli-Arab conflict. It affects all aspects of life, particularly the relationship between the Jewish majority and the Arab minority. The current research examines the patterns of political tolerance and intolerance in each of these groups. These patterns are largely structured by the larger conflict, as the most important sources of political tolerance generally lie in political processes. Tolerance means indulgence for ideas and groups differing from or conflicting with one's own. Political tolerance requires a willingness to apply political democratic rights, such as freedom of expression, organisation, and representation, and equality before the law, to groups or individuals that one finds objectionable.

The test of tolerance for an individual as for a society is therefore in the context of a serious objection, often in the context of a perceived threat. The Arab-Israeli conflict, on which the Jews and Arabs in Israel obviously disagree, puts both groups in such a context, which makes the Israeli case a most interesting one for the general study of tolerance.

The political context is well known. The Arab-Israeli conflict defines the major issue dimension in Israeli domestic politics. Indeed, it is the dominant feature of Israel's existence, despite the peace agreement with Egypt. It is characterized by a permanent state of war that erupts into major war from time to time. This is part of the Israeli situation and mentality and is reflected in all spheres of life. Demographics are also an important aspect of the conflict. Israel's population at the end of 1982 numbered 4,063,600 of which 3,373,200 were Jews and 690,400 were Arabs. Israeli Arabs constitute a minority of about one-sixth, yet they are part of the Arab majority in the Middle-east, where the Jews are a tiny minority.

Given the parameters of the conflict, both groups-the Jewish majority and the Arab minority- find themselves in a threatening situation. In the face of five major wars, numerous terrorist attacks and attempted attacks, and hostile neighbours, the Jewish perceptual consensus is that the conflict is a matter of life or death, that if Israel loses one war "the Jews will be thrown into the sea, "as the Arab slogan goes. The mentality is one of "siege" and "no choice." Being the majority in Israel, the Jews define the character of the state. Jewish nationalism-Zionism-is an important attribute clearly not shared by the Arab minority. It entails views and policies contrary to the wishes and interests of the Arab minority.

Some such policies concern them directly, such as the Law of Return, which encourages Jewish immigration; the expropriation of Arab land; and the imposition of military government over specific zones in the country between 1948 and 1966. More broadly, the Arab minority dissents from Jewish attitudes and policies toward the Arab states, the occupied territories, and the Palestinian problem.

The Israeli Arabs are put in a situation that makes it almost impossible for them to define their identity and their loyalty: "How to be loyal Israelis and remain true Arabs". In the context of the conflict, they identify to a large extent with the nation's enemy, and they are perceived by the Jews as a hostile minority, even as a fifth column, although there is no support for such a claim. Although they have been incorporated into Israeli society in some ways, and despite guaranteed equal protection under the law, asymmetry in Jewish-Arab relations is eminent.

Social, economic, and political inequalities, widespread segregation, political control, and cultural differences are still the dominant features of such relationships. Growing radicalisation among the Arabs has been noted by Jewish experts and laypersons. It is coupled, however, with a factionalism that is less often noticed. Given the Arab-Israeli conflict and the ensuing majority-minority relations among Jews and Arabs in Israel, it is instructive to investigate the climate of political tolerance within the Jewish majority and the Arab minority in order to further our understanding of Israeli society and of the dynamics of tolerance more generally.

IDEOLOGY AND TARGETS FOR INTOLERANCE

The data for our analysis are from a national survey conducted in the fall of 1980. The survey examined a (non proportional) stratified sample of the Israeli population, with 913 Jewish and 300 Arab respondents. We asked our respondents to select, from a list of unpopular groups, the one they liked the least, in order to identify the political targets of intolerance. The list of groups presented to the Arab sample was somewhat different from that presented to the Jews. Several groups that are on the Jewish agenda are not on the Arab agenda, and vice versa. All respondents are also given the option of naming a group not appearing on the list, but very few did so. Given the preeminent place the Palestine Liberation Organisation (PLO) occupies on the Israeli agenda with its terrorist, political, and international roles, we expected a large number of Jewish respondents to choose it as their least-liked group.

Yet we attempted to make a clear distinction between the PLO, an outside group with no legal or political standing in Israel, and "groups in Israel that support the PLO." This distinction is important because we are interested in tolerance and intolerance toward groups operating within the system. Thus the PLO as such does not qualify. In the Jewish sample we did not specify these groups (which support the PLO) but left the issue to the respondent's interpretation and understanding. In the Arab questionnaire we specifically named the one best-known such group that outspokenly describes itself as supporting the PLO: Bnei Hakfar, Sons of the Village. Very few Arab respondents selected this group as a target, but 35 per cent of the Jews chose the groups in Israel supporting the PLO as their least-liked group, with 22 per cent more choosing them as their second-least-liked group.

The next most common target among Jewish respondents is Rakah, the Israeli Communist Party, which has four members in the Eleventh Knesset. Of the respondents, 29 per cent chose it as their least-liked group, and 24 per cent chose Rakah as their second-least-liked group. Rakah is basically an Arab party in terms of its voters and activists. It is anti-Zionist, its positions are perceived by many Jews as supporting the PLO, and its communist message is much less salient than its Arab nationalistic message. Among the Arabs only 5 per cent selected Rakah as least-liked. In addition to groups in Israel supporting the PLO and Rakah, several Jewish groups are defined as extreme, unpopular, and left-wing in Israeli politics.

We listed four such groups in the Hebrew questionnaire and one (Sheli) in the Arab questionnaire. Mazpen is a small extreme Jewish group, with an anti-Zionist and Trotskyist ideology. It was selected by 5 per cent of the Jewish respondents, with an additional 8 per cent selecting it as second-least-liked. Sheli is a political party that had two representatives in the Ninth Knesset, but it received less than 1 per cent of the vote in the 1981 election and, by 1984, had joined another political party. It is composed of and obtains most of its support from Jews, but is also active among Arabs.

It was formed out of several leftist splinter groups, including the Jewish members of the Communist Party, which split in 1965 basically along Arab-Jewish lines. Peace Now is another Jewish leftist group, acting as a pressure group on the issues of the occupied territories, peace with Egypt, and the recent war in Lebanon. The main definition of all these groups is along the Arab-Israeli conflict dimension, although at least the first two have a wider left-wing message. The Black Panthers' most salient definition is ethnic, and their protest has been against injustice and discrimination toward the Sephardic Jews. They also belong to the left wing of the Arab-Israeli conflict and of Israeli politics more generally. Very few respondents selected these last three groups.

Three right-wing groups were mentioned as least-liked: Kach, Gush Emunim, and Hatchia. All three are defined along the Arab-Israeli cleavage. Gush Emunim, the Block of the Faithful, is the group behind many of the settlements in the West Bank. Most of its members are orthodox and religious, believing in the Jewish right to the land of Israel, and in their messianic mission to inhabit and build it. Gush Emunim acts as a pressure group, and its members work through several political parties. Hatchia is a political party with five representatives in the Eleventh Knesset and is closely aligned with Gush Emunim. Kach, Rabbi Kahane's group, is much smaller but has similar views, even calling for forced Arab emigration from Israel and what Kach calls the "liberated territories."

Kach ran for Parliament in 1981 but received much less than the minimum 1 per cent needed to obtain representation. By 1984, however, it obtained one seat in the Knesset. About 7 per cent of the Jews selected one of these groups as their least-liked target, but fully 65 per cent of the Arabs did so. Finally, we listed two religious groups. Neturei Karta, the third most popular target among Jews, is an ultra religious group that one would be hard put to define as left- or right-wing. It is anti-Zionist and does not recognize the state of Israel, but most references to it relate to its religious extremism and coercion. Thirteen per cent chose it as least-liked. Among the Arabs, 7 per cent mentioned the Young Muslims, a Muslim orthodox religious as well as nationalistic group that recently gained support in several townships, calling for a return to Islam.

Beyond the details of the targets Jews and Arabs select, the results point to two major conclusions. Arab and Jewish selection patterns are very different, but for both populations, most disliked groups stem from one and the same cleavage dimension, the Arab-Israeli conflict. Fully 79 per cent of the Jews select groups belonging to this dimension, and 72 per cent of the Arabs do the same. Indeed, if we disregard respondents who did not answer the question, the figures are even more impressive: 83 per cent and 90 per cent, respectively. But the specific choice of groups is very different, representing a mirror image.

Arabs overwhelmingly select Jewish right-wing groups; the ratio is 65 to 7 in the whole sample and 82 to 9 when "no response" is disregarded. Jews select left-wing groups, primarily groups perceived as Arab. The ratio between the left-and right-wing groups is 74 to 7 and between Arab and Jewish groups it is 64 to 30. The results are very clear: The Jewish-Arab cleavage is dominant with Jews and Arabs on opposite ideological sides. Arabs dislike right-wing (nationalistic) Jewish groups, whereas Jews dislike left-wing (nationalistic) Arab groups. To complete the picture we may look at the ideological self-identification of our respondents. We asked them to define themselves as left-wing or right-wing along a 7-point continuum, from extreme left to extreme right.

Of the Arab sample, 50 per cent define themselves as left-wingers and only 15 per cent as right-wingers. In the Jewish sample 20 per cent are left-wingers and 44 per cent are right-wingers. The Jews are on the right of the political spectrum; the Arabs are on the left. This spectrum is largely defined in Israel along the Arab-Jewish conflict dimension, more so than on economic matters, and the close identity of the left with compromising views among Jews and Arabs and of the right with Jewish nationalism is clear.

These results reinforce those of Smooha and Peretz, who examined Arab and Jewish attitudes toward the Israeli-Arab conflict. They showed that Israel's Arabs as a whole reject the Jewish national consensus. The Arabs support and the Jews oppose a Palestinian nation, Israeli withdrawal to the pre-1967 borders, recognition of the PLO as a representative of the Palestinians, formation of a Palestinian state on the West Bank and Gaza Strip, repeal of the annexation of East Jerusalem, and the right of repatriation of the Palestinian refugees.

THREAT AND POLITICAL INTOLERANCE

Israeli society is highly polarized on these issues. The spectrum of political groups active in Israeli politics, and the pattern of groups that Jews and Arabs dislike and to which they object, is one manifestation of this polarisation. Indeed, when we examine the objections of our respondents to the groups they dislike, they are overwhelmingly political, ideological objections. We asked our respondents in an open-ended question why they disliked the specific group they had selected. Jews often accused their least-liked group of being anti-Israel, anti-Zionist, or pro-Arab (46 per cent of the responses). Many Arabs accused their least-liked group of being against the Arabs (24 per cent), but 55 per cent of them referred to the group's actions, methods, and tactics as the reasons for disliking it (compared to 19 per cent in the Jewish sample). Violence, discrimination, settlements, and land expropriations were frequently mentioned.

The objections raised on both sides are highly relevant to the political situation. These are realistic, serious political and ideological objections, most of them revolving around the Arab-Israeli conflict. The opinions (selected more often by Jews) and the action (selected more often by Arabs) of the disliked groups are viewed as threats to one's own rights, particularly national rights. An objection is a necessary precondition for tolerance. It obviously exists here. But objections are not identical to threat. Logically they are different, although empirically-in particular, in this political context-they are likely to be closely related. We expect Israelis, both Jews and Arabs, to be greatly threatened by the political groups they mentioned.

Although it is difficult to assess objectively the degree of actual threat posed to Arabs and to Jews in Israel by their least-liked groups, we expect Arabs to perceive a greater threat than Jews. The source of this expectation is the "hostile minority" status of the Arab community in Israel; their close kinship, socially and ideologically, with the Palestinians in the territories occupied by Israel in the 1967 Six-Day War, and the fact that most of their targets are Jewish right-wing groups that have extreme nationalistic views with regard to those territories, their inhabitants, and Arabs more generally.

The fact that the Arabs often mentioned the deeds of their least-liked group as the reason for disliking it may also suggest that Arabs perceive a greater threat than Jews. This is indeed the case. We measured threat in two ways. First we presented to respondents a series of semantic differential items about the group in question. They were asked to rate, on scales ranging from 1 to 7, their least-liked groups on each adjective pair. On all items, Arabs see their disliked group as more threatening than do the Jews. In particular they perceive their targets as more dishonest, violent, and untrustworthy, and as bad.

We also asked our respondents to what degree the group posed a personal or regime threat, and on those questions both Arabs and Jews perceive the threat more as a regime threat in political, collective terms than as a personal threat. Across all these measures of perceived threat, an average of 56 per cent of Jews, but fully 68 per cent of the Arab sample, were highly threatened. Both percentages are considerably higher if we exclude the important-unimportant adjective pair and the question about personal threat. Clearly, then, both sets of respondents are highly threatened, but the Arabs more so, as one would expect given the fact that the Israeli Jews are the ruling majority in the state of Israel.

In fact, on the first five adjectives, an average of 88 per cent of the Arab respondents feel threatened. We could hardly expect results closer to unanimity. Jews who select Jewish targets and Arabs who select Arab target groups are far less threatened than the Jews who select Arab targets or the Arabs selecting Jewish targets. The differences are substantial and are greater for the Arab respondents. These differences are also most pronounced in terms of the adjectives "dishonest," "untrustworthy, " "bad, " and "dangerous." Still, the Jews who selected Arab targets were more threatened than the Arabs who selected Arab targets, and so being an Arab in Israel does not guarantee a greater level of perceived threat than does being a member of the dominant ethnic group.

Among Arabs the Jewish target groups are perceived as very threatening, particularly in terms of violence, danger, and badness. They are also seen as posing a much greater regime threat, and a somewhat greater personal threat, than the Arab target groups do to those Arabs who chose them as least liked. This national and ideological polarisation is coupled with high levels of perceived threat and leads to an expectation of very low levels of political tolerance in both sectors, which is what we find.

We measured tolerance by asking respondents a series of questions about the group they selected as least liked: whether members of the group should be allowed to become prime minister; whether the group ought to be outlawed; whether members should be allowed to hold public rallies; whether members should be allowed to make speeches in public and appear on TV; whether members should be allowed to teach in public schools; whether they should be allowed to study at universities; and whether they ought to have their telephones tapped. Individual respondents are therefore asked questions of tolerance with reference to particular target groups, overcoming the shortcomings of previous measures of tolerance, which ask all respondents about a specific group without inquiring whether an objection toward that group exists at all.

Here, objection is ensured by allowing each respondent to choose a least-liked group. This is particularly important in the current instance, as we cannot expect Israeli Arabs and Jews to dislike the same, or similar, extremist groups. The typical Israeli, whether Jew or Arab, is intolerant, on the average. Arabs are slightly less tolerant than Jews. The average percentage tolerant across seven items is somewhat higher for Jews, and they achieve a tolerant majority on two of the items, while Arabs do so on none. A similar percentage of Jews and Arabs gave tolerant responses on becoming prime minister, holding rallies, and free speech.

Arabs were more tolerant on one item, teaching in public schools. This is probably the problem closest to their personal concerns as an Arab minority; the other items are more hypothetical and of less direct relevance to them. Jews were more tolerant on the other three questions: outlawing the least-liked group, phone tapping, and university studies. Jews who selected Jewish groups as least-liked are more willing to tolerate them than are Jews who picked Arab groups. The average difference in tolerance is 20 percentage points. Indeed, among the Jews who pick some Jewish group as least liked, a tolerant majority obtains for four of the seven items, and on two more items the percentage tolerant is over 40 per cent.

These relatively high levels of tolerance stand out in comparison to all three other columns. Jews who select an Arab group as least-liked are much less tolerant, achieving a tolerant majority on only one item. Among Arabs-both those who chose an Arab group and those who chose a Jewish group-the level of tolerance is close to that of Jews who pick Arab groups. They do not achieve a tolerant majority on any item in either category, although tolerance toward Arab groups is somewhat higher than tolerance toward Jewish groups. Among Jews at least, the willingness to apply the democratic rights to a group one opposes is largely a function of whether the target is Jewish or Arab. The two Arab groups come very close in their ideological position to the leftist Jewish groups, yet the Jews' willingness to tolerate them is much lower.

Dissent when it is voiced by Arabs is considered less legitimate and is not as likely to be tolerated. Both Jewish and Arab sectors in Israeli society are characterized by "focused intolerance." Both sectors are in general politically intolerant (Jews mainly toward Arab groups) and the targets for intolerance are highly concentrated. Considering that Jewish public opinion is the one that affects the regime most directly, its characteristics are probably more relevant with regard to system-level manifestations of intolerance. But there is a dynamic feedback relationship between these two publics and intolerance on either side no doubt breeds intolerance on the other.

NORMS OF DEMOCRACY AND TOLERANCE

Intolerance often arises from perceptions of threat. Most citizens will be intolerant toward a group if they feel that this group threatens important values or constitutes a danger to the political regime. In an individual-level (multivariate) analysis, we found that perceptions of threat are the most important determinant of political tolerance among Jews and Arabs.

The one factor that has been found to offset threat and to induce tolerance is a strong belief in the abstract norms of democracy. The stronger the belief in these norms, the more people is willing to act on these norms and to apply them in concrete and threatening situations. The fact that tolerance is one value that at times must be weighed against other values that are believed to be at stake finds its expression in various legal doctrines. The "clear and present danger" concept of American liberal legal thought sets one limit on tolerance.

Other doctrines, more influential in European political thought and practice, set more severe limits on it easily compromising tolerance in the presence of threat, probably because threat was and is more real in those polities than in the United States. In Israel the most important and often-cited reference to this issue is the High Court of Justice ruling in the Al-Ard case. Al-Ard was an Arab leftist, nationalistic group that operated in the late 1950s and early 1960s. In 1964 it was refused official status as an association, and the Supreme Court, sitting as High Court of Justice, upheld this decision. In its rejection of the group's appeal, the court stated:

It is a very important rule that only extremely weighty considerations may prohibit the registration of an Association. The freedom to organize is one of the mainstays of the democratic regime and one of the basic rights of the citizen. Heaven forbid that we should revoke this right and proscribe as Association simply because one or another of its aims is to aspire toward a change in the legal situation existing in the State. The present situation might be in need of reform from this or another point of view and a movement wishing to organize public opinion in the State in order to bring about reform of the situation may do this within the framework of an Association registered by law, but no free regime can give its hand and conscience to a movement which undermines the regime itself.... This restriction is essential. It has often happened in the history of states with democratic regimes that fascist and totalitarian movements of various kinds have arisen against them, and utilized those selfsame rights of the freedom of speech; press and organisation granted them by the state in order to conduct their undermining activities under their protection.

Whoever saw this during the period of the Weimar Republic will never forget the lesson learned then.

And further:

It is the elementary right of any state to preserve its liberty and very existence in the face of foreign enemies and their collaborators within the camp. As my learned friend has said, no administration should be required to authorize in the name of the freedom of organisation, the establishment of a fifth column within the boundaries of its state. On the grounds of the material before us there is a sufficient basis to fear that the Association which the claimant wishes to register has indeed gone on this perilous way, destroying the allegiance which every citizen owes to the state in which he resides.

Just as in court decisions the values of political tolerance and other values, such as the constitutional order or national security, are evaluated and counterbalanced, so are they also in individual decisions. In the absence of a strong threat, belief in abstract norms of tolerance will constrain responses to specific instances in which citizens' tolerance is tested. The stronger the commitment to these general norms, the more tolerance one expects in specific instances despite the threat they may entail. If the threat is strong enough, however, it may override these abstract beliefs. It is important, then, to examine the status of democratic norms in Israeli society. Israeli democracy is well established, yet its origins are Eastern European.

The early Jewish immigrants were from Eastern Europe, and they left a lasting mark on Israèli political and social organisations, from the political parties and the Histadrut labor union to the moshavim and kibbutzim. Lacking the Anglo-Saxon liberal tradition, Israeli democracy puts more emphasis on majority rule and equality and less on civil liberties and minority rights. One therefore expects differential levels of support for these different aspects of democracy among the

Jewish public. If Anglo-Saxon liberal values are not expected to be rooted in Jewish political culture, they surely are not expected to be part of Arab political culture. The Arabs did not have much of a democratic heritage at all before 1948. On the other hand, since they are a minority, the belief in such abstract norms of democracy would be extremely functional for them. Ideals such as free speech and minority rights can only serve to protect the rights and political actions of a minority such as Arabs in Israel.

The level of support for these principles is generally high and only partly corresponds to our expectations. Almost 90 per cent of the Jews support the principles of majority rule (89 per cent), the right of criticism (89 per cent), and equal legal rights (88 per cent). Over 80 per cent support free speech. Only on the question of minority rights does this overwhelming majority shrink. It is a considerably reduced majority, down to 63 per cent. Among Arabs, we see an overall high level of support for liberal political values of minority rights and free speech. Most important to our concerns is the difference between Jews and Arabs in support for minority rights and for majority rule. Jews have a stronger belief in majority rule than do Arabs (18-point difference), whereas Arabs believe more strongly than Jews (9-point difference) in minority rights.

Recent findings from studies of the citizen orientations of Israeli adolescents show the same pattern. Of an Arab sample, 31 per cent rated "being tolerant of others' views" as important for good citizenship, compared to only 5 per cent of a Jewish sample. The abstract norms are not, then, purely abstract, and belief in them is at least in part a function of the group's minority or majority status. We may note that among Arabs the support for these two norms is about equal (about 70 per cent), but among the Jews there is a difference of 26 percentage points between support for majority rule and support minority rights. On the issue of free speech, 83 per cent of the Jews and 89 per cent of the Arabs are supportive, but only 38 per cent and 40 per cent (a difference of 45 and 49 percentage points, respectively) are willing to allow it to their least-liked group. Such discrepancies are a well-known phenomenon in political research, but their magnitude is greater here.

Furthermore, when we relate support for these abstract democratic norms to the degree of tolerance expressed by respondents, we find that belief in these norms does not predispose Israelis to be more tolerant politically toward unpopular groups. Among Jews we find a weak positive impact of general norms on tolerance. Belief in these general values makes Jews only slightly on political tolerance.

INDIVIDUAL DIFFERENCES IN TOLERANCE

The pattern of "focused intolerance" that characterizes the Jewish as well as the Arab public in Israel is estructured largely by the Arab-Israeli conflict. We have emphasized the mirror image we obtain, with high intolerance in both sectors, targeted predominantly toward Jewish right-wing groups among Arabs and left-wing Arab groups among Jews. We further examined the perceptions of threat and the degree of commitment to abstract democratic norms in the two publics, and suggested that these too were the by-product of this conflict, as well as of the minority-majority relationships stemming from it.

Up to this point the analysis has been mostly on the aggregate level, focusing on the frequency distributions in the two groups. In this section we will present an individual-level analysis, in order to elaborate on the effect of the political context-mainly the Arab-Israeli conflict-on the dynamics of tolerance in Israel. We have already noted that subjective perceptions of threat are a major determinant of political tolerance. This is true of both Arabs and Jews. In both instances, the direct impact of threat on tolerance is the strongest of any independent variable we have examined. This is true of the United States as well as, for example, New Zealand, although in these two societies belief in the general democratic values can, to some extent, offset the effects of perceived threat. In Israel, among both Jews and Arabs, the norms do not serve this protective function.

Ideology also plays a central role in Israeli politics. Beyond its importance, the content of the ideological dimension and of the left-right labels is crucial. Zionist nationalism is the major component of ideology, and on it, if on anything, there is widespread consensus among Jews. Although contributing a major common element to ideology, views and interpretations of nationalism, as they relate to the Arab-Israeli conflict, also provide the major and most salient sources of ideological variance within the Jewish majority and between Jews and Arabs, as we have shown earlier for the patterns of target group selection. The relationship of ideology to political tolerance is therefore immediate.

Among Jews, tolerance is explicitly part of left-wing ideology, which is one of relative accommodation of Jewish and Arab nationalism. The right-wing position is nationalistic and less accommodating toward the Arab world, and takes the position that peace can be assured only through military strength. The leftists are more willing to risk concessions for what they believe could be a lasting peace with the Arabs. Thus almost by definition the two competing ideologies should differ in tolerance, as the major cleavage dimension along which target groups are selected is that of the Arab-Israeli conflict.

The same is true for the Arabs, but in the opposite direction. For them the labels are reversed: The left-wing position emphasizes Arab nationalist concerns, whereas the right-wingers are more accommodating in terms of their attitudes toward their minority status, the Jewish state, and the Jews themselves. Among Jews, left-wingers are more tolerant, whereas among Arabs the right-wingers are. Left-wing Jews and right-wing Arabs are the least nationalistic, come closest to each other on the ideological continuum, and are the most accommodating and therefore the most tolerant. But they are minorities in each sector. In their study of Jewish and Arab attitudes on the conflict, Smooha and Peretz report that 72 per cent of the Jews scored toward the hawkish end of their index and 60 per cent of the Arabs toward the non hawkish end.

"This bimodal distribution leaves only 29 per cent of the Arabs and 28 per cent of the Jews in the broad middle, sharing compromising views". Eliminating a causal model that explains political tolerance (using maximum likelihood confirmatory factor analysis), we found that in the Jewish sample ideology has a direct effect on tolerance (independent of perceptions of threat). In the Arab sample the impact is more indirect, through threat perception, and is of course in the opposite direction. Left-wingers are more threatened by their targets than right-wingers are by theirs, and the more threatened one is, the less tolerant one becomes.

The degree of political tolerance toward a disliked group can be a largely cognitive, reality-based response to the way one perceives a complex political world. The Israeli-Arab conflict is the major factor shaping the political context of Israelis, and as such it is the source of the public climate of intolerance we found in the Jewish majority and in the Arab minority. Similarly, differences in orientations toward the conflict and perceptions of it, as measured by political ideology and perceived threat, are the principal sources of variance in tolerance among individuals in the two groups. If we might be allowed the luxury of speculation, we suggest that these political sources of intolerances are, in the final analysis, the most critical.

We have shown elsewhere that the social and psychological forces that underlie political tolerance and intolerance are largely uniform in democratic societies but that the political context varies greatly in its impact on individual levels of tolerance. In examining political tolerance in different societies, the primary differentiating agent is not different personality types in the various societies, but rather the vastly differing political context in which the citizens must live and conduct their political, as well as their everyday, lives. What we suggest is that, should the context change, levels of tolerance among Jews and Arabs could well change, even though their personalities and social characteristics are unaltered. Even more important, in apparently tolerant societies a changing political climate with requisite threats to the values and interests of the citizenry can readily undo such a seemingly solid basis for a democratic regime.

2

The Struggle for Civil Society in El Salvador

The armed conflict that wracked El Salvador January 1992 began 1980 to the signing of the Peace Accords in January 1992 began and ended in a struggle over civil society: over what expression civil unresolved struggle over civil society would be allowed to take, over its influence in public debate expression civil society would control it, and how. If the Right fought to take, over its influence in public debate over who would economic power it, and how. If the Right fought first of all on the ground of civil society, own economic power, it fought first of all means available to subordinate, or subdue, the ground of civil society, unleashed via the wave of organizing by church groups, unions, all means available to subordinate, or subdue, the forces unleashed via the wave of organizing by church groups, unions, and the eruption of civil war in the 1960s, were preponderantly representatives.

The targets of the famous "death squads," which emerged well society: union leaders, teachers, community organizers, health workers, catechists. While political militants have been the eruption of civil war in 1981, were preponderantly representatives prominent among recent victims of the violence civil society: union leaders, teachers, community organizers, health workers, catechists. While political militants have been the struggle going on in E1 Salvador today is essentially a struggle over the character among recent victims of the violence civil society out by resurgent death squads, the struggle going on in the war and the Peace Accord today is essentially a struggle over the character and direction of the new civil society that has arisen in the wake of the war and the Peace Accords.

This struggle has been scarcely visible in the debates over the reemergence of the death squads, over compliance with the recommendations of the Truth Commission or the Accords themselves, or in the posturing of political parties in the wake of the elections of 1994. Nevertheless, it is a struggle that carries profound ramifications, including electoral ones, for the parties of the Right, principally the Alianza Republicana Nacional (ARENA), and of the Left, principally the Frente Farabundo Martide Liberacion Nacional (FMLN) and the breakaway, "social democratic" faction led by Joaquin Villalobos (now the Partido Democratico).

It is a struggle rendered especially visible by a series of battles, initiated well before the end of the war, over the role of community organisations, and the non-governmental organisations (NGOs) with which they are linked, in the process of reconstruction and reconciliation. The United States Agency for International Development has played a key role in this struggle. This chapter examines the development of the controversial sector of NGOs and its role in post-war reconstruction in an attempt to illuminate both the complex process of accommodation, in which El Salvador is now engaged, and the current question regarding the role of "civil society" in the construction and maintenance of viable democracies.

THE IDEA OF CIVIL SOCIETY

The collapse of Communist systems in Europe, continuing criticism of the social welfare state in the North Atlantic polities, and the striking emergence of new community organisations and nongovernmental organisations in the developing world have all contributed to a sense that we must look to the texture and quality of civic life, above all to its organized expression in "civil society," for solutions to the problems of governance, participation, and social welfare that confront modern societies.

According to the Tocquevillian version of the argument, the denser the web of civic associations, the more vital the democracy will be and, even, the more apt the society to experience rapid and equitable development. In Latin America, civil society has been viewed not only as the chief carrier of democratizing forces, but also as a prominent actor in the transitions to democracy which have swept the region since the late 1970s. Despite varying assessments as to the precise role that civil society played in these events, there is broad agreement that a vibrant civil society means a more democratic society. In the process, "civil society" has increasingly come to have been identified with the welter of non-governmental organisations (NGOs) and grassroots organisations (GROs) that have sprung up over the last 20 years.

The new optimistic equating of civil society with political democracy demands a more critical look. The current enthusiasm for civil society mirrors an earlier enthusiasm for "pluralism" as the basis for effective democratic governance, without taking into account the numerous critiques of the earlier formulation. As E. Gyimah-Boadi has argued in the case of Ghana, civil associations may play a variety of political roles, not all of which are necessarily constructive for democracy. Robert Putnam finds "civil community" to be at the root of the superior performance of Italy's regional governments in its more modern North as compared to that of their counterparts in the South. However, he traces the tradition of civic associations in the North back to the late medieval era: scarcely 50 years of democracy attest to the power of civil society to produce good government.

Moreover, the new rhetoric of civil society tends to assign functions to the latter that not even the pluralists had imagined for, we are told, civil society can (a) replace an incompetent and overburdened state as the guardian of social values, (b) serve as the source of inspiration for civic action, and (c) operate as the provider of social services. In Latin America, not only in rhetoric but in practice, international lending agencies and bilateral development organisations have increasingly insisted on the need to channel funds through NGOs, strengthening their ability to assume functions formerly reserved for state agencies. At the same time, international donors have pushed their new partners to adopt "professional" standards and become "self sustainable."

Nevertheless, large doubts persist about the capability of NGOs and community organisations to play the new roles, to generate funds on their own, or to assume the representative functions which have often been assigned to them or which they may have arrogated to themselves. In El Salvador we are witness to the reconstruction of civil society in the wake of a terrible civil struggle, one which began with an attempt to eradicate the most vital elements of that society in the name of "anticommunism." The new civil society now emerging is marked by that struggle. As civil organisations attempt to adjust to the new situation, they face important questions about their autonomy from political forces, their ability to advance the interests of their constituents, or clients, under ever-tightening economic circumstances, and the possibilities for reconciliation in a thoroughly divided polity. Under such circumstances, the warnings of John Keane are appropriate: "civil society can also degenerate into a battlefield ... Under extreme conditions; civil society could even hemorrhage to death".

Though El Salvador has not yet reached such extremity, the continuing struggle for civil society now going on there should alert us to the difficult process of construction which new democracies face and help us to reconsider some of the claims made for, and about, civil society, democracy, and democratisation. Because NGOs have played a central role in this process, both as civil associations per se and as promoters of civil association, the account that follows looks closely at their development during the civil war, and then at the challenges they face in the subsequent peace.

Three questions will occupy our attention here: First, what has been the effect on the peace process of the resurgence of civil society since 1984? Has a resurgent civil society moved El Salvador closer to reconciliation and democracy, or has it simply recapitulated, and reinforced, the polarisation which contributed to civil war? Second, what is the character of the civil society which has emerged? Are we witnessing a "democratisation" of society or a continuation of the vertical patterns that characterized both wartime and prewar El Salvador? Finally, what is the role of outside actors, and of the United States in particular, in the construction of a new civil society? What has been constructive, and what destructive, in the work of US and European agencies and NGOs?

CIVIL SOCIETY AND CIVIL WAR

The wave of terror that engulfed El Salvador just before, and for several years following, the coup of 1979 obliterated the "popular front" organisations of campesinos, trade unionists, students, women, and non-governmental organisations that had emerged during the 1970s to confront an increasingly repressive state. Many of the constituent organisations were similarly obliterated, "decapitated," or driven increasingly repressive state. Many of the constituent organisations were similarly obliterated, "decapitated," or Gonzalez, who had been in one time, themselves.

The late Victor Gonzalez, who had been, at of the ecumenical coalition Diaconia, recounted the dark days director of the ecumenical coalition Diaconia, recounted the dark days of 1986 when the organisation, created to serve the hundreds of thousands of internal refugees displaced by the war, could count on only two staff members, with the rest too afraid to come to the office for fear of being detained by a government which viewed such efforts as "subversive". The US State Department aided in such persecutions, carrying out public relations campaigns among international donors against such organisations as Tutela Legal, the human rights arm of the Archdiocease of San Salvador, The Human Rights Commission of El Salvador (a non-governmental agency), and Diaconia. Few individuals thought it worth their while to organize themselves into civil associations of any kind during the first years of the war.8 Only the international spotlight, plus considerable financial support from abroad, allowed organisations associated with the churches and the Left to begin building in 1984.

THE PRIVATE SECTOR INITIATIVE

Starting in 1983, however, a new sort of organisation began to arrive on the scene. The Fundacion Salvadorena para el Desarrollo Economicoy Social (FUSADES) was created in 1983 by a group of wealthy Salvadoran business people. The United States Agency for International Development (US-AID), driven by the Reagan administration's enthusiasm for private enterprise and committed to creating a string of business organisations throughout Central America to support export-oriented policies, played an important role in FUSADES' rapid growth.9 The modest sums put up by its wealthy sponsors(about $1,600 apiece) were quickly supplemented by AID largesse. In its first year, FUDADES obtained a $185,000 contact from AID to promote the Caribbean Basin Initiative (CBI). In 1984, the year following, it received the first disbursement of what was eventually to be a contract of $50.46 million as part of AID's "Industrial Stabilisation and Recovery Program."

Though AID still considers this program its "lead vehicle for facilitating non-traditional exports and investment", the government share of the contract was only $2.56 million. Over the next 10 years, FUSADES became the main outlet for AID monies in the civil sector. By 1992, the disbursements planned reached as high as $156,849,000. Though AID would cease to fund the operating expenses of FUSADES in 1994, a scheme worked out in 1991 provided FUSADES with a minimum income of $5 million a year, from 1994 onwards, in interest earned from credit programmes funded by the AID.

FUSADES grew rapidly, becoming the most influential think-tank in El Salvador. The organisation's Department of Economic and Social Studies drafted the structural adjustment plan which became the basis for the economic program of the new ARENA government in 1989. Former President Alfredo Cristiani and several of his cabinet members were among the founding members of the organisation. FUSADES also spawned a whole family of new organisations with major encouragement and help from AID. In 1986, FUSADES spun off the Fundacion Industrial para la Prevencion de Riesgos Ocupacionales (FIPRO, or Industrial Foundation for Prevention of Occupational Hazards), the Fundacion HABITAT (no relation to Habitat International), and the Fundacion Empresarial para el Desarrollo Educativo (FEPADE or Business Foundation for Educational Development), the latter with funds from the AID program called Fortalecimiento de Asociaciones (FORTAS or Strengthening Associations).

All three organisations rapidly became major recipients of AID funds, and all three have continued to be major channels through which AID provides funds for national reconstruction. Other AID-funded organisations in the private sector include Junior Achievement, Fundacion Antidrogas de El Salvador (FUNDASALVA, El Salvador's Antidrug Foundation), the Comite Coordinador para el Desarrollo Economico de Oriente (COMCORDE or Coordinating Committee for the Economic Development of Eastern El Salvador), and the Centro de Apoyo a la Microempresa (CAM), an organisation to help small business.

The explicit aim, particularly in creating FUSADES, was to promote a package of economic policies that the administration in the United States felt was needed to foster political stability and economic growth. While the AID had the support of the World Bank, the International Monetary Fund (IMF), and the Inter-American Development Bank (IDB) in this project, it lacked that of the Duarte government, then in the early stages of its administration. The most remarkable aspect of the AID strategy is the extent to which it involved itself in building the political power and influence of a segment of the Salvadoran business class to accomplish its purposes.

It was almost as if AID officials had decided to take seriously the claims of dependency theory about the "weakness of the domestic bourgeoisie" in Latin America, turning those claims into prescriptions for action. In fact, however, AID appeared to pursue a dual strategy: on the one hand, it supported the government in its attacks on organisations that it associated, whether rightly or wrongly, with the Leftist opposition; on the other hand, it was able to dominate those elements of the Salvadoran business elite that it viewed as "progressive" by building up a new type of organisation, heavily financed by the United States.

Whether AID officials worked out of a coherent vision of the sort of civil society El Salvador required or acted on implicit assumptions about the kinds of organisations most likely to serve US purposes remains unclear. Still, interviews conducted with AID officials suggest there was an implicit vision behind the massive effort of the 1980s, and into the early 1990s that was designed to influence the character of Salvadoran society. When asked why AID insisted on building and supporting organisations led by the wealthiest members of a class divided society, one official close to the Private Sector Initiative (as AID calls the program) replied matter-of-factly that these are the sorts of people most capable of keeping civic organisations afloat: they can raise money, they have "good business sense," and they wield influence.

In this model, economic power should be wedded to social activism in creating a nonprofit sector capable of "getting the job done," whatever that job might be. Not only do those who wield the greatest economic power have an obligation to serve society through such organisations, but they are also uniquely qualified to lead and manage an "independent sector" that mirrors, in personnel and practice, the standards of recruitment and efficiency of the business world from which boards of directors and managers alike are drawn.

In wartime El Salvador, this model - which is not entirely a caricature of the worldview of the major US nonprofits - was probably all the more attractive because it provided a base from which it would be possible to fill a social space that would otherwise be occupied by community activists identified with the political Left. The FUSADES group of organisations, however, was scarcely capable of reaching the levels of society to which the FMLN, its allies and sympathizers, and other elements of the opposition appealed. As new political spaces opened up under the Duarte administration, so organisations from the "popular sector" quickly emerged to take advantage of the new opportunities.

THE REBIRTH OF THE POPULAR SECTOR

At the time that FUSADES came into being, few civic organisations were alive and operating. Thanks to the demands of the war, the Red Cross had sprung to life after years of serving as little more than a ladies auxiliary to the hospitals of San Salvador, work that was soon supplemented by the arrival of a "Blue Cross" and a "Green Cross." Also responding to the war situation, a small group of churches and older NGOs came together to form a consortium called Diaconia to manage relief funds for the thousands of refugees who, fleeing the war, had crowded into San Salvador.

Nevertheless, Diaconia found itself the target of a fierce repression which stemmed from the fact that it lent visibility to a problem which both the Salvadoran and US governments wished to downplay, i.e., the fact that the military's campaign in the countryside was having a devastating effect on the country's rural population. Diaconia was also vulnerable because most of the population it served had roots in rebel territory, and many were identified, in one way or another, with the rebels. Some of those displaced were, in fact, members of the FMLN, and their work within Diaconfa made the organisation vulnerable to both political manipulations by the Frente on the one hand and to repression by the government on the other.

In 1983, representatives of what was then the Ecumenical Committee for Humanitarian Assistance, the Archdiocese of San Salvador, and the Episcopal, Lutheran, and Baptist churches met secretly with leaders of the FMLN in Mexico City to forge an agreement that succeeded in ending interference by the FMLN, at least for a time; but it did not end the repression. By 1985, however, Diacona and the few international NGOs that remained to aid refugees displaced by war were gradually being replaced by a new set of organisations, many with ties to the FMLN, but all dedicated to protecting the civilian populations affected by the war.

The new organisations - community organisations in the war zones and among the slum dwellers of San Salvador; confederations of these as well as of cooperatives, both old and new, in the countryside; and NGOs set up to provide services (development assistance, health care, and education) for local populations and aid in the repatriation and resettlement of refugees and those displaced by the war - arose in response to local needs and tactical considerations. In both territories held by the FMLN as well as in the "transition zones" marked by hard fighting, civilian populations were under enormous pressure. In some areas, from which the bulk of the population had fled, those who stayed behind had to sustain a living in the face of the government's attempt to "empty the ocean to catch the fish."

In other areas, civilians organized themselves in an effort to preserve their right to remain, to provide themselves with the basic necessities of life, and in an attempt to better their precarious lives, either on the land or at the margins of San Salvador. The uniting to form confederations arose as a way to coordinate the efforts of communities that were otherwise isolated and scattered and to serve as advocates on behalf of their members. The NGOs acted as domestic counterparts to those international agencies, mostly European, who were still willing to try to reach this population, and they channeled funds, material goods, and technical assistance to the communities to the best of their ability.

This was also the era of AID-sponsored "civic action" programmes and the US Military Advisers Group, which were aimed, in an attempt that was only partially successful, at putting an end to the sort of Salvadoran military operations that produced the massacre at El Mozote and winning the hearts and minds" of the rural population. The FMLN viewed the efforts at civic action, as well as the new Municipalities in Action (MIA) program (designed to coordinate and give a "civilian face" to the project), as a threat to its own political control of, and expansion in, the contested regions. Thus, some of the new community organisations assumed the tactical jobs of staving off government efforts at "development" and muting the effects of civic action campaigns, while the new NGOs provided the resources necessary to give community organisations and organizers credibility in the face of government initiatives.

However, the most dramatic manifestation of the new "popular sector" civil society was the repopulation movement, which commenced in 1985 with resettlement of 187 internal refugees at Tenancingo and reached its culmination, from 1987 onwards, with organizing the massive resettlement from the Mesa Grande and Colomoncagua refugee camps in Honduras. Although this effort received widespread support, from the Archdiocese of San Salvador across a broad array of civic organisations and international donors, it had to overcome serious resistance from the Salvadoran government, which viewed resettlement as an effort to restore to the FMLN a population base in areas which government forces had previously "cleansed," via saturation bombing and terrifying military sweeps, over the preceding 5 years.

Still, resettlement went forward, with groups of refugees and displaced persons reclaiming villages and towns that had been abandoned years before or squatting on private land whose owners had long since fled. Each group had its community organisation; most organisations were tied to one of the parties of the FMLN (though the FMLN itself was not initially supportive of the repopulation effort); and each organisation was linked to an NGO that could provide logistical support and a small, but vital, flow of international assistance in the years that lay ahead.

The logic of organisation, especially once communities were reestablished in what still combat zones were, was "vertical", approximating a "war communism" in which community decision making, though founded on participatory principles, was subordinated to the exigencies of the war effort. These, then, were the actors who emerged to reconstitute civil society in El Salvador during the course of the war. Most such organisations were born, to one degree or another, out of the logic of war. With the winding down of the war, community organisations and NGOs of both the Right and the Left began to make plans for the peace. However, and despite the hopes of many, the peace has often appeared to be little but "war by other means."

MAKING PEACE: THE NEW STRUGGLE FOR SOCIETY

The peace that culminated in the signing of thc last of the Peace Accords was made by politicos, not by Salvadoran society as a whole. It was negotiated behind closed doors, and its terms responded to the demands of the participants and their immediate constituencies: the Army High Command and the Salvadoran elite, in the case of the Salvadoran government, and its soldiers-in-arms, in the case of the FMLN.

Deals were struck with other politicos to achieve election reform, an agreement on land distribution (for ex-combatants of the FMLN and the civilian population in its zones of influence, including, especially, the repopulation movement), and new mechanisms for negotiating social and economic reforms. But the core institutions of the Salvadoran government remained untouched, and the core interests of the FUSADES wing of the ARENA party were guaranteed, at least until the next election. The organisations of civil society played no role in the negotiations, and almost no role in the deliberations of the rival parties, except to remind all sides that peace was a necessity. If this was a "negotiated revolution," it was a very limited revolution indeed.

CIVIL SOCIETY AND THE PRIVATE SECTOR

Virtually invisible in the political maneuvering of those who were party to the Accords, however, was the tremendous ferment in Salvadoran civil society and a continuing struggle for its control. US-AID continued to fund FUSADES lavishly, along with its offspring, incorporating them into programmes aimed at the "reinsertion" of the former combatants and reconstruction of the war torn parts of the country despite their scant cxperience with this population. Up through 1993, AID also supported efforts of the Salvadoran government to prevent the channelling of reconstruction funds through the largest, most experienced of the FMLN-related NGOs, using a variety of excuses which were belied by the continuing confidence which the European donors, including the European Community (EC), displayed in those same NGOs.

AID continued to create "private sector" NGOs, with its $10 million investment in the Centro de Apoyo a la Microempresa (CAM) being the most recent example. Despite severe cutbacks in funding, those AID officials to whom I spoke referred wistfully to the possibility of helping to create an organisation that would be dedicated to "civic education," somewhat along the lines of the League of Women Voters and, presumably, with the same reliance on the richest, brightest segment of Salvadoran civil society which has characterized all their efforts to date.

Meanwhile, FUSADES has struck out on its own. In the latter part of the 1980s, AID had attempted to push FUSADES into organizing FORTAS, originally funded to promote the development of business associations, its "social arm." When it appeared that FUSADES was moving too slowly in this matter, AID cut off funding. Nevertheless, the former director of FUSADES, Eduardo Nunez, pushed ahead, creating a series of mini-foundations to institute and carry out social services in rural areas. Each foundation is headed by 3-4 local coffee barons, with the participation of other wealthy property owners or business people in the area.

Although the actual work of the foundation is confined to the environs of a rural town, the address of its headquarters is located, almost invariably, in one of the wealthier San Salvador suburbs, where the coffee barons have their permanent homes. Each foundation starts with a small endowment raised from its members. It then seeks to establish local projects of benefit to the area: e.g., a dispensary in an isolated community, a school building where people have had to do without schooling, perhaps a basketball court or soccer field. The foundation uses the influence of its founders to bring in funds from the government and only more rarely seeks external funding; finally, the project is donated to the community.

Nunez himself was personally committed to the project and convinced, as he put it, that this is why we had this terrible war," because those with money had never done anything for "their" people. He started by going to an area and calling upon the "people with influence," the richest property owners and business people in the area, lecturing about the consequences of neglecting "their" people. He then offered the full support of FUSADES and Project FORTAS in getting their foundation off the ground. Unlike the foundations and NGOs created by others, the foundations that come under the aegis of Project FORTAS sail through the process of official registration.

What Nunez failed to mention was that these foundations have been established throughout the best coffee-growing region of the country, where they supplement the traditional (and traditionally effective) political repression which kept the area relatively tranquil during most of the war - and safely within the ARENA camp through what has now been 6 elections. Nor did he allude to the favors which government officials have begun to bestow in the form of providing international donors with highly partisan lists of "eligible" NGOs, including the new foundations, for projects in the area.

Although AID has not provided any assistance to Project FORTAS since 1991, when the new effort began, the AID officials who were interviewed looked upon the initiative with favor. One official who was closely associated with the Private Sector Initiative, described above, observed that he had initially been skeptical of what even he viewed as a paternalistic approach. Nevertheless, he reported, he had gradually "come around" because the foundations served to "open the eyes" of their members, who, in many cases, had previously had no idea of the seriousness of the needs around them.

Furthermore, he went on to say, these groups don't have a passing interest in the area: they grew up there, have roots there. While a development agency may have only a finite interest in the area, the foundation members are there for the long term. In the end, he noted, it also comes down to a matter of who has the power to get things done. Indeed, it is also a matter of who has, and keeps, the power in the local communities. Civil society, FORTAS-style, reproduces and reinforces the top-down structure of political and economic power in the communities where the foundations are located, including the very individuals who have always wielded that power.

It is true that such institutions have their counterparts in the nonprofit worlds of the United States and Europe, but, in the Salvadoran context, and from a political point of view, Project FORTAS is designed to maintain past power alignments and ensure continuance of the power status quo. The pious hope, as expressed by the AID official quoted above, that the "middle class" would gain access, sooner or later, to the governing boards of these institutions suggests a remarkable *naiveti*. What is even more remarkable is that it took the Salvadoran ruling elite 500 years and a civil war to discover paternalism.

THE POPULAR SECTOR AND RECONSTRUCTION

On the other hand, when it comes to the NGOs with links to the FMLN, it would appear that AID is far less willfully blind to the political consequences of development assistance. According to the terms of the Peace Accords, the "National Plan of Reconstruction" was to have been drawn up through consultation among representatives of government, the NGOs, and community leaders and financed through a fund administered by the United Nations Development Programme (UNDP). Instead, government bureaucrats, with the support of AID, drew up a plan that placed heavy emphasis on rebuilding infrastructure, with the bulk of the funds, both for local relief and redevelopment, being channeled through the municipalities (still largely in the hands of ARENA mayors).

It also put administration of the program into the hands of the Comision Nacional de Restauracion de Areas (CONARA), an agency that had originally been established to strengthen the government's control over the contested areas. However, the European donors balked at this plan due to CONARA's history of counter-insurgency. When the government responded by creating a new agency to implement the National Plan (the Secretariat for National Reconstruction), not only did the Secretariat take over CONARA's offices and equipment, but it also hired CONARA's former staff and was headed up by CONARA's last director.

In the face of pressure from the United States, combined with the intransigence of the Salvadoran government, the UNDP was excluded from overseeing disposition of the funds. In fact, the efforts of the UNDP to coordinate the work of the various United Nations agencies with the work of the opposition NGOs almost led to a diplomatic break with the Cristiani government. Up until late 1993, the European donors boycotted the Secretariat, which left AID as its principal source of funds. Even recent grants by the European Community and others have been more on the order of joint ventures and have carried the stipulation that a significant portion of the funds be channeled through NGOs.

In the first year of the Secretariat's existence, what funding that did go to NGOs went, almost invariably, to those considered "safe," i.e., NGOs with ties either to AID or to some FUSADES-affiliated group. Excluded were the federations of cooperatives, whether associated with the FMLN or the Christian Democrats; traditional NGOs, like the Fundacion Salvadorena dc Desarrolloy Vivienda Minima (FUNDASAL), which the administration considered too wedded to community organizers; and NGOs with links to the FMLN.

The grand exceptions were "umbrella" projects run by Catholic Relief Services (CRS), which works through a wide range of local NGOs and community organisations, many of whom have ties to the FMLN. Officials at AID were quick to point to the CRS projects as evidence of the Agency's willingness to work with the FMLN, though the projects are supposed to be under the direction of the Secretariat, not of AID. No matter who takes credit for the liberality of the official reconstruction effort, it seems clear that CRS is the exception that proves the rule. None of the 5 older, national-level NGOs with ties to the FMLN have obtained more than minuscule sums from the Secretariat. Both AID and the Secretariat responded by raising doubts about the "capacidad" of the organisations to handle the funds, a reservation which prompted one adviser of a European-funded project to observe:

When an organisation has been handling competently some millions of dollars annually for 7 or 8 years, you have to conclude that they have the capacity to handle at least that much in the future. Even the smallest of the "big 5" manage $1-2 million in project monies yearly; and all have adopted professional accounting procedures over the last few years. Former UNDP liaison for NGOs, Carlos Locares, has similarly argued that these NGOs were particularly well suited to work with the populations targeted by the National Plan of Reconstruction:

They are the ones who have the mystique necessary to do the sort of field work required with this population. Of course they have deficiencies, but these are deficiencies which could and should be worked with.

The enthusiasm of AID for the Municipalities in Action component of the reconstruction program had abated somewhat by the time of my interviews, as it became clear (1) that municipal authorities were ill-equipped to handle much more than small, straightforward projects, and (2) that municipal institutions hardly allowed for the sorts of community participation that government and AID propaganda had been touting. Conflicts between municipal authorities, NGOs, and community groups over priorities and policies were written off to politically motivated incidents (which, in many cases, they were), without any serious efforts being made to develop new approaches for resolving disagreements or new institutions to enlarge participation. Indeed, when the mayor of Suchitoto (a member of ARENA) joined in one such effort, he was attacked by officials of his own party when the central government, apparently with the support of AID, balked at NGO members with ties to the opposition taking any extensive part in the municipal planning.

ALTERNATIVE VISIONS

By contrast, several European donors, including the European Community (EC), have promoted innovative schemes for the governance of regional development projects that provide for a broad range of participation on the boards of directors of new regional authorities: municipal officials, heads of government agencies, representatives of NGOs, and community leaders. In one case, the European Community has created a large-scale development corporation to administer regional projects; the corporation will be governed by a board made up of representatives of the EC, the communities involved, government officials, and investors.

Although this project has been criticized for its top-down approach, efforts have been made to coordinate the work of NGOs in the area and to incorporate all interested parties in the governance of the corporation. In placing technical personnel in the communities, the program's director was careful to choose individuals who shared the political affiliation of the communities and went well beyond his mandate to include populations not formally covered by the EC commitment, a flexibility notably lacking in AID projects. In Suchitoto, Nejapa, parts of Chalatenango and San Vicente departments, and elsewhere, local officials (including ARENA mayors) have made efforts, supported by US and European NGOs or party-based networks of NGOs, to bring together community leaders, NGO personnel, and officials from both local and central government to plan for, and coordinate, local development initiatives.

When Director Charles Costello assumed direction of the AID Mission in Fall 1993, AID's familiar complaint that NGOs and community organisations in the "popular sector" were "over-politicized" began to moderate. In this, they had not been far wrong. However, what the judgment was missing was any appreciation of the enormous vitality, and variation, that exists among these organisations, from the grassroots on up through the hierarchy. The wartime chain of command - which assigned each FMLN party its own territory of operation, each territory its community organisations, and each organisation its NGOs - is coming apart in bits and pieces as these constituent parts have begun to pursue their own interests, following their own individual logic.

The major NGOs with ties to one or another of the five FMLN parties display considerable variation in the closeness of that continued association, though all have striven for greater professionalism and greater transparency, even where party connections remain strong. The political structures built by the parties, the so-called gremios, are also in turmoil. Those with deep roots in the communities they represent appear to be more stable than those whose representation" was more fictive than real, more a product of tactical considerations than of responding to any felt need within the community itself.

Moreover, the NGOs and gremios alike face increasing independence on the part of communities who demand control over their own affairs, including the freedom to choose their own benefactors and allies. Although complaints abound regarding the overbearing nature of political structures that still control some funding, many only reflect the restructuring that is taking place. A European development worker pointed up the difference between two communities that were once tied to the Partido Revolucionario de los Trabajadores de Centroamerica (PRTC) or Revolutionary Workers Party of El Salvador: Sisiguayo as opposed to Las Marias II and Los Molinos. Sisiguayo is a community made up of former FMLN combatants and hacienda workers who settled on two former haciendas on the Bay of Jiquilisco, in Usulutan.

Sisiguayo had the luck to be organized. They say who can come and who can't. An NGO approaches them, they say, "What can you do for us?" If they like the project, they talk terms. What are your rules of operation? These are ours. How much are you going to spend? How long are you going to be here?" Sisiguayo was originally organized by the PRTC. They had the luck that the PRTC used a model of organisation in which the theology of liberation had played a big role; they had read some books of Freire, and participation was important. So eventually, people told the PRTC, "Look, you're fine as politicians, but we want to run our own affairs." And the PRTC, to its credit in this case, withdrew.

They've gained politically from it; they gained credibility in the area. They're doing quite well, as are the Communists, who have also known how to let the communities decide for themselves. The PRTC failed in the north, in Las Marias II and Los Molinos, where the local comandante decided he was judge and jury and ended up killing a couple of people. He was withdrawn, but he was never sanctioned, and people there say that, as long as the PRTC isn't going to give them justice, they want nothing to do with them.

By and large, the parties and the "popular sector" NGOs have to accommodate to the communities. In the polarized atmosphere at war's end, and with clear evidence that the government's intentions were still hostile, the organisations tied to the FMLN took the attitude that no one would be allowed to enter "their" communities without their approval. Some people still speak this way. Nevertheless, throughout El Salvador today, government and AID projects can be found operating alongside those sponsored by the gremios and cooperative associations and the NGOs to which they are tied. Communities that still feel the need to check with their gremio or NGO before agreeing to anything are told to "Go for it." And NGOs linked to the FMLN work under AID and government contracts.

This does not mean, however, that conflict is at an end. On the contrary, both the style of development assistance and the character of civil organisation associated with the so-called "popular sector" differ markedly from the model created by AID and the Salvadoran elite; and those differences have been exacerbated and politicized even more by the continuing polarisation of El Salvador. Warning! OCR inputs differ greatly long historical development in the United States has served MEANS: COMpVG MODELS OF identify nonprofit organisations with the twin characteristics of long historical development in the United States headship and public service.

For a variety of reasons, similar notions shape the debate over the new organisations with the twin characteristics of El Salvador. In both counteract non partisanship and public service. For a variety of course, the reality is more complex, reasons, political polar notions shape the debate over the new organisations in El Salvador has sharpened the political El Salvador. In both countries, of an organisation and how reality is more complex, but political what NGO or civil group in El Salvador has sharpened the political import political connotation, even when the organisation and how it is perceived. Thus, who works with what NGO or civil group in El Salvador conveys avoiding political entanglements.

As we have distinct political connotation, even when the very configuration of the NGOs spun question FUSADES, under the tutelage of AID, bespeaks a concept of civil successful in avoiding political entanglements. Even though traditions FUSADES, under the tutelage of philanthropy and nonprofit giving are very weak a concept of civil society elite, the NGOs created under AID auspices draw on which economic elites play the leading role. Even though traditions almost exclusively for their board members and executive person profit giving are very weak among Salvador's Not only do these arrangements make use of the NGOs created under talent auspices draw on business elites influence of such individuals, but they also reinforce their board members and executive personnel political only do these arrangements make use of FUSADES members in the considerable talent and administration is once of such individuals, but they also reinforce example.

Board membership gives either social and access to political position. The US officials, FUSADES well as control over in the Cristiani administration is only one example. Board membership gives chosen to endow the new institutions. Such power, which should be familiar enough to politicians and US officials, as well as control over the considerable sums of US foundations, with which AID has chosen to end by the presence of elected officials and representatives of the community institutions. Such power, which should be familiar enough to observers of Community Chest, is not balanced by occur in the presence of elected States. Nor is it officials and repree from the temptations of corruption. The community in overarching bodies, micro enterprise lending project established by AID in 1992, the Community Chest, as may occur in the United States. Nor is it free from the temptations of corruption.

The multi-million dollar corruption scandals involving project established by AID its directors, so carefully chosen 1992, the Centro de Apoyo a la Microempresa (CAM), has twice business wracked by The starkness of the politicisation scandals involving its directors, so carefully chosen from perhaps best illustrated by the small handful of organisations that have Those deliberately, to of the politicisation in Salvadoran route. Nearly all society boards of directors who are made up of professionals from the upper mall handful of organisations that have chosen, deliberately, to go the none is partisan route. Nearly well-endowed.

Some have been able to use their connectors who are made up of professionals from the Right, or with AID, to garner government class. None is particularly well-endowed. Some have been able to use their connections on the Right, or with AID, to garner government funds; yet all maintain their right to select their projects independently. One example is El Buen Ciudadano, a relatively new organisation that is identified with ARENA by outsiders. However, the board of directors of El Buen Ciudadano is made up, almost exclusively, of professionals. One of its founders made clear the organisation's distance from the group sponsored by FUSADES: as far as he was concerned, FUSADES was established to promote the recuperation of big capital." As he put it: if you look at the directors of their projects, all are children of the economic elite; as for their training programmes for workers, whom did they train, if not workers for their own factories?

El Buen Ciudadano was founded to promote democracy and acceptance of democratic institutions by encouraging people to share in democratic values. To date, their biggest project has been the voter registration program that was funded by US-AID through the Southwest Voter's Research Institute. El Buen Ciudadano and other civic organisations were able to see up close the foot-dragging and inefficiency with which the ARENA-controlled Tribuno Supremo Electoral (TSE) approached the process and were witness to the magnitude of the problems that beset the elections. When they protested the way in which the TSE handled UNDP monies designated for transporting voters to the polls, the TSE summarily banned them from taking part in any further cooperative efforts.

Even organisations that make a special effort to remain "neutral" must walk a fine line or risk banishment from government channels that provide access to projects and funding. Another "middle-of-the-road" NGO is the Comite de Integraciony Reconstruccion para El Salvador (CIRES), which was generated out of the staff and infrastructure left behind by the International Rescue Committee when it departed El Salvador at the end of the war. Perceiving it as a "safe" NGO, the government approached CIRES even before the Secretariat for National Reconstruction was created to draw up a proposal for funding under the National Plan for Reconstruction.

Though dependent on funding from both the Secretariat and AID, CIRES has tried to steer a non-partisan course, siding with NGOs of the Left on most refugee issues and attempting to deal with all communities regardless of political affiliation. Eileen Rosin, formerly Executive Director of CIRES, recounted their first year: At the time the first proposal was formulated, we had named a number of communities with which our technical people had contacts. By the time we got the money and got back to those communities, they had all been organized by the FMLN. There was a good deal of suspicion of us, of what we wanted, of who we stood with. We gradually worked out a relationship with each of the gremios involved. Each was different.

In the north of San Miguel, where we were working on a PROSAMI project [an AID-sponsored maternal and infant health program], we dealt with the local gremio, which was controlled by one of the factions of the ERP [then a party of the FMLN, but also coordinated with FASTRAS, the national-level development NGO linked to the ERP]. FASTRAS was very helpful and basically left it with the gremio, with which we worked out a relationship: they helped find promoters for each community ... In Usulatan it was another story... Relations varied tremendously. In one community we ended up not working because nothing we could do would satisfy the suspicion of the gremio. One community was part of COMUS [agremtol, which was linked to FENACOA [a cooperative association], so we had talks with them.

It wasn't just a matter of asking "permission"; we are also concerned not to duplicate efforts or compete. Nevertheless, CIRES' staff concluded that they would not work through the gremios in the future but would go to the communities directly: We have no intention of competing with the gremios, we're not interested in community organisation, except to strengthen existing structures, help with the formation of the committees necessary for the program, etc. But we don't want to be in a position of having the gremio drain off the money we bring in, or filter it back to the party. Torn between the need for coordination and the knowledge that political manipulation often accompanies organisation, CIRES has chosen an uncomfortable, technically defined middle way, delivering projects with as much community participation as possible, but leaving community organisation to others.

If the handful of nonpartisan civil organisations represented by El Buen Ciudadano and CIRES illustrate possibilities that were largely foregone by the efforts of AID to strengthen civil society, the organisations of the so-called popular sector are the polar opposite of the FUSADES model, at least in theory. Hundreds of community organisations have grown up in El Salvador as a result of the war. They range from community fora for thousands of rural settlements and urban barrios to informal cooperatives to more formal, local arms of political parties. Most are members, in one form or another, of larger gremios or regional political organisations. Ranged alongside the community organisations are NGOs of one degree of professionalism or another.

Some are simply gremios that have assumed the task of generating funds and projects for constituent communities, while others operate at the national level with professional staffs and manage millions of dollars of aid annually. In contrast to both the FUSADES and the Buen Ciudadano models, the more formally organized NGOs in the popular sector generally are governed by a board of directors or general assembly composed of representatives of the communities served, of the cooperative associations, of the unions, and of the smaller NGOs. All depend upon external funding, though some generate money-making projects of their own, drawing on government contracts to cover operating expenses, or finding work on the side as commercial consultants. Many of the community organisations and most of the NGOs can confidently be associated with one or another of the original five parties of the FMLN, though such political ties are weakening.

To the extent that political ties remain strong, they carry divisions among NGOs with them, not to mention the occasional infighting. For example, the dismissal of the respected director of FASTRAS, Andres Gregori, in early 1994 was a direct result of the reorganisation that took place within the Expresion Renovadora del Pueblo (ERP), the faction of the FMLN led by Joaquin Villalobos. With this political blow, the European sponsor withdrew support and FASTRAS' innovative Programa Ecologico de Tecnologia Apropriada folded. Among the highly organized communities of the Fuerzas Popular de Liberacin (FPL), complaints continued to be heard in late 1994 regarding the party's imposition" of political leaders.

The end of the campaign season in 1994 reportedly brought a flood of personnel into the NGOs, securing employment for dubiously qualified activists after months of political work. Nevertheless, principles of community self government and popular participation arc well-entrenched in both the rhetoric and the philosophic outlook of many community members, NGOs, and political leaders. Meanwhile, and paradoxically, "professionalisation" has given NGO staffs greater autonomy *vis-a-vis* boards, parties, and the communities they serve. In theory and, to a large degree, in practice, the "popular sector" is quite organized in sharp contrast to the exclusive organisations sponsored by AID and the business elite.

However, this sector's vision of development is also in sharp contrast to that of the government and the FUSADES circle. The most common denominator among these organisations is their explicit advocacy of the principle of community participation in the design, development, and implementation of their projects. Beyond this demand, by now a commonplace of international development rhetoric, many of the popular organisations share a vision of establishing networks of economic enterprises among poor communities to provide the basis for genuine economic power and sustainability in the "new popular economy" model, as it is called. This vision, which is shared to one degree or another by most of the Left and many of their allies in the churches, certainly represents a challenge to the economic program advocated by FUSADES and by the patrons of FUSADES in Washington.

Whether it genuinely subverts the "gains" of the latter's program for the Salvadoran economy, as the Salvadoran elite evidently feel, is another question. From an objective point of view, those gains appear more illusory than real. The expansion of non-traditional exports, into which AID poured so much money and effort, has scarcely made up for the collapse of coffee, still the country's chief export. What sustains the economy today are the nearly $1 billion in remissions from Salvadorans living abroad, mostly in the United States. Now the North American Free Trade Agreement (NAFTA) and the rush to win terms of trade similar to that of NAFTA for Central America as a whole threaten the viability of much of El Salvador's industry. The privatized banking system has already seen its first failure.

With official US investment in rapid decline, and other sources of foreign aid apt to follow suit in the near future, there are few signs that the economic model embraced by the government will sustain the shock of greater integration into the world market. These realities put in question any Salvadoran project, whether driven by notions of "subsidiarity" and the free market, or by the alternative of solidarity and "market socialism."

HIS inquiry began with three questions: (1) what has been the effect on the peace process of the resurgence of civil society since 1985, and, in particular, has a resurgent civil society moved El Salvador toward reconciliation and democracy, or has it recapitulated and reinforced the polarisation which contributed to civil war? (2) What is the character of the civil society which has emerged? Are we witnessing a "democratisation" of society or a continuation of the vertical patterns that characterized both wartime and pre-war Salvador? Finally, (3) what has been the role of outside actors, particularly the United States, in the construction of a new civil society?

The answers are mixed on all three questions. Though the organisations of the new civil society have learned to work together at times, past and continuing politicisation has rendered minimal the effects of that cooperation which does exist. The government continues to direct its resources, almost overwhelmingly, to inefficient and, at times, corrupt government agencies, ARENA party mayors, and the "private sector" NGOs. On the other hand, NGOs in the "popular sector" continue to harbor jealousies of their party rivals, not only between the Left and Right but also within the Left as well. In general, the "dense web of civil associations" that has emerged in the new El Salvador has not been notable either for reducing tension or promoting reconciliation.

At times, indeed, the very fact of organisation has tended to heighten tension and lead to conflict. This is not altogether bad; in any society, genuine grievances must find organized expression before they can be addressed constructively. The "optimistic equation" is not so much wrong about the virtues of association as it is mistaken about the mechanisms for democratic amity. While the organisations of civil society might serve as vehicles for self-help in resolving problems and promoting cooperation, they must also do battle with the state, from time to time, on behalf of their members, as well as with other forces that stand in the way of solutions. The simple truth is that "civil associations" are important to people not only for the cooperative solutions they offer, but also for their ability to serve as advocates and combatants in behalf of their constituents.

Whether they make a positive contribution to democracies in the process of development depends more on the larger context and, in particular, on the response of the political system than it does on the reach, or nature, of the organisations themselves. The second question can be answered in a more positive vein, though with similar qualifications. To the extent that the people of El Salvador have organized representatives, intermediaries, and interlocutors to represent their interests, so will they be able to get their voices heard which will, in and of itself, help to further democracy. It may well be that what they have to say will be stifled or suffer distortion at every level, but only through organisation will it be possible for individual sentiments to be multiplied, reinforced, and strategically launched.

In this sense, then, democratic forums have multiplied, particularly in the former combat zones, where the FMLN approach to local organisation has carried over into communal assemblies, communal decision making, and some, apparently increasing, degree of accountability. The multiplication of NGOs has given people and communities choices and has helped to break down, at least in some cases, the party monopolies imposed by the war. The NGOs themselves have been forced to confront demands for accountability from a number of quarters, thereby reinforcing the participatory philosophies they espouse, if not always practice.

At the same time, not all NGOs advocate community development, democratisation, and accountability as central values; and not all that do profess such commitments carry them out. The mini-foundations of FUSADES' Project FORTAS are notably paternalistic, and there is no reason to think that a democratic civil society will quickly emerge out of them. Many of the "middle-of-road" NGOs also practice a top-down approach that places more of a premium on bringing projects to fruition than to community development and "democratic participation." The work they do, their ability to remain politically neutral in a highly polarized setting, as well as their professional approach is all important, but their overall contribution to the democratisation of Salvadoran society is primarily indirect.

The community organisations and NGOs of the Left continue to be plagued by partisanship and political manipulation. While circumstances and political philosophy push them to exhibit greater professionalism and respect for the autonomy of the communities and individuals with whom they work, political polarisation between, and within, both Left and Right continues to feed the demand for control. In short, while civil society in El Salvador today displays some vigorously democratic shoots, of equal vigor are those elements that reinforce the power, privilege, and control of the few, whether it be the economic elite of the Right or the political elite of the Left.

That the "dense web" of Salvadoran civil society consists of anti-democratic, as well as democratic, strands should come as no surprise. The equating of associational life with democracy, made by Alexis de Tocqueville in 1840, was premised on the existence of a political system that was already democratic; it was also notably free of economic or political polarisation. However, if de Tocqueville naively oversimplified the egalitarianism inherent in early US society, he also underestimated the forces that would lead to civil war in just a few short years. The truth is that associations may serve a variety of purposes. Though they arise from societal needs and aspirations, associations can quickly take on a life of their own, one that may be characterized by specialisation and strict accountability or by opportunistic expansion and unresponsiveness, by independence and autonomy from political forces or by tight integration into ongoing political struggles.

Moreover, the character of a society's associations may reflect the character of the rest of the society, so that their contribution to democracy will be only as strong or weak as the democracy itself. For Salvadoran civil society to be democratic, Salvadoran parties and the Salvadoran state will have to become more democratic. Democratisation of El Salvador cannot depend solely on the democratisation of civil society: parties, state, and civil society must all be democratized together. The democratic forces in civil society may contribute to that process but, ultimately, must be carried forward and ratified at the political level.

These answers anticipate the answer to the third query: what have foreigners contributed to the emergence of civil society in El Salvador? The evidence suggests a clear distinction must be made between the contribution of European donors and international NGOs on the one hand, and that of the United States government on the other. Whereas, throughout the war and afterwards, the European states and European Community helped support the community organisations and NGOs of the Left through a variety of channels, the United States, along with the Salvadoran government, waged war on them, even after peace was established.

While Europe used its influence on the ground, in the United Nations, and in such organisations as the United Nations Development Programme to promote an inclusive model of reconstruction and reconciliation, the United States preferred to deal exclusively with the Salvadoran government, a small band of US-sponsored NGOs and consulting firms, and those NGOs which US-AID had helped to create and nurture. While the European donors took an active part in developing pluralistic models for municipal and regional reconstruction, USAID refrained from doing so, preferring to endorse the Municipalities in Action program, operated by the ruling party, and backing the government in its hostility to multi-party participation. If AID did begin to soften its approach after 1993, this was clearly a case of too little, too late;" meanwhile, FUSADES and its NGO satellites have continued to be the favored recipients of AID largesse.

United States policy toward Salvadoran civil society was, by its very nature, designed to exclude: AID financed the development of an important segment of civil society, controlled and directed by elements of the business elite, with no provision for, or intent to include, any other elements of that society. It was also, by its very nature, a politicized policy: initially conceived as a counterweight to the economic policies of the Duarte government, it quickly served to bring business supporters of ARENA more into line with the views of the United States on a number of issues; however, it was carried out at the expense of the Left, through systematic isolation and harassment, and of those in the political center who supported alternative policies.

It was a polarizing policy as well: confident of US approbation, Salvadoran government and business leaders alike continued to exclude the Left from all development efforts (both government-affiliated and private), while they moved, at the same time, to consolidate their power over significant social institutions at both the national and local levels. Indeed, the wave of assassinations which followed the elections of March 1994 might lead one to give credence to the (privately expressed) view of one European development official, to the effect that "In El Salvador, what AID is doing is laying the groundwork for the next civil war, which I would guess we'll see in five or six years." Such an evaluation may be extreme, both in its prediction for the future and in its assessment of AID's role in the process, but it points up the very real dangers inherent in the policy that the United States chose to pursue.

If the AID approach did encompass a long-term vision, it was undoubtedly mistaken. A healthy civil society cannot be created via institutions designed to serve only one segment of society, nor through policies which operate to exclude, systematically, other significant sectors. Any choice of partners by external donors implies, ipso facto, a certain selectivity regarding the sorts of organisations and efforts that ought to be supported. There is no doubt that, for peace to be sustainable in El Salvador, the privileged classes had to feel well represented, if not secure, in the new postwar world. For peace to continue, they must continue to be represented. "Civil society" is, and should be, an enormous catch-all, where interests of every kind are free to come together, to organize, and to make their voices heard (if not felt).

In that sense, the AID strategy served an important purpose. It did not, however, serve well the process of reconciliation, which depends on isolating intransigent elements on both sides, privileging cooperation, and creating channels that resist political manipulation by any party. In choosing the weaker side, European donors and NGOs also helped to maintain the bases for polarizing organisation in civil society. But polarisation depended (and depends) overwhelmingly on the way in which the state and the parties manage power. The Europeans have striven to find ways to bring the parties together and ameliorate conflict, at least at the local level.

Ultimately, however, as our answers to the first two questions have already suggested, democracy in El Salvador depends on making a commitment to democracy at every level of society: at the state level, in its decision making and use of state resources; at the national political level, in the electoral arena and in the relations not only among parties, but between the parties and civil society; and, finally, at the local level, within civil society itself. Though foreign actors may continue to play a limited role, the requisite commitments to democratic principles can only arise from practice - from conflict, contestation, and cooperation in multiple arenas, over multiple issues large and small, and over much time. El Salvador's civil society will be an important protagonist in such experiences, but, reinvigorated though it may be, it cannot carry the whole burden of political change in what is still a much-divided society.

3

The ANZUS Conflict and New Zealand Politics

On July 14, 1984, New Zealanders voted into office a Labour government committed to banning nuclear-capable ships from visiting their country's ports. With that electoral verdict a major conflict between New Zealand and the United States over nuclear ship visits and the meaning of the security arrangement between the two created by the ANZUS treaty would soon erupt. Additionally, a complicated set of interactions involving the public, pressure groups, and political leadership in the policy-making process of New Zealand would become quite evident. As noted upon reflection by New Zealand's former Prime Minister David Lange, "our scrutiny of the [ANZUS] alliance with the United States caused a great deal of domestic controversy". This chapter examines the nature of this international conflict and the effect that it has had on politics within New Zealand.

Before the Labour government's ban on nuclear ship visits, thirteen nuclear-capable vessels-all of them flying the U.S. flag-had berthed in New Zealand waters between the first such stopover in April 1960 and the last in March 1984. It is the United States' view that the ANZUS Security Treaty, which was signed by Australia, New Zealand, and the United States in San Francisco in September 1951, requires its alliance partners to permit port access to United States warships, whether they are nuclear-capable or not. Before its change in nuclear policy, New Zealand, especially when governed by the National party, essentially endorsed the U.S. (and Australian) position that membership in ANZUS, and the security benefits that it provided, meant allowing all classes of U.S. warships into the country's harbors.

Prior to the recent controversy between New Zealand and the United States, relations between the two countries had been quite amicable. One of the most surprising aspects of the ANZUS controversy lay in the fact that it was so uncharacteristic of New Zealand foreign policy. Apart from a gesture of independence in the League of Nations in 1938 under the first Labour government, New Zealand had had an exemplary record as a faithful ally. Originally a colony of the United Kingdom, New Zealand supported Britain loyally, as a member both of the Empire and of the Commonwealth, whether in the Boer War or in the two world wars.

The statement of a Labour prime minister at the beginning of World War II-" where Britain goes, we go, where Britain stands, we stand"-was worn like a badge of honor. When, despite the pleas of the British government, Australia withdrew its troops from the Middle East Theater in 1942 to counter the Japanese threat in the Pacific, New Zealand remained steadfast in its commitment, even at the possible risk to its own shores. In the 1960s the New Zealand flag flew alongside those of its Australian and American allies in Vietnam. As recently as 1982, New Zealand dispatched a frigate on station in the Indian Ocean in order to support its old ally Britain in the Falklands War.

Despite its remoteness, New Zealand is virtually unrivaled for its participation in wars during the course of this century. Until 1984, constancy, reliability, and predictability were the watchwords of the country's external relations. What led to such a radical change in this long-established pattern of behaviour?

At the outset there is a need to distinguish between support and deference. For all of its minor differences with what was still widely referred to as the "mother" country, New Zealand's support of Britain in time of need was familial and unquestioning. The relationship with the United States, although close, tended to the deferential.

There is also the danger of being unable to distinguish between the formal ANZUS treaty and New Zealand-U.S. relations in general. For New Zealand, these relations were based upon common cause against Germany and Japan in World War II. Never was it intended for the United States to become the prevailing power in New Zealand's region of the Pacific Ocean. The 1944 Canberra Pact between Australia and New Zealand demonstrated "Australian and New Zealand determination not only to seek a full part in the final campaigns against Japan and in the peace settlement that would follow, but also to resist American domination of the post-war South-west Pacific". For the antipodean countries, ANZUS was the price extracted from the United States for its agreement to the Japanese Peace Treaty.

The secondary role of the ANZUS alliance for New Zealand was clearly illustrated during the 1956 Suez Crisis. Forced to choose between its traditional ally, Britain, and its new, immensely more powerful ally, the United States, New Zealand remained doggedly loyal to Britain, however ill-judged the venture. For its part, the United States initially appeared to have little enthusiasm for the treaty, showing "no eagerness to make ANZUS more than a means of exchanging views and information and of fostering a common approach to problems, and suspicions grew in Australia and New Zealand that the Eisenhower administration in Washington was cool towards the alliance".

Following the debacle of Suez and the later visit by the British secretary of state for Commonwealth relations in 1961, during which New Zealand was told of Britain's plan to gain entry into the European Common Market, with the consequent threat this action posed to New Zealand's economy, the center of gravity shifted. New Zealand had to recognize its more direct dependence upon the United States, which, as a result of the Korean War and the French collapse in Indochina, was evincing much greater interest in the affairs of the Pacific. For a time, it seemed that this direct dependence might be mitigated by the existence of the South-East Asia Treaty Organisation (SEATO), in which Britain was represented.

Such hopes were illusory, however. There was considerable controversy, for example, over how much New Zealand's commitment to Vietnam owed to the SEATO pact and how much of it arose out of ANZUS. It was not until the 1970s that ANZUS came to be recognized as the principal treaty that provided an external security blanket for New Zealand. Even so, New Zealanders envisioned ANZUS as only a party of its overall relationship with the United States. They tended to view the pact more as an alliance than as a binding formal treaty arrangement. It is arguable, for instance, that New Zealand's willingness to send troops to Vietnam was more the product of this alliance sentiment than the result of a specific treaty obligation.

Fundamentally, this was the cornerstone upon which in 1984 Prime Minister David Lange built his case for continuation of New Zealand's membership in ANZUS, but without nuclear ship visits by its treaty partners. What the Labour government failed to appreciate, however, was that although it might be possible to develop an alliance without a formal defense treaty, once a treaty was in place it would become virtually impossible to nullify its central provisions (whether specific or implied) without affecting the basic nature of the alliance.

The antinuclear thrust of New Zealand's position was nurtured in the activities of a myriad of pressure groups that dot the country's landscape. For a country with only three million people, New Zealand is lavishly endowed with an extensive pressure group system. Contrary to the central arguments of Mancur Olson, many of the strongest of these groups are driven by incentives that promote their view of the collective good of the country. Certainly this has been the case with peace and environmental organisations. Throughout the 1960s and 1970s in particular, environmental and peace groups worked steadily to educate the public about the dangers of nuclear energy and, especially, nuclear weapons. Local governing bodies were lobbied, usually effectively, to declare themselves nuclear-free zones-a cost-free exercise. As the various pollution-related problems of the Northern Hemisphere mounted, the relatively pollution-free environment of New Zealand became more prized.

The testing of nuclear weapons in the South Pacific by France served as a proximate reminder that nuclear issues were not all that far removed from New Zealand. In 1971, a public opinion poll found that 82 per cent of New Zealanders opposed French testing. A year later nearly 49 per cent supported a trade ban imposed on the unloading of French ships by New Zealand's leading labor union organisation-the Federation of Labour (FOL)-as a protest against nuclear testing in the region, even though the FOL was not very popular among most of the public. In the mid-1970s, 60 per cent approved of the Peace Media Foundation's sending of a flotilla into the French nuclear test zone.

Visits by nuclear-capable U.S. warships to New Zealand's ports became a direct target of antinuclear activists. Such forays into the country's waters were readily seen as an unwanted and unnecessary intrusion into the nuclear-free environment of New Zealand. In a country that appears to flourish on protest movements, protestors baiting these monsters on the waters in their dinghies, rowboats, and surfboards became a highly visible national sport. A large minority of the public endorsed the message of these protests. Several polls conducted between 1976 and 1983 show that a fairly constant 40 per cent of New Zealanders were opposed to the presence of nuclear-armed vessels in their country's harbors.

Despite the smallness of the New Zealand contribution, the Vietnam War too left deep scars on New Zealand society.. Although New Zealand troops in Vietnam were all volunteers and not conscripts as in the United States, young New Zealanders emulated their peers in the United States in mass protests and demonstrations on a scale rarely seen in their country. Law and order itself came to be on trial as the legitimacy of the state was questioned. The effect was to stimulate anti-Americanism, or, more accurately, strong opposition to U.S. foreign policy entanglements. For many New Zealanders, especially the young, U.S.-dominated alliance systems began to be viewed as a source of disharmony.

With the advent of the Vietnam War the pressures upon New Zealand to conform to U.S. policies clearly increased. As the costs of alliance participation mounted, questions were raised over the overall cost-benefit ratio of the alliance system, both domestically and internationally. Subsequently, a U.S. examination of attitudes in Australia and New Zealand described such views in detail. The alliance, it reported, could be seen as "potentially entrapping, pushing the two countries into unwelcome and yet unavoidable American adventures".

The questioning of discipline and authority that characterized the younger generation was not limited to internal politics but extended to great-power decisions, which began to be viewed as decidedly fallible. One consequence was that New Zealand's remoteness in the South Pacific, for so long widely considered as a source of weakness and vulnerability, came to be accepted as a source of strength. Thus, the effects of the Vietnam War served to reinforce powerfully the strains of the nationalism stimulated by Britain's blunt warning in 1961 that

New Zealand would have to stand on its own feet and learn to trade elsewhere.

By the early 1970s, with the initiation of Labour Prime Minister Norman Kirk's "moral" foreign policy and the protests against French nuclear testing in the Pacific, New Zealanders became growingly conscious of the reality of their position as an isolated, small South Pacific island-nation rather than as a part of the large whole that had once been the British Empire. The seeds of nationalistic independence were firmly planted as the pressures of ANZUS membership reminded New Zealanders of their dependence on the United States. Translating this uneasiness about alliance relations into public policy became the mission of members of the Labour party of New Zealand.

It should be borne in mind that, by and large, party government is live and well in New Zealand. That is, political parties are the principal mechanisms through which ideas are converted into public policy. The election of a party frequently means the transformation of that party's platform into government policy in New Zealand. At first, it was the left-wing members in the Labour party who questioned the meaning of alliance relations, especially with the United States. However, to attribute the acceptance of New Zealand's current antinuclear policy totally to these activists is unduly flattering, for the process of which they were a part was far more complex. It involved an intricate web of actors, the most important of whom were members of Parliament, pressure groups, and the public, as well as the Labour party.

The ban on nuclear ship visits is a classic example of Lindblom's "muddling through" rather than a clear-cut policy, resolutely pursued. Ineptitude, miscuing, and outright mistakes offer a less dramatic but far more convincing characterisation of this policy process than a conspiracy organized by left-wing radicals. A consistent thread in the process was to be found in the internal organisation of the Labour party. Calls at the party's annual conferences to withdraw from great-power alliances, such as SEATO and ANZUS were regular features on the agenda from at least 1956 onward. Although initially little more than of nuisance value, the Vietnam War, in particular, spurred a steady rise in the curve of support from delegates for these measures.

Party leaders and members of Parliament, however, were aware that the opinions of delegates, although well argued, were frequently highly spiced emotional appeals not shared by the bulk of the general public. Non-nuclearism, like pacifism, was generally regarded as an impractical ideal. Nevertheless, support also grew gradually for remits opposing the establishment or extension of nuclear facilities, whether in the form of ships, submarines, missiles, or navigational aides. In fact, no nuclear ship visits took place between 1965 and 1975; because of doubts relating to legal liability should any of the ships have a nuclear accident while in port.

During this interlude ANZUS, however, was not affected by any important precedent in Labour party thinking. When nuclear ship visits resumed in 1976, the issues of ANZUS and such visits were firmly fused in the minds of conference delegates, although important Labour officials, such as shadow defense minister Michael Connelly, remained tightly tethered to the principles of ANZUS-including the propriety of nuclear ship visits. However, the Labour leadership position on visits by nuclear-capable vessels and ANZUS was steadily being undermined from two directions. On the one hand, the rank and file of the party organisation was strengthening its hold on the policy-making machinery.

On the other, an attack on former Labour Prime Minister Bill Rowling by his National party successor, Prime Minister Robert Muldoon, was to eventually have the effect of elevating the prohibition of the nuclear ships issue from conference resolution to official party policy. When David Lange became leader of the Labour party in 1983, he suggested that the party's defense policy should be altered to conform to that of its Australian counterpart, which allowed for the passage of nuclear-propelled, but not nuclear-armed, warships. At that time, Lange made no secret of his belief that Labour's nuclear weapons-free zone could only be achieved realistically if a Labour government accommodated visits by nuclear-powered ships. In Lange's words: "My objective is to get as much assurance of an absence of nuclear weaponry as possible". Lange was bluntly informed by the president of the party, Jim Anderton, however, that the leader had no power to modify party policy. The party thus contested the 1984 election on a policy banning nuclear ship visits in any form.

Ironically, during New Zealand's relatively short campaign period, it was the then-sitting Prime Minister, Sir Robert Muldoon, who mostly sought to make nuclear ship visits an election issue. Muldoon insisted that banning such visits would lead to an end of the ANZUS alliance. The Labour party countered that New Zealand could adopt an antinuclear policy and still have the protection of ANZUS. Two of the country's more important minor parties supported Labour's ban. Indeed, the espousal of that policy by the New Zealand party - widely regarded as a right-wing or libertarian -oriented party -helped make the call for a ban politically respectable.

Labour's electoral victory in July 1984 did not necessarily guarantee that its antinuclear pledge would become governmental policy. Given the propensity of New Zealand's political parties to make a multitude of election promises, many of which are broad and unspecific, no government ever succeeds in implementing all of them. Promises that may either be too difficult to implement or politically embarrassing may be dropped well down the list of agenda items. Because of the irreconcilable nature of Labour's pledge to be in a nuclear-free ANZUS, banning the visits of nuclear-capable vessels seemed a likely candidate for such treatment. Moreover, Labour's counterpart party in Australia backed off its promise to restrict nuclear-armed warships from its country's waters after Bob Hawke became prime minister.

THE CONFLICT

The night after his victory Prime Minister-elect David Lange met with Secretary of State George Shultz in Wellington. What exactly transpired at this meeting is open to interpretation. Lange contends that he steadfastly reaffirmed his party's intention to implement its "no nukes" promise as soon as the Labour government was in place. U.S. officials claim that Lange refused to either confirm or deny whether his campaign pledge would be honored. This hedge was taken by the Americans as an encouraging sign that an acceptable accommodation could be reached. Regardless, it was made clear to the New Zealand prime minister-elect that a ban on nuclear ships would be adjudged by Washington as a serious breach of the ANZUS alliance and sanctions would follow such an action.

The situation soon began to clarify. In November 1984, the United States requested and was granted blanket permission for visits of any of its non-nuclear-capable vessels. This was in line with the general policy of the New Zealand government which specifically "welcomes visits by naval vessels that are not nuclear armed or powered". Indeed, between 1958 and 1984 there had been more than 150 visits to New Zealand (not counting multiple port calls by the same vessel) by nonnuclear American ships. With regard to nuclear ship visits, Lange, speaking at the end of 1984, appeared to minimize any potential problems by suggesting that the Americans would not seek port access of such vessels because they would not want to be rebuffed by New Zealand. He believed that Washington officials were intelligent, perceptive, and reluctant to engage in some needless, provocative incident: "We have the utmost co-operation on this matter".

This optimism quickly faded. In early 1985, after a series of private meetings between members of the New Zealand and U.S. governments, it was decided that the United States would seek permission to berth the *USS Buchanan* in New Zealand. The *Buchanan* was a rather old destroyer with, in all probability, no nuclear capability. New Zealand countered that the visit would be permitted only if the government could be fully assured that the *Buchanan* was not nuclear armed or powered. Given Washington's refusal to divulge such information, it became the responsibility of the prime minister to determine the nuclear properties of the *Buchanan.* Lange's inability to totally rule out a nuclear quality to the *Buchanan* led to a denial of port access and the cancellation by the United States of the proposed visit.

This sequence of events turned out, in retrospect, to be the breaking point in U.S.-New Zealand relations over the nuclear ships issue. As noted by McMillan, "if the United States had not requested access for the *USS Buchanan* and if New Zealand had not refused access, the worst of the dispute between the two countries might have been avoided." Why did the proposed visit of an old non-nuclear-powered ship cause such difficulties? It seems clear that the request for the *Buchanan* visit represented a genuine attempt by the Americans to accommodate New Zealand's interests. There was considerable speculation at the time of the request that this ship was chosen in order for the United States to test whether New Zealand's new policy could accommodate the strict American code of neither confirming nor denying the presence of nuclear weaponry aboard its ships.

There was also reason to believe that Lange had been given an unofficial assurance by Washington that the *Buchanan* would not be nuclear armed and that, accordingly, the Americans expected no difficulty with their request for a visit. True, the prime minister has emphatically denied any suggestions about a secret assurance, but, curiously, he was also reported as saying:

"Had the *USS Buchanan* come to New Zealand...the United States would have moved strenuously to ensure it was not carrying nuclear weapons". A subsequent statement by the U.S. ambassador to New Zealand, H. Monroe Browne, that the New Zealand government had refused the visit "apparently because it could not satisfy it that the ship was not nuclear armed" can also be read as supporting this viewpoint. Certainly in private conversations with U.S. officials both in the State Department and in New Zealand, the overwhelming impression received is that Washington had done everything possible to accommodate Lange's requirements.

Rightly or wrongly, U.S. officials believed that there had been a tacit understanding with the prime minister that the *Buchanan* would be admitted. Consequently there was a deep sense of betrayal when the request was denied. The mistrust of Prime Minister Lange was further exacerbated by the fact that he was absent on a private visit to the Tokelau Islands at a crucial stage of the proceedings. What had hitherto been a policy controversy now became, for the Americans, a matter of duplicity. On the other side, Lange could well have experienced a disjunction between what he could promise as leader and what he could perform as prime minister.

Recall that as the newly elected leader of the Labour party in 1983 Lange had unsuccessfully sought to restrict official party policy to banning only nuclear-armed vessels. The main problem, however, was the nuclear ban itself. Just as the original election manifesto promise to prohibit nuclear ship visits and to retain ANZUS was an improbable combination, so too the evolution of the policy to "trust me" (meaning Lange) to make an independent assessment of the nuclear capability of U.S. ships based upon New Zealand intelligence reflected little more than political naivetı. Regardless of the justification, as of February 4, 1985, the proposed visit of the *USS Buchanan* to New Zealand was off. The United States immediately held New

Zealand in violation of Article II of the ANZUS treaty, which calls for "the Parties separately and jointly by means of continuous and effective self-help and mutual aid [to] maintain and develop their individual and collective capacity to resist armed attack."

Sanctions were swiftly invoked. The United States cancelled an invitation previously extended to New Zealand to participate in scheduled naval exercises. The amount of military intelligence supplied to New Zealand by U.S. sources was substantially reduced. New Zealand was denied the right to purchase equipment for its defense forces at specially discounted prices. Meetings between high-level officials of each country's government were deliberately voided by Washington. Furthermore the Reagan administration moved to hurt New Zealand's economic base by dropping its opposition to Congressional legislation trying to restrict agricultural imports (upon which New Zealand depends so heavily) into the United States, withdrawing support for New Zealand's butter sales in third countries, reducing the quota of beef imported from New Zealand, and using American influence in Europe or Japan to encourage a reduction in the purchase of New Zealand dairy products. The nuclear ships conflict was at its zenith.

DOMESTIC REACTION

The public reaction to the Labour government's ban on nuclear warships was swift and enthusiastic. In August 1984, less than a month after the government announced its policy, 76 per cent of New Zealanders noted their approval of the ban on the entry of nuclear weapons into their country. A year earlier, without such a prohibition in effect, only 46 per cent of the public disapproved of visits by nuclear-armed warships. Hence the government's antinuclear policy received a wide round of applause from most of the New Zealand public.

As has been argued elsewhere, this massive swing behind the government's policy suggests a consolidation effect. That is, the New Zealand public appears to have rallied behind their government as the conflict with the United States developed. Cleavages that structured nuclear opinion before the ANZUS controversy erupted disappeared as the public closed ranks in support of their government. In 1983 disapproval of nuclear ship visits was manifested more among women than men, more among the young than the old, more among higher- than lower-status New Zealanders, and more among Labour and third-party supporters than partisans of the National party. After the antinuclear policy was proclaimed, these differences faded.

Across the board, gender, age, socioeconomic status, and party affiliation became less important in differentiating nuclear opinion. For instance, in 1983 when the National government permitted nuclear ship visits, only 23 per cent of that party's faithful opposed this policy. A year later, even though their party had just suffered a rather humiliating defeat in the 1984 election, 63 per cent of National identifiers supported the Labour government's ban. This 40 per cent movement in opinion was the largest shift recorded among political and social groups in New Zealand between 1983 and 1984. Such public rallies behind government policies in times of international conflict are not uncommon.

Foreign policy initiatives in the United States and Britain usually are followed by public consolidation in support of these endeavours. There is an abundance of social, psychological, and anthropological evidence demonstrating that external threat breeds internal group solidarity. Indeed, Darendorf concludes that this asymmetrical effect constitutes a "general law." As the ANZUS conflict intensified, public consolidation, at least on the surface, remained intact. Immediately after New Zealand rejected the proposed *Buchanan* visit and the United States responded by invoking sanctions, the public stood firm in its support of the ban on nuclear weapons.

A poll conducted on February 9, 1985-four days after the *Buchanan* visit was cancelled-found 73 per cent of New Zealanders agreeing with the Labour government's prohibition. Some five weeks later, after thc U.S. threats and sanctions had been aired, the public approval score had improved to 77 per cent. Moreover, a critical, defensive attitude developed among the ban's supporters. For them, New Zealand was being treated unfairly by the United States. Their country had not neglected its treaty responsibilities. If it came to the point of choosing between allowing nuclear ships port access or breaking defense ties with the United States, most of these New Zealanders preferred the latter course of action.

In many ways the public's solidarity limited the Labour government's maneuverability during the ANZUS crisis. Peace groups could legitimately talk of a consensus of antinuclear feeling in New Zealand. Any perceived deviation from Labour's anti nuclear policy on the part of government officials, including the prime minister, could be resoundingly criticized by these activists. Moreover, leaders of these groups had direct access to Labour MPs. Indeed, several of these MPs were openly sympathetic, if not politically indebted, to these groups. When, for instance, it was thought that the prime minister might be softening his antinuclear stand in his discussions with the Americans over the request for the *Buchanan* visit, peace activists and a handful of Labour MPs sternly reminded Lange of the widespread public support for his government's ban.

Even its adversaries pressured the government to conform to its antinuclear commitment. In 1985, for instance, the deputy leader of the Democratic Party, one of New Zealand's more successful third parties, introduced a bill to enact the "no nukes" policy into law, as promised in Labour's election manifesto. The purpose of this action was, of course, to embarrass the government and to emphasize the lack of progress that had been made in moving toward creating the promised legislative backbone to the nuclear ships ban. Hence, through a variety of means, the issue was kept before the public. The matter was, after all, official public policy and support for it by members of the parliamentary wing of the party and some ministers meant that the government had scant room even for agenda manipulation.

For example, Lange's search for a means by which New Zealanders could be assured that the *Buchanan* was not nuclear-capable could not cross a threshold of public acceptability. Evidence, such as a ship's point of departure or the nature of its delivery systems, could have been offered as proof. However, without U.S. confirmation or denial such information could have been held by the public to be suspect. Considering that Washington was resolute in sticking to its "neither confirm nor deny" policy, New Zealand was left to trust that the United States would not send a nuclear vessel. Given the widespread perception among New Zealanders that the Americans had violated its promised embargo on allowing nuclear weapons to enter Japan's water, the Labour government would have been publicly ridiculed if it had accepted a Japanese-style solution based upon trust.

The prime minister-particularly a Labour prime minister-whatever his personal inclinations or the pressures brought to bear by a super-power ally, had little alternative but to give priority to domestic considerations. Moreover, the government found the nuclear ships issue to be very useful in trying to maintain its appeal among its natural constituents. For a myriad of reasons, Labour, once in government, embarked upon a domestic economic program that contravened the preferences of many segments of its coalition base. More specifically, the government launched a market-oriented approach to solve the economic and financial problems plaguing New Zealand.

Privatisation of state-owned assets, restructuring of government departments, user pays in a wide variety of areas, including tertiary education, and tax packages designed to stimulate business growth were pursued aggressively by the government. Such policies ran counter to the ideological tradition and the thrust of the Labour party, leading to growing uneasiness and restlessness among many of its traditional members and supporters-especially those in trade unions. Thus, the government needed a high-profile, popular policy that would clearly signal that this was in fact a Labour government, standing on Labour principles. Here, the nonnuclear policy provided the obvious, necessary trade-off.

With public support in full swing, the government entered into the post-*Buchanan* phase of the ANZUS conflict without much room to change the direction of its policy. After several failed attempts at negotiation, the United States declared in 1986 that by sticking to its nonnuclear policy New Zealand had, in effect, withdrawn from the ANZUS treaty arrangement. The United States would no longer guarantee the military protection of its once close and faithful ally. For its part, the Labour government in 1987 went further by enacting its policy into legislation, thus requiring any future government to change the law if it wanted to revoke the antinuclear ban.

The Labour government appears to have gained a great deal of electoral mileage out of its nuclear ships ban. The Labour party went into the 1987 national election riding the crest of a wave of widespread popularity. Indicative of this phenomenon is the fact that the National party, hitherto the only party to welcome nuclear ship visits, shifted ground during the 1987 campaign in order to accommodate public sentiment on this issue. National's leadership began to argue in favor of no nuclear weapons in the country, stressing that it would trust Washington not to request port access for vessels carrying such armament into New Zealand.

Moreover, there is some evidence showing that Labour's nuclear position served, on balance, to constrain wholesale defection by voters who were disenchanted with the market direction of the government's economic and social policies. Hence the consolidation effect precipitated by the initial conflict that flared over the nuclear ships ban had a great influence over the conduct of domestic policy making and politics in New Zealand. However, the lasting importance of this consolidation remained problematic for two reasons. First, the structural scope of the antinuclear attitude was limited. It only encompassed views toward nuclear weapons and criticism of the U.S. treatment of New Zealand during the height of the controversy.

Opinion toward visits by nuclear-powered vessels and the overall public commitment to membership in ANZUS were not fully enveloped within this attitude structure. Second, there were signs that the solidarity that had emerged among all groups of New Zealanders in the initial phase of the conflict was showing signs of disintegration. On the first point: New Zealanders-both before and after the conflict- showed a greater willingness to accept the berthing of nuclear-powered ships than nuclear-armed vessels. In 1982, 38 per cent opposed port visits by nuclear-propelled ships. Within a month after the 1984 controversy occurred, that figure had increased only 8 per cent (to 46 per cent).

Public disapproval of visits by nuclear-powered ships increased as the conflict intensified in early 1985. But even after the cancellation of the *Buchanan* visit and the imposition of sanctions by the United States, the public disapproval of nuclear-powered vessels reached only 52 per cent, some 25 per cent less than the number of New Zealanders rejecting the entry of nuclear weapons into their country. Moreover, many New Zealanders continued to value ANZUS membership even at the height of the nuclear ships conflict. A nationwide poll conducted in February 1985 uncovered widespread support for continued membership in ANZUS: 78 per cent of the public approved of New Zealand's participation in the alliance, while only 12 per cent disapproved.

In both March and October of that year, New Zealanders were evenly divided when forced to choose between breaking defense ties with the United States and allowing nuclear-armed ships into their country's ports. A year later, most (44 per cent) preferred a nuclear-free ANZUS to being in ANZUS with nuclear ship visits (37 per cent), and to no such ships and no ANZUS membership (16 per cent). When pushed to choose between a nuclear-free policy and ANZUS membership, a majority (52 per cent) stated-albeit, for some, quite reluctantly-that they would prefer being in ANZUS *with* nuclear ship visits to having a nonnuclear policy and withdrawal from the alliance (44 per cent).

On the second point: As early as February 1985, some cracks in the foundation of the consolidation effect were becoming evident. Cleavages in opinion toward the ban on nuclear weapons emerged along much the same lines as had existed in 1983 before the ANZUS conflict. Specifically, age, gender, and party identification again came to structure opinion. By February 1985, nearly 10 percentage points separated the support given to the ban on nuclear weapons by New Zealanders under and those over age 40. Six months earlier, this age division did not exist. However, a similar age difference was evidence in 1983, a year before the outbreak of the ANZUS conflict.

A generational gap in opinion on nuclear matters is not uncommon in many capitalistic, industrialized societies. In New Zealand this age division, by and large, reflects pre- and post-World War II experiences and socialisation. Younger New Zealanders have been raised largely free from a major war commitment, the ravages of the great depression, and a dependent orientation toward Britain. They have been urged to be independent-minded and assertive. They had also benefited from the availability of higher education and a beneficent and broad set of social welfare policies. As the post-World War II baby boom came of political age, self-confident, idealistic youth became increasingly effective in its questioning of long-established positions and attitudes.

Many young people tended to view an alliance system dominated by the United States as a source of disharmony. Not surprisingly, they were more likely to accept the ban on nuclear weapons. Interestingly, Prime Minister David Lange, in his early forties when the ban went into effect, clearly identified with this generation. Many in the older generation attributed the stopping of the Japanese occupation of the Pacific before it reached New Zealand's shores during World War II to the United States. For them, the ANZUS alliance provided a guarantee of New Zealand's security, a unique entree into the counsels of greater power, and a continuation of a long tradition of New Zealand internationalism making a contribution to the overall peace of the world.

Gender also reemerged in early 1985 to structure views on the ban on nuclear weapons. By March a 7 per cent difference in opinion between men and women had replaced a nil gap in August 1984, when the consolidation effect occurred. This difference was the same as that which had existed prior to the ANZUS conflict. A great deal of research shows that women are more likely than men to be antinuclear and pacific in outlook. New Zealand women fit this pattern well. The combined effects of gender and age on nuclear opinion are quite pronounced. This is especially the case for young women and older men. In March 1985, there was a 25 per cent difference between these two groups in reaction to the Labour government's nuclear ships ban. Young women overwhelmingly approved of the policy, while older men mostly rejected the government's position.

This age/gender separation existed in 1983 before the controversy, but it became muted immediately after the initial conflict erupted in July 1984. Party identification normally plays a major role in structuring opinion about issues in New Zealand politics. The previously noted dampening of differences in nuclear opinion between partisans that occurred in the immediate wake of the ANZUS controversy soon began to change. By March 1985, Labour and National loyalists were divided by 37 per cent in their views of the ban. In May 1986 this separation had increased to 43 per cent. Studies of voting behaviour in the 1987 national election revealed that support for the government's nuclear policy was strongly associated with party affiliation.

Hence, as the ANZUS conflict wore on, age, gender, and party again exerted influence on nuclear opinion. The consolidation effect was most intact immediately after the initial announcement of the ban on nuclear ships was made in 1984. It began to show signs of slippage as the controversy continued, despite the escalation of the war of words between Wellington and Washington that transpired in early 1985. Moreover, by May 1986 the overall public support for the government's policy had shrunk some 11 per cent, from nearly 77 per cent in March 1985 to 66 per cent a year later. The consolidation effect appeared on the brink of disintegration.

The United States could take some heart in the likelihood that public support for the ban was beginning to soften. This might account for the development of a low-key approach to the problem by Washington as the conflict continued. For instance, the United States terminated New Zealand's involvement in the alliance rather quietly. It limited its punitive sanctions mostly to military and intelligence matters, leaving direct economic embargos largely out of the recrimination program. Furthermore, it maintained and even expanded its commitments and presence in the country along other fronts. Finally, it surely hoped that, if New Zealanders elected a National government in 1990, a more agreeable ships policy would be put into place.

While all official contact with Labour government leaders was routinely shunned, Washington publicly courted members of the opposition. For its part, the National leadership-until early 1990-openly came to advocate a ships policy based on trust. Keeping in mind the Japanese approach to nuclear ship visits, National leaders announced that they would have the utmost confidence in the United States not to send vessels carrying nuclear weapons into New Zealand's waters. In the meantime, some disturbing counter-evidential events were widely publicized in New Zealand. The Chernobyl explosion in the Soviet Union not only was a vivid reminder of the danger of nuclear accidents; it also economically benefited New Zealand, the home of noncontaminated agricultural products.

In 1989, it was revealed that some twenty five years earlier, a U.S. fighter airplane equipped with a nuclear bomb had fallen from an aircraft carrier that had just visited Japan. The news raised questions about whether a Japanese approach to nuclear-free waters would be honored in practice by the Americans. This incident, coupled with reports of a series of fires and faults aboard nuclear vessels throughout the world in the first half of 1989, probably reinforced public concern over the risk of nuclear accidents at sea. Indeed, earlier polling had recorded that fear of accidents was one of the major reasons given by New Zealanders when they were asked why they opposed nuclear ship visits to their country.

New Zealand's nuclear ships policy was thrust back onto the center stage of domestic politics on April 25, 1989, when then-Prime Minister Lange delivered a lecture at Yale University in which he fully discussed the ANZUS crisis. In his address, Mr. Lange "raise[d] the issue of whether New Zealand should give formal notice of withdrawal from the ANZUS Council". The speech was roundly criticized in the New Zealand press as a transparent attempt by Lange to shore up this sagging popular support at home; as inappropriate, coming as it did on ANZAC day, a day of remembrance of New Zealand's participation in past wars; and as a sign that Lange was out of step with his own cabinet, which had not been consulted prior to his announcement of the threat to withdraw New Zealand from the ANZUS Council altogether.

Missing from this environment of cross-signals over the nuclear ships controversy was information about the New Zealand public's view of the matter. Had the consolidation effect totally unraveled? Or was there still substantial support for New Zealand's antinuclear stand? Popular sentiment about these matters had not been measured since 1986. To gauge the current state of opinion, we commissioned the Heylen Research Centre, one of the country's foremost polling organisations, to survey a national representative sample. Personal interviews took place on June 10, 1989.

Support for the "Labour government's policy to ban the entry of nuclear weapons into New Zealand" was at 83.5 per cent, the highest approval score yet recorded on this policy. Only 3.5 per cent had no opinion of the matter. Moreover, public opposition to visits by nuclear-powered vessels had also strengthened. By 1989, 63 per cent of New Zealanders approved of the government's ban on these vessels, an 11 per cent increase in approval since the question was last asked in 1985 at the height of the ANZUS dispute. Finally, on balance, New Zealanders-by a margin of 51.6 per cent to 39.7 per cent-preferred breaking defense ties with the United States to allowing nuclear-armed ships into their ports. When forced to choose between a "no nukes" policy and the military protection of the ANZUS alliance, the public chose the former.

Positive feelings about New Zealand's antinuclear policy have crystallized as time has elapsed. Even though the conflict has come off the international boil and the United States has replaced overt threats with low-key diplomatic inducements, there is still widespread public support for the nuclear ships ban. It is difficult to argue that this outlook is simply a continuation of the consolidation effect that resulted when New Zealanders rallied around their government in response to external pressure. Some variations in nuclear opinion between social and political groups existed in 1989. Party identification divided public sentiment sharply. On average, 85 per cent of Labour supporters approved of the ban on nuclear-armed and - powered vessels, as well as leaving the alliance in order to preserve a nuclear-free New Zealand.

While consistency prevailed among Labour partisans, such was not the case among their National counterparts. The latter supported the ban on nuclear weapons, but their approval declined in the case of nuclear-powered ships, and it did not extend to abandoning the alliance. As a result of these inconsistencies, the average score on the three nuclear questions for National supporters was 47 per cent. These findings had some clear policy implications. The Labour government would have found it most difficult to retreat from its antinuclear stance. By 1989, this was probably the only policy area widely endorsed by the New Zealand public.

Along virtually all other policy fronts, the government had become very unpopular during its second term in office. Specifically, it received low ratings in its handling of economic, educational, health, and race relations issues. Only a small fraction of the public - about one in five-considered the government's overall performance to be satisfactory. The government's credibility was such that even to hint at a break from its antinuclear policy would have been fatal to its chances for reelection. Thus when a change of leadership took place with the resignation of the Prime Minister, David Lange, in August 1989, his successor, Deputy Prime Minister Geoffrey Palmer, immediately announced that there would be no alteration in the country's antinuclear policy.

Meanwhile, the National party was receiving mixed signals from the public. The widespread growth in public support for a nuclear-free New Zealand made promising an early return to the alliance (and the possibility of renewed nuclear ship visits if the party became the government) an electoral risk. A strong element of National supporters approved of the ban on nuclear weapons. However, many of these partisans preferred being in the alliance to sticking with the ban, thus putting some interesting cross-pressure on the party leadership. Men and women across the spectrum of socioeconomic status approved of the prohibition of nuclear-capable ships. Age, however, differentiated nuclear opinion in 1989.

The younger the New Zealander, the more the support for a ban on nuclear-armed and -powered vessels, even if such an endorsement meant breaking defense ties with the United States. Conversely, older New Zealanders were the least supportive of these positions. The age-related patterns become even more interesting when gender is added into the picture. Younger (under age 40) women were the most supportive of the government's antinuclear policies, followed in order by younger (under 40) men, older women, and older men. By and large, the younger the gender group, the greater the antinuclear support. For instance, 85 per cent of the youngest (age 15 to 24) women in the sample approved of the ban on nuclear-powered vessels, while only 46 per cent of men over 55 agreed with this position. This 39 per cent difference in opinion indicated a wide gender/age gap on nuclear matters in New Zealand.

Antinuclear opinion in New Zealand went from minority status to a widely supported public policy in a very short period of time. The initial ANZUS conflict resulted in a widespread public rally behind its government. Interestingly, apart from some heated political rhetoric, the conflict-as far as international conflicts go-was rather mild in nature. No shots were fired. No invasion occurred. Direct economic sanctions were threatened but not comprehensively carried out. Regardless, the U.S.

reaction to New Zealand's ban on nuclear ship visits precipitated a consolidation of public opinion behind the government's position.

The internal dynamism of New Zealand's political system affected this transformation of minority opinion to popular policy. Most of the country's leading parties promoted the antinuclear view. Peace groups tenaciously pursued the acceptance of antinuclear policy, both at the elite and mass levels. Labour members of Parliament kept a watchful eye on the party's leaders to prevent any waver in the implementation of this policy.

The widespread support for the Labour government's stand against berthing nuclear vessels gained it valuable public support at critical junctures as it systematically introduced a controversial market-oriented approach to the country's economic problems. Conversely, the government had limited scope for maneuverability in its attempts to resolve the nuclear conflict with the United States. As a result, the government refused requests for ship visits and the United States withdrew its military support for New Zealand and cut intelligence links. The ANZUS treaty soon became a dead letter for New Zealand although a bilateral connection with Australia remained.

It was not until March 1990 that any sign of a thaw in the frozen relations between the two countries was signaled. At that time, Secretary of State James Baker announced that the United States would welcome talks with high-ranking officials of the New Zealand government, although he reaffirmed Washington's opposition to the nuclear ships ban and its intention not to provide New Zealand with military intelligence and equipment. The Labour government responded favorably to this development, but quickly emphasized its continued commitment to the nuclear ban.

The consolidation in public opinion regarding the nuclear ships ban appeared to weaken as the controversy wore on. By

1986, some slippage in support for the ban on nuclear ships had occurred. Moreover, as early as 1985, social and political points of cleavage among New Zealanders began again to differentiate nuclear opinion. Party identification especially divided the public. The opposition National party-along with the U.S. government-could take hope in the growing number of supporters coming to oppose the ban. However, a subsequent round of opinion testing indicated that approval of the ban and its implications for breaking alliance ties had firmed.

The firming of widespread and consistent endorsement of this position suggests that antinuclear sentiment was becoming a mainstay of the country's political culture. In many ways, the commitment to anti nuclearism appears to have transcended partisan politics and has become a national symbol, one that may have been initially created in response to outside pressure but that now exists as a signature of New Zealand identity. Young New Zealanders are coming to political maturity overwhelmingly socialized into this outlook.

Indeed, the last bastion of opposition to anti nuclearism resides among their older counterparts. Not surprisingly, in March 1990 the National Party-the last major political organisation to oppose Labour's ban-switched its position on nuclear ships visits and announced that, if it formed the government, it too would not accept such vessels into New Zealand's ports, regardless of ANZUS. With that proclamation all political elites in New Zealand became totally synchronized with popular sentiment. Consequently, it is hard to envision the day when nuclear-capable ships will again come into New Zealand's waters.

4

The Sartrean Account: The Look and its Conflicts

At the center of his ontological treatise, *Being and Nothingness*, in a section titled "The Look," Sartre creates a small narrative moment of dubious virtue in which he is able to resolve one of the truly vexing problems of phenomenology up to his time. It is the problem of the Other. How is it that one can apprehend the Other as subject? Previously, philosophy had sought to understand the other through reflection or attribution. But to regard the other as a reflection of oneself ends in an obvious solipsism: all others would be only reflections of oneself. To define the other as a subject simply because one saw a person standing there reduces subjectivity irretrievably to object status. And to attribute subjectivity to the other as an extension of experience with oneself as a subject renders one a source of mere doctrine through which to see others. Yet to proclaim the other to be unknowable as a subject leaves no basis upon which to speak about personal and social relations.

In the context of twentieth-century Euro-American society, characterized by alienation and a closing down of public or political space, each of these possibilities (reflection and attribution) becomes egregious in providing a mechanical solution to the question- collaboration with that sense of alienation. Hence, the importance of Sartre's argument. A coherent response to the question of the Other as subject that avoids the classical traps renews the necessary sense that in others there is someone there, and that one has the possibility of real interaction.

Sartre's account of the look, of one's visibility to another, reverses the terms of the problem. For Sartre, the Other-as-subject is a subject known not through oneself but as a disruption 0f oneself, One confronts the Other in a space that is both one's own and not of one's choosing; and in that space, one apprehends the Other as subject in one's becoming an object for that Other, i.e., through the Other's effect on oneself. It is this sense of becoming an object for another that de-centers the egocentric emphasis of traditional Western phenomenology and opens an exterior space between persons, where dialogue becomes possible. The question of what constitutes dialogue has become an important issue, in the US especially.

Priding itself on maintaining the eighteenth-century notion of "freedom of speech," which resides at the heart of the concept of civil liberties and thus of the modern nation, the "US ethos" has lost sight of the fact that freedom of speech is a monologic concept. It does not provide for social interaction or for the existence of a political space of cooperative participation through speech. It simply says that one may say what one likes (with certain exceptions). In an era in which the means of dissemination of speech and information are themselves monopolized by corporate structures and commercial interests, the guarantee of freedom of speech does not extend to a guarantee of channels of expression that matter.

Indeed, corporate control of the media has in effect rendered the freedom of speech an empty right- that is, an empty rite that may seek solidarity, but only within the sound of one's voice. It would serve us well, in that case, to revisit and examine Sartre's ontology of the look and, in particular, his extension of it to what he calls being-for-others, in order to approach an ontology of dialogue, and the ethics contained in it, as relevant to our relation to public space and thus to political life. If, as Wilfred Desan has said, Sartre's philosophy represents "the most extreme form of freedom the history of philosophy has ever presented," then it behooves us to see if it will provide a mode of freedom beyond that of ritualistic freedom of speech.

Yet Sartre's account contains an obvious problem, which has already served to obstruct just such a project. If one apprehends the Other as a subject through having been rendered an object for the Other in the look, when one reciprocates, retrieving one's own subject hood by returning the look, one thereby renders the Other an object for oneself in turn. And the ensuing oscillation of successive objectivisations signifies an unending conflict as the originary nature of this process of interaction. An uneasy balance of subjectivities can be achieved as a contingent mutuality, but it is an unstable structure, continually on the verge of breakdown.

Each individual lives in peril of the Other's re-objectivizing look; both stand ready with a pre-emptive look in order to preserve their own autonomy, subjectivity, and freedom- a kind of ontological Cold War. This contingent mutuality is what Sartre calls one's being-for-others. As a pragmatic inter-subjectivity (or what Levinas would call an example of philosophy's "ontic style"), being-for-others "appears as a pure irreducible contingency"; one makes the Other be, and at the same time apprehends the Other in situation as who one has to not be. But in that sense, being-for-others cannot be intersubjectivity, since each subjectivity exists only through the cancellation of the Other.

To reveal oneself as a subject implies reducing the Other to an object in order to do so. For the Other to be a subject to whom to reveal oneself, one must submit oneself to becoming an object in turn. As a project toward ontological intersubjectivity, being-for-others is self-defeating. Being-for-others "represents the negation of any synthetic totality," a seemingly irresolvable arena of disunion between individuals. As Sartre puts it, "conflict is [its] original meaning". For an array of commentators, the irreconcilability of this conflict, implicit as it is in the absoluteness of Sartrean freedom, presents a political problem.

It appears to render social solidarity or collective responsibility all but impossible. Desan, for instance, argues that because Sartrean freedom is absolute, one is confronted with an essence of human reality that is not preceded by its existence. Desan thus suggests that Sartre is defining an essence for freedom, that the absoluteness of freedom that Sartre posits must imply that it has no essence, no bounds- that it must remain indefinable. In effect, not only does consciousness take on the limits of definition, but it is a source of ultimate separation from all others, in the sense that there is no necessity for connection across the disparity between separate freedoms.

Thomas R. Flynn notes correctly that what Sartre calls the "we-subject," the sense of acting together with someone else in a common project, remains in the realm of the psychological. Since the look cannot be plural, "relations of solidarity or equivalence are simply a translation into the plural of quite individualistic phenomena". Flynn points out those ultimately subjective or psychological relations are not social at all. And Ronald Aronson argues that if no ontological foundation is provided for superseding the adversarial essence of one's being-for-others, then each person remains the "relentless enemy of each and every other": "A society of free men treating all other free men as free is thus impossible". In effect, Sartre's notion of freedom works against itself; in its absoluteness, it becomes "so sweeping as to be meaningless."

Sartre argues, of course, that the "us-object" (possible even for a large group, such as an exploited class) can establish itself as a collective consciousness, but only contingently, only in the continued presence of an enemy. Even in the Critique of Dialectical Reason, in which Sartre describes a collective subject, it is still situationally produced in response to an external threat. That is, the collective subject, the group-in-fusion, also marks the eviction of solidarity from the realm of the communal, where Aronson wants to locate it, to the realm of the confrontational. In his article, "Materialism and Revolution," Sartre allows the possibility of a solidarity based on the "recognition of other freedoms" and the demand for reciprocated "recognition on their part." Aronson adds, however, that Sartre's sense of solidarity still contains a disguised adversarial bargain; if one asks, "Solidarity in the face of what?" an enemy seems again implied.

Aronson, seeking the ontologically collective, concludes that Sartre's ontology of individual freedom does not provide for a subjectivity that could support true solidarity for its own sake, as a humanisation of society. Nevertheless, there is often a confusion of ontological and ontic freedom that waylays many commentators. For Sartre, though one is confronted with constraints in one's everyday social relations that are oppressive or alienating, the positionality one can establish for oneself between acquiescence and rebellion, between passivity and the invention of forms of resistance, is undetermined.

Though the situation may not be of one's choosing, it remains contingent precisely with respect to the absoluteness of the freedom that can apprehend it as one of constraint, which is part of one's determining who one is to be in that situation. When Desan says, "[O]ur freedom is grounded in our concrete situation", he is speaking of ontic freedom, where ontologically, for Sartre, the for-itself has no ground. Freedom cannot be reduced to ontic constraints. Constraints become constraints only to the extent that freedom is absolute in its ability to see them as constraints, as well as to choose to transcend them or not. What is grounded in our concrete situation is our worldly existence, in which we must choose who we are.

In terms of this confluence of problems, let us reconsider the look. It is possible that some commentators, in seeking an account of social intersubjectivity, have conflated the concept of solidarity with an ontological "collective subject" in a manner that rehearses the confusion of ontic and ontological freedom. It may be that solidarity, whether against an enemy or toward a process of cultural transformation and community construction, resides at a different level of ontological praxis and presupposes a different moment of value. I will argue that because Sartre's account of the look, his vision of the interpersonal as a subject-object relation, is couched within the realm of the visible, it takes the form of conflict. It will be my contention that being-for-others takes on a different character when articulated in terms of the spoken or "audible." And this difference will have certain socio-political ramifications.

THE LOOK

Sartre begins his account of the look with the Other as object. The Other, seen in the distance, is an object for me; yet different because the things of my world are also objects for that Other. The Other "sees what I see"; my world is present to the Other's eyes without distance. Seen as seeing, the Other presents an animal center (complete, like an object, yet hidden in its autonomy) that de-centers my own relation to the world. My world "flees" toward the Other, precisely because the Other sees and appropriates it; its immediacy to myself is replaced by an immediacy to the Other.

The Other is defined not as the absence of a consciousness in relation to the body which I see but by the absence of the world which I perceived, an absence discovered at the very heart of my perception of this world. Thus, "a clement of disintegration" is added to the world. Though nothing has changed, and the world still exists, it now has other meanings. The objects of my world drain away, not into a future (because they are already past), but to a temporal elsewhere. The Other-as-object transforms a world written by and for myself into what must now be read, and I am transformed in turn from a writer of my world to a reader of a world.

In Sartre's account of the look (which is again, in his text, a first-person narrative), the visual relation is reversed. On entering the real or imagined perceptual field of another, one becomes oneself "present to the eyes without distance", like all objects. In Sartre's famous example, he is peeping through a keyhole, wholly and pre-reflectively engrossed in this act. When he hears footsteps and realizes that he has been seen, the object of his own attention becomes the Other's look for which he is the scene. He finds himself the shameful object of the Other's attention. In thus becoming an object for the Other, he grasps the Other as a subject, a freedom.

That is, rather than apprehends the Other-as-subject through an attribution of subjectivity, one encounters and knows the Other in oneself as an attribution by the Other- not through the attribution's content, but through its enactment. Three transformations occur to the self-as-object. First, one is given a nature, an "outside"; the self (the "I") finds its foundation beyond itself, in the Other-as-subject. Second, there is a loss of project, of instrumentality in the world; one understands oneself as the Other's project. And third, there is a loss of mastery or autonomy; the once autonomous self finds itself no longer self-determining. Its foundation is elsewhere, lost to the Other's hidden apprehension. Through loss of self, one gains a knowledge of an unknowable Other because one becomes the Other's knowledge. One is transformed from person to personage and becomes an aspect of a situation that is by and for the Other.

The Other's look makes me be beyond my being in this world and puts me in the midst of the world which is at once this world and beyond this world. One is given (twice), by the Other as the content of the look and by oneself through the

Other, and withheld (twice), in losing one's apprehension of oneself and as the Other's hidden knowledge and project. One is written by the Other as the Other's knowledge in the act of being read. And in reading the Other's look, one is transformed from being a writer of one's world to being part of the world written. The self becomes a form whose content is elsewhere, and a content whose form is absent. The look is always accompanied by shame- the shame of having been rendered an object.

However, it is important to understand that by this, Sartre means an existential rather than a moralistic shame. Existential shame is the situation of being stripped of one's autonomy as an object for another; it names a formal relation. The content of this relation may indeed be morally shameful, such as being caught peeping through a keyhole, but it is not restricted to such situations. Sartre conflates them in his example, perhaps for purposes of starkness; but other examples are instructive. One might be speaking to another intensely, and suddenly encounter the Other's look as one of longing or intimacy. Intimacy is as legitimate a content for the look as reprobation at discovering a peeping Tom.

One discovers oneself to be the object of that intimacy or longing, as knowledge whose content (project) remains hidden yet directed at oneself as its object. One might blush, though not because it is a morally shameful situation. Rather, it is the loss of subjectivity as existential shame that would produce the blush. In such a circumstance, to return the look of intimacy does more than reciprocate its objectivisation. Returning a look of intimacy is an undertaking under the aegis of the Other's apprehended intimacy, a desire to maintain a tenuous balance within one's being-for-others, to preserve the aura of desire or closeness as a project, without descending into "originary conflictuality."

Indeed, this tenuousness suggests why subtle social phenomena- love relations, for instance- require elaborate discursive and narrative extensions, such as the love stories of novels and romance magazines, the formulation of marriage rituals, methodologies of divorce, etc. The ephemerality of longing looks requires prior narrativisation to ensure commonly understood significations, that is, to be experienced in common as events that defer the conflictuality of alternating objectivisations to a detente. Though Sartre devotes some attention to conflictual or non-mutual cases of desire- mapping a spectrum from masochism as the project to be an object for the Other, to sadism as the project to render the Other all object for oneself- there is a difference between such cases and the desire to maintain a mutuality of desire (or intimacy) in the exchange of "looks."

The former obviate mutuality as a project, while the latter projects a contingent mutuality; but it does so only with certain assistance from beyond the signification of that exchange. In the former, subject-object relations are worked out in their immediacy. In the contingency of mutuality, there must be mediation, a structure of discourse and narrativity that adjoins the interaction, perhaps even rendering it non-concrete in its social interactivity. Three questions are thus raised that must be more carefully elucidated within the purview of Sartre's account: first, the nature of the project for mutuality; second, the role of narrativisation in that project; and, third, the relation between the ontological project for a mutuality in Sartre's narrative and the role of narrativity in Sartre's ontology.

THE STRUCTURE OF MUTUALITY

In apprehending the Other as subject by having become an object for them, it is not the Other one encounters, but rather the look of the Other that one apprehends. The Other becomes "the one who delivers me to myself as unrevealed but without revealing himself". The Other's subjectivity is thus not a metaphor for oneself. In being delivered to oneself, in becoming knowledge for the Other, one obtains an outside, a nature, in exchange. But this interchange is not unidimensional. Though retrieving one's subjectivity by returning the look, and transcending the Other's transcendence at the expense of the Other's subjectivity, something else is exchanged. There is one aspect of the Other th es to be". Rather than refusing the Other being, one refuses to be the Other, apprehending the Other as a being-in-situation, for which one is, oneself, the situation. That is, one chooses oneself as a freedom while remaining the object one had been for that otherness. This means one acts as having to be oneself as not being the Other in detaching oneself from the Other, who one makes be a Not-Me-not-object.

In effect, one recovers oneself as a subject that apprehends itself as having been given a nature, but also as having been the situation in which there is another who one must refuse to be. The Other whom I recognize in order to refuse to be him is before all else the one for whom my for-itself is. In short, one's own infinite possibilities and the transformation of the Other into what is not-lived-by-me become each other's context. Being-for-others thus has two parts: the existence of one's own factical "oneself" as a responsibility for the Other, and one's responsibility to the Other that one lives as a "oneself" retrieved as subjectivity. It is the boundary of an internal division that both separates and renders inseparable.

Avoiding oscillating objectivisations, and embracing as a choice of possibility the Other as subject, one adopts the project of maintaining the Other as the subject one apprehended in the Other's look, but now as one to whom one turns as such. That project shifts one's apprehension to the situation of the Other being-a-look seeing oneself, and grasps the Other as the center of an alternate, reintegrated world. Through there being being-for-others, one can confront the Other as subject. In this face-to-face encounter, which is an internal mode of being (I-and-the-other) rather than an external relation, one grants to the Other the subjectivity apprehended through her/his look as a project for oneself, as a subjectivity that had discovered itself as a facticity, a "oneself" through the Other's look.

But the granting of subjectivity to the Other is a gratuitous (contingent) grant, whose return cannot be other than the subject-subject encounter itself. For the Other to return the look would not be to re-objectivize oneself, but rather to re-enact and reconfirm the project of being-for-the-other through that look. As an abandonment of oneself to the nature given to oneself by the Other- as well as an abandonment to the Other for whom one's for-itself is, in reciprocity- being-for-others remains a gratuitous gift. It is not a question of solidarity, since it does not arise out of an agreement that would make a conceptual object of the interchange, wholly enacted within factical mutuality.

And it has its limitations: each individual is a limited and limiting consciousness for the Other. But these limits as mutuality are like a dance, a sense that it occurs as something the Other does for which one is responsible and which one does oneself for which the Other is responsible. As Sartre puts it, to adapt oneself "to the human order" (the order of meanings), one "set[s] up a dialogue with the Other". It is this unspoken dialogue that is plumped into the air between persons in the exchange, perhaps at a cafe table, within looks of intimacy and desire. In Sartre's invocation of this dialogue, he is telling a story of silence and recognition (his text is actually about responding to meanings and directives already inscribed in social space).

Nothing need be spoken, because the look is recognized, and the project of relating to the Other as subject, of embracing the objecthood the Other has bestowed upon one as a gift that is itself desirable, becomes a project that enacts its mutuality simply out of familiarity with the nature of intimacy, while being at the same time a choice to apply it toward the Other. It is not a common project, but a mutuality of recognition and choice.

The issue of recognition now brings us to the question of the source or origin of recognition. In Sartre's invocation of dialogue, he is himself recognizing the signifying nature of interaction, which then must include the trace of the sources of its significations, as well as of recognition itself. It is the signifying nature of an interaction, as a mode of mediation that will relate a sense of "dialogic" interaction to Sartre's description of exchanges of the look.

THE ROLE OF NARRATIVITY

Narrativity plays an important role for Sartre, beyond constituting mere philosophical examples. As he says in one interview, philosophy misses the singular- what transpires for or happens to the individual. Sartre turns to drama and fiction to resolve or investigate questions that cannot be investigated in the generality of the philosophical. Narrative preserves the specificity of the subject, while at the same time signifying what is generalizable (including the necessity of narrative to preserve that very specificity). In that sense, the vignettes used throughout Being and Nothingness do more than serve as examples; they function philosophically in form, formally describing the subject in his/her particularity, and signifying that the subject is always particular, always an individual.

Not only is Sartre's account of the look centered around a narrative of discovery, its inner structure can be read as a highly complex structure of narratives. In Sartre's example (of the peeping Tom), the "story" is of a man looking through the keyhole, hearing footsteps, and discovering himself discovered by a (real or imagined) Other. Juxtaposed to this is the formal arrangement of the ensuing dramatic situation, consisting of the fact of the Other's look and the fact that this "look" is one of discovery, for which the man at the keyhole becomes the object, who then apprehends himself as an object. If the scene is a discovery of voyeurism, the protagonist of the "story" is the voyeur who discovers himself as discovered with a sense of moral shame, which constitutes the substance of the story.

Sartre's ontological interest is the formal transformation in the voyeur, insofar as he apprehends his discoverer as a subject by finding himself the object of the discovering look. But this formal arrangement breaks down without an additional narrative dimension, which is likewise formal and whose actual terms do not matter. At the moment of discovery, the Other has not spoken, nor does s/he need to speak. The voyeur, as discovered, tells himself what the Other is telling her/ himself has been discovered. If the voyeur feels reprobation as the object of the Other's knowledge, that knowledge, which contains reproach as its content, is the link that gives the discoverer subjectivity.

Yet that knowledge is nothing but the content of a narrative about the discovery that the voyeur tells himself about the discoverer. Similarly, the longing look that renders one an intimate object for the Other is a story whose substance, as the Other's longing, one tells oneself at the moment of discovering oneself as its object; that is, one tells oneself that one is being looked at with a sense of longing, or that the Other's look is one of intimacy. Let us abstract this structure a bit. In Sartre's story, told in the first person, there is a narrator (an "I"), who is caught at the keyhole, and a character, an Other (real or imagined), who comes upon him there.

Though the narrative of self-discovery as an object is told in the "same" first person, the center of consciousness for it shifts to the "eye" (the "I") of the Other, for whose freedom the first "I" has become an object. The narrator's existential shame (the same for both reproach and intimacy) arises from being seen by that Other (as an Other-as-subject, a character in the narrator's narrative), who, in making the discovery (seeing), has a secret, unplumbable knowledge of what he has discovered.

Nevertheless, the narrator tells us in part what that knowledge is. It is himself, an object for the Other, yet an object "as" something (a thing of moral reproach). In the eyes of the Other, the narrator enacts that Other's knowledge. The "I" narrating, having been discovered at the keyhole and being appropriated by the Other's knowledge as an object, is at the same time enacting the narrative of what the Other has discovered- as an (ethical) meaning. Thus, where the first narrator had narrated a character discovering him, he now becomes a character in turn in an appropriative story of reprobation in which the Other is the narrator.

Yet this second story, whose narrator is the discoverer, is told for the discoverer by the first narrator. In effect, the first narrator arrives at knowing the Other as a subject by rendering the Other a narrator in turn, whose narrative provides the content of the objectivisation of the first narrator in the first story. In other words, the "cover" story of being discovered is a recta-narrative. The character (Other) in that meta-narrative is the narrator (Other) of a second narrative in which the first narrator ("I") becomes a character ("I"), and the story that the Other (as character) narrates is the enactment, with its ethical value, narrated by the "I" as narrator, through the Other- that is, through a narrative given to, and told for, the Other (character) by the first narrator. The "I" and the Other are narrator and character at the same time, two narrators and two characters that are distinct and conflated, doubled and changing places- each becoming the other's narrator and the other's character.

What reveals the Other's subjectivity is not his being, or the fact of being a character in a story, but rather his being given the role of narrator for a story in which the "I" as meta-narrator is a character (object). The meta-narrator (the "I') is written by the Other's apprehension (discovery), while writing that Other's apprehension himself; in the look, one loses authority as an object for the Other only through one's own authorship. And now we see that Sartre's account of the look does contain a moment of attribution to the Other. One's own shame appears to oneself in the form of the Other's narrative, but one attributed to that Other; and one feels the shame narrated by the Other because one recta-narratively attributes to oneself a character hood in that Other's narrative. Thus, the meaning of one's action is at once an attribution to oneself through the Other and an attribution to the Other through oneself. It is not an attribution of subjectivity, but an attribution of meaning to oneself through the Other-as-subject.

To that extent, however, Sartre's account deconstructs. Its meaning is not where he places it. It is an account whose self-assumed meaning is non-attribution, but whose form is a story of attribution. Though the specific content of the Other-as-subject's discovery (and objectivisation) is immaterial to this double-narrative structure, the fact of narrative is not immaterial to Sartre's account of subjectivity. Furthermore, the discursivity of this ontological "scene" overflows. While the meaning given to the "I" (as object) by the Other-as-subject is a story the Other tells in a story the "I" tells, the source of the story the "I" tells the Other telling comes from beyond the ontological relation. To discover oneself in reprobation or intimacy is to have already known and recognized that meaning from elsewhere and to discover it "here" in "this" double narrative.

That elsewhere- as the general source for the narrative's (contingent) content (whether reprobation, longing, etc.), as the source of recognition- is a certain social given ness, which, in appearing as the content of a double narrative, is never the object of an intention. As the meaning of an experience, it comes from elsewhere and is then given back to an elsewhere (an Other), in order for one to submit oneself to it. Indeed, it must come from elsewhere as a narrative; insofar as it is assumed to be a common experience (reprobation or intimacy can be given to the Other-as-narrator only through the assumption that the Other feels it in common with oneself).

Only a narrative can render experience a common experience, because only narrative can reveal the hidden ness of consciousness to others. Neither activity nor mere gesture can present experience or feeling to others without their having been narrativized in common first- hence, the social necessity of narrative as the epitome of social discourse. And in this inversion, the look then becomes a special case of tacit dialogue, unspoken yet doubly narrativized in terms that are given by the social order, to which one adapts oneself in order to interact. Adapting oneself to the social order and entering a dialogue with the Other are two sides of the same coin, for which the account of the look, and an apprehension of the Other-as-subject, is both an abstract case and a special case.

DIALOGUE

Having adumbrated the look in this fashion, can we still say that conflict is fundamental to the look? Or must we now admit to an alternate trajectory? Let us look at Lacan's version of Sartre's account of the look, his own notion of the gaze, not as offering an alternate trajectory but as providing a differing, mismatched account, whose difference might elucidate this question. Lacan juxtaposes two accounts of the look in his text. For him, the gaze, like the look, is centered on "being seen." But rather than being something to which one submits, it is a prior condition. The gaze is the "pre-existence to the seen of the given-to-be-seen". It is an element of how one is already given to the eye of the other- a moment of Heideggerian fore-having- rather than how one is discovered.

[The other's] eye is only the metaphor of something ... prior to his eye. What we have to circumscribe ... is the pre-existence of a gaze- I see only from one point, but in my existence I am looked at from all sides. For Lacan, the subject is not passive; the gaze is solicited. There is a desire for the gaze, a desire that the other's eye be the eye that gazes at one and sees one in a particular way. As an activity of the imagination, the gaze engineers being seen through an already desired form of recognition (and thus self-recognition). It is a function upon which the subject depends, an "I" embodied as the eye of another, rather than in an encounter.

For Sartre, the effect and the knowledge incurred in the look are wholly immediate, while for Lacan, the gaze abandons the immediate for a past and a future (a pre-existence and a desire). That is, in Sartrean (ontological) terms, the Lacanian gaze would appear as part of one's project, while in Lacanian (psychoanalytic) terms, the Sartrean look would participate in the imaginary. Beyond the disparity between ontological and psychoanalytic language, the gaze is not the Sartrean look. But, in fact, Lacan does use the structure of the look- not with respect to seeing or being seen, but as fundamental to dialogue. He begins his account of speech by discussing what he calls "empty speech" (as Sartre begins with the Other-as-object), a theoretical opening of permissibility.

In the psychotherapeutic situation, a subject engages in "empty speech" when addressing someone who is not there, but whom s/he desires to address because s/he desires his/her recognition. In such situations, one's speech doubles itself. One speaks to an other (the analyst), who is there, and to an Other (the imaginary), who is not there. Lacan calls this therapy-speech empty because "the subject seems to be talking in vain about someone who, even if he (the analyst) were his spitting image, can never become one with the assumption of his [the subject's] desire". But by addressing a present other, one discovers the meaning of the desire to address the imagined (absent) Other.

One says things that are heard, in actual statements, and things that are to be heard, which constitute the (linguistically unconscious) content or truth behind one's statements. For Lacan, "the unconscious is that part of the concrete discourse ... that is not at the disposal of the subject". It is what one "wants to say" (vouloir dire), the language in which one speaks one's real meaning, rather than what one actually says. Indeed, to speak is already to imply that there is a truth somewhere and that the subject's speech has somehow, whether positively or negatively, invoked it: "Even if it denies the evidence, [the subject's discourse] affirms that speech constitutes truth".

Similarly, in subjecting oneself to the other's look, in discovering oneself in it, the truth of who one becomes, the nature one is given in the content of that look (given narratively by/in the "social order"), is incontestable. However, for Lacan, speech produces its meaning because there is also a reply, even if that reply is not forthcoming. In conveying the subject's truth, the subject's speech "always subjectively includes its own reply". If the subject solicits a response already contained in his/her speech, it is a reply pre-existing its solicitation (the unconscious as "elsewhere"). In addressing the other, one discovers the meaning that one's speech already had (the prior unconscious truth) insofar as the other hears and responds, sometimes preferably in silence. (Indeed, should the analyst respond in speech, it would be only to an actual statement, rather than to the subject's unconscious truth.)

For the subject to confront his/her hidden truth, there simply has to be an auditor, an ear. Through listening, the analyst allows the silent reply to give the subject's speech its meaning as addressed to the imagined absent Other. For Lacan, this gets generalized (in social situations) in the following way. When I speak, the other hears me twice: in my concrete discourse and in nay hidden truth. The other is doubled between the symbolic other (objet a), and the imaginary Other from whom I seek recognition (objet A). As other, the one who hears, the one whose response I solicit, that other "hears what I say"; and as Other, the one spoken to, the one to whom my hidden truth and desire are addressed, and whose recognition and desire I desire, that Other "hears what I hear."

The symbolic other gives my speech the meaning it has contingently, and the imaginary Other gives my speech the meaning it already has, and must have. When Lacan says, "[M]an's desire finds its meaning in the desire of the other", it is in this sense of response as prior meaning, e.g., the desire to be recognized by the other. Speech is the desire for a response, not a reaction, and desire is speech for recognition as desire. The enactment of speech constitutes the subject as whom and what is to be recognized. In speaking, the subject is referring him/herself to the response and the recognition of the other.

On the other hand, in hearing me, the Other (object A) becomes the one who catches me in the pre-reflective moment (at the keyhole). In apprehending my truth, my meaning, the Other's ear (at the moment of hearing me) renders me an object of recognition, the object of the Other's desired desire, the desired desire subjectively implied in having spoken to the imaginary Other. Speech, enacted to constitute the subject as whom/what is to be recognized, also constitutes the subject as an object of recognition for the other, through the response solicited from the Other. The Other's ear, by hearing, makes me an object for it, as does the Other's eye by seeing.

It is analogous to Sartre's look; having-been-heard is structurally the same as having-been-seen. And similarly, there is a loss of autonomy, of project, to the other's silent apprehension of my "truth." As Lacan suggests, I identify myself in language in order to lose myself in it- to become what I will have been for the response. Furthermore, in finding myself discovered at the auditory keyhole, in speaking in order to produce the other's discovery, I discover myself as the self given by that speech, but one already imagining (narrating) the condition for its self-objectification through the Other.

The object I become in the other's hearing is the myself, the object I as subject have called forth for myself by speaking (by manifesting my desire for the Other's desire, for the other's response). That is, the meaning of my concrete discourse lies between myself as subject (soliciting a response from the symbolic other) and myself as object (of recognition by the imaginary Other). Thus, there are two different narratives in which I find myself narrator and character. The first (the desire for response) is contained in the act of speaking, and the second (the desire for recognition) is imagined for the Other in which I find myself a character.

That is, the Other who hears becomes the "character" from whom I desire a response, and the other whose recognition I desire is already a narrator of that recognition of which I am the object. Thus, the overall narrative structure is the same as Sartre's look. However, one speaks not only to be heard, not only to solicit a response, but to receive one in fact. One must speak in order for the other to capture and recognize one's being in one's speech, as an ear; but the Other must reply in order for one to "realize ... what I shall have been" by speaking. For Lacan, one speaks to the other as an act of bestowal upon her/him, as well as an act of becoming for oneself.

If I call the person to whom I am speaking by whatever name I choose to give him [an object], I [a subject] intimate to him the subjective function that he [becoming a subject] will take on again in order to reply to me [an object], even if it is to repudiate this function.

That is, I address the other (thereby rendering myself an object for him/her) in order to give him/her the subjective function of responding in speech to me, an object, even though thereby repudiating his/her subjectivity and becoming an object for "I" who hear him/her. I speak in order to confer subjectivity and to hear a response that will return my subjectivity to me. Reciprocally, my hearing the other's response becomes a recognition and abolition of the Other as a subject, and my response to the other becomes a restitution of subjectivity for the Other. Each response to the other simultaneously becomes recognition and a constitution of the Other as subject; each act of listening becomes the objectivisation of the Other, a reciprocated "look."

One speaks to be heard at the same time one engenders a subject to hear, and one listens to become again a subject. This continual exchange of speech constitutes the structure of concrete dialogue, and in its reciprocity, it has the structure of being-for-others. The structure of the look straddles the gap between Sartre's ontology and Lacan's psychoanalytics. Sartre uses it to solve the existential problem of the Other-as-subject, and Lacan uses it to solve the psychoanalytic problem of the Other's desire as the meaning of desire. Both are governed by doubled narrator-character relations, and both rely upon an elsewhere- a social given ness for Sartre, and an unconscious for Lacan.

In sum, dialogue is homologous in form to being-for-others. Though Lacan invokes Sartre's notion of the look in his own account of the gaze, the element of Lacan's discourse that is most homologous to the Sartrean look is in fact Lacan's account of dialogue. And if Lacan has transferred Sartre's structure to a theory of dialogue, it is a transformation not alien to Sartre's own thinking.

Language is not a phenomenon added on to being-for-others. It is originally being-for-others; that is, it is the fact that subjectivity experiences itself as an object for the Other. In a universe of pure objects language could under no circumstances have been "invented" since it presupposes an original relation to another subject.

Yet in what sense are these two separable? If (in the Sartrean structure) I become an object for the Other's discovering or longing look, it is ultimately I who choose the narrative content of that look, and thus I who desire that choice. If I speak to obtain a certain recognition from the other (in the Lacanian structure), as an object for him/her, from whence did a recognizable sense of recognition come, if not from a prior interaction or prior social experience? Thus, there is at least a realm of overlap. Yet at the same time, there is an inversion between the two.

For Sartre, one seeks to reveal oneself as a subject to the Other-as-subject, and instead becomes an object; for Lacan, one desire to become the object of desire for the other spoken to, but only has one's own subjectivity returned in the other's speech. But if the Lacanian structure is homologous to the Sartrean, than that inversion must also find itself inside the Sartrean structure as well. That is, the Lacanian homology suggests that Sartre's being-for-others contains the desire to confer subjectivity as one of its possibilities.

THE SARTREAN DIALOGIC

In the Sartrean paradigm, one is seen when one speaks, and one is caught in the look by speaking in the presence of others. In the Lacanian paradigm, one speaks to be seen and rendered an object by the one who listens. Insofar as speaking is an intentional act, and speaking is purposive, whose purpose is to be beheld, to be seen and heard, we confront a situation in which being-for-others represents more than the project to maintain the Other's subjectivity; it is a relation of being-for-others engendered intentionally for that purpose. The intentionality to appear contained in the act of speaking to others envelops the situation. One's words represent intending the situation in which one seeks (intends) to be objectivized in the look, to be beheld by the Other, as a matrix for their meaning.

In other words, beyond being the situation in which the other is granted being, or refused being, as a being-in-situation, one intends that situation through speech, as a structure accompanying speech, to grant the other being as a project and to refuse objectivisation of the other in order that there be a subject there. To speak is to take responsibility for being the situation in which to apprehend the Other as a subject, before the fact. The meaning of what is spoken remains what it is, the discursive or semiotic dimension of the situation, its interior. But around it, the look as listening has provided a different priority for a subject-to-subject relation.

Ultimately, what one's words mean will be discovered in the other's response, to which one returns the look in listening. When the other responds, the look goes the other way. One is seeing the Other in the Other's intentionality to be seen. Sartre approaches these two domains, the semiotics and the ontology of dialogue, in his dialogues with Benny Levy in Hope Now, but he does so from a different direction than the one we have taken. Having hired Levy as a secretary, the blind Sartre (no longer able to "look") found himself immersed in a generation of thought that was not his, yet not not-his, through Levy's full participation as co-thinker.

Hope Now surprised a number of people because it seemed to represent a departure of sorts from some of Sartre's former political thinking, for instance, replacing the cathartic sense of violence that Fanon had theorized with a recognition that neo-liberal strategies of debt starvation, paramilitary terror, and gratuitous police violence left no clear target, and violence no longer presented itself as liberatory. But the political thought of those dialogues came from two sources, and ended as a single discourse that had its own trajectory. Having approached each other in the seriality of a business arrangement, the dialogic substance of the interaction between Sartre and Levy created an affinity transcending seriality. For Sartre, it represented a "reciprocal abandon" to a "thought created by two people." Sartre found himself the recipient of thinking from beyond himself and Levy both.

Sartre then characterizes dialogue as "a plural thought," one with a meaning that "each person approaches in his/her own manner" and produces on "different bases, premises, and preoccupations". Each participant determines only a share of its substance, leaving the dialogue to produce its own character, independent of the specific intentionalities that compose it. The plurality of the thought is not the dialogue itself but the process emerging from relinquishing control over one's meanings. As it proceeds, a participant must coordinate three disparate moments continuously: his/her own thought, the thought represented by the speech of the Other, and the substance of the dialogue itself as a detotalized (and self-detotalizing) totality.

Each person enters the dialogue as serial (speaker), as being-for-others (listener), and as a (micro)group-in-fusion- a group of two (or more) brought together to defend themselves collectively against forgetting what had transpired between them and lapsing again into seriality. In that sense, though Sartre approached the structure of dialogue in Hope Now from a direction other than that of being-for-others, it contains the latter. He began with its semiotic content and moved from that toward what the ontological basis upon which it unfolded might be. The confluence of ontological states he positions in it contains a mutual sense of autonomy of its participants, a mutuality of recognition as engaging the same project toward being-for-others, and a sense of responsibility toward the dialogue as an entity.

But it is already a self-detotalizing totality toward the Other through that entity, arriving at an acceptance of the Other as subject for having listened in order to preserve that subjectivity in the Other by speaking in turn. The confluence of these three aspects guarantees the singularity of each dialogue, within the exchange of(listening) looks in response to speech. Finally, it is also the acceptance of a knowledge emergent from the elsewhere of the dialogue itself that removes the possibility of a proprietary relation to what one knows, by entering that knowledge into the public space of the dialogue.

Today, freedom of speech has been commodified to the point where a proprietary relation to what one says lurks behind each saying. Yet to speak in dialogue is to have one's knowledge, as a contribution to the dialogue, changed by being recontextualized in what had preceeded, and what others will respond to what one has said. Because dialogue proceeds as precisely the transformation of each knowledge brought to it by recontextualisation in itself, a proprietary relation to one's own knowledge reveals itself to obviate dialogue, and thus to be an imprisonment in one's own alienated thought.

THE SOCIAL DIMENSION

To see being-for-others as a dialogue in which one has a sense of responsibility, a mutuality of recognition, and a mutuality of autonomy that guarantees its singularity requires a re-evaluation of the conflict central to being-for-others. Being-for-others is a failed project of the subject if it is understood as an ontological moment. But in its narrativity, it takes on a different character. While the object one discovers oneself to be in the look is a recta-narrated character, the subject to whom one loses it is a character narrated by one- in both cases deploying narratives from one's social context or environment. In a dialogue, with its particular content of speech and response, speech itself becomes a boundary across which both see each other as characters mutually narrated within one meta-narrative.

And in this case, it is a meta-narrative that does not have a socio-cultural content (as does reproach or intimacy). What gives content to the meta-narrativity of the dialogic situation is the existence of spoken language itself, that is, the very foundation of cultural being, including the totality of narratives that provide the social meanings of the language spoken (not just natural languages, either; the narratives of interpersonal relations in New York City are quite different from those of the Virginia Piedmont). Within the realm of dialogue, conflict is no longer an original meaning.

The desire to bestow subjectivity upon the Other ceases to be a special case of being-for-others and becomes a more general matrix, precisely because both the look and the dialogue depend upon a meta-narrativity that precedes specific socio-cultural attitudes by engaging being-for-others in the exchange of social meanings through language itself. Though one's objectivizing look engages a conflictuality, each objectivizing act of listening engages a project of mutual subjectivisation because speech, which has semiotic meaning, already implies a response in its having obtained semiotic meaning through responsiveness in the first place.

Each act of speech is autonomous and singular, yet not separable from the historicity of the language that the interlocutors speak, with its multi-narrativities and vast cultural background. If response is the general case- by which meaning is heaped upon the present through its cultural past- then the project within the structure of being-for-others of retrieving one's subjectivity in a way to preserve one's having been an object for the Other-as-subject becomes the general case of one's being-for-others, for which the conflictuality of a returned objectivizing look is a special case.

That is, if meta-narrativity is a concomitant of subjectivity and a condition for a factical (as opposed to ontological) intersubjectivity, a certain priority is given the structure of dialogue as more than merely one of the possibilities of being-for-others. The ontology of dialogue, which repeats the structure of being-for-others in terms of being-heard rather than being-seen, reverses the priority of the visible and the discursive, and transforms the Lacanian priority of desire into the desire to confer subjectivity.

This is perhaps the great attraction in Sartre's overall ontology that it contains, within its individuated investigation into subjectivity and intentionality, a sociality that constitutes the lurking general case, the ocean in which Sartre's specific narrativities of the subject and its ontological states are the fish. Or as Levinas has said, "[T]he relation to the other is ... not ontology ... [it is a] bond with the other which is not reducible to the representation of the other, but to his invocation [voice]."

Levinas uses the term "religion" to name this "bond," but he characterizes it as indicating "the relation between men [sic], irreducible to understanding, [that] is by that fact distanced from the exercise of power". He is looking at what ontologically precedes power and conflictuality in a relation to an event in which the Other is indispensable, as the very being of that event. The dialogic structure of responsibility is not simply a "relation to the other." Representation takes on a form of materiality that is not its meaning. It is a relation with the other under the aegis of responsibility rather than toward a telos.

Within the Sartrean framework, all interpersonal relations, including those of solidarity, must differentiate (or individuate) themselves through chosen narratives. The narrative of solidarity need be nothing more than an indexical ("here," or "are we together in this?"). But situationally, solidarity is always already a discursive phenomenon: solidarity for what, against what, in the name of what must be specified. As such, it must entail more than just speaking in solidarity (as one can speak intimately); it involves speaking in a sense that brings the narratives of solidarity into the meta-narrativity of the dialogue, as an enactment.

Each must become a character in a narrative of solidarity that the other can recognize, in order to be recognized as such. One becomes an object in solidarity by grasping the Other as a subject in that solidarity, a narrator of a common performance, in such a way that one can be recognized as in solidarity, as and by one's response. In what besets us politically, the relation of intersubjectivity as facticity rather than as ontological category is a necessary transcendence of the "right to flee speech," which becomes meaningless in the context of corporate-controlled public space. It is at the very fundamental level of dialogue- and with an understanding of dialogue as containing a sense of responsibility, responsiveness, and recognition, without proprietary hold on what one has said- that an essential dimension wherein to begin to reconstruct a form of public space reveals itself.

5

The Analysis of International Territorial Disputes

Explanations of international territorial dispute settlement tend to be dominated by state-centric approaches that usually depart from a realist conceptualisation of international politics. Such approaches, by definition, take the nation-state to be the primary, or dominant, actor in international territorial dispute settlement even if it is not conceived as a unitary one. The tendency to adopt state-centric approaches to territory and territorial disputes is evident in a study of the territorial dimension of conflicts by Goertz and Diehl. Acknowledging the valuable empirical work carried out by geographers and historians on specific case studies, the authors argue that adequate theoretical work on the significance of territory is missing from such studies

Even so, they tend to fall into what Agnew and Corbridge call the "territorial trap." For Goertz and Diehl territory is both a "facilitating factor" and a "subject" of conflict but its disposition is still dominated by nation-states. In recent years, most analysts adopting a state-centric perspective have assumed the state should be at least partly deconstructed in order to account for patterns of influence on decision makers operating within the framework of the nation-state. Even such deconstructed explanations, however, tie subsidiary political action to nation-state decisions and behaviour.

Challenging such orthodoxy are several new approaches that may be applied to understanding territorial disputes put forward by contemporary geographers and sociologists. A far more nuanced view of human territoriality, for example, is developed by geographer Robert Sack. Sack conceives territoriality "....as the basic geographic expression of influence and power,... an essential link between society, space, and time .... For humans, territoriality is ... a complex strategy to affect, influence, and control access to people, things, and relationships." Territoriality can be used as a strategy of control for political or non-political purposes, and it can be used beside non territorial strategies.

Furthermore, while modern nation-states have attempted to reify the central authority of states by employing territoriality, the theory of human territoriality shows that in fact there are many different kinds of territorial (and non territorial) behaviour and a great many territorial possibilities in our human societies. Sack perceives "territories" as "socially constructed forms of spatial relations and their effects depend on who is controlling whom and for what purposes". Used in this sense, territoriality may be applied to a whole range of human agents, institutions and examined at different points in space and time. The theory of human territoriality enables us to examine the relational and contingent aspects of the exercise of political power.

Congruent with Sack's approach but far more comprehensive in its theoretical scope is Structuration Theory (or ST), an approach pioneered by sociologist Anthony Giddens. By comparison with traditional power politics approaches that explain dispute dynamics on the basis of a preponderance of national economic or political power or as the result of international agreements sustained by a strategic coalition of domestic and foreign policy decision makers, Structuration theory conceives power and influence more fluidly, placing greater emphasis on both the context and the subjective aspects of decision making.

To demonstrate Structuration theory's utility for understanding the dynamics of international territorial dispute settlement, this study applies Structuration theory and two rival explanations, dependency theory and strategic coalition theory, to the analysis of a well-known territorial dispute, the case of El Chamizal. The chapter begins by specifying the key assumptions of each rival explanation, including Structuration theory, followed by a narrative of the El Chamizal dispute and a synopsis, drawn from the case literature, of how each rival explanation explains the Chamizal settlement. The conclusion summarizes Structuration theory's analytical merits and points to several potential applications in developing better explanations of the dynamics of international territorial disputes and regional conflicts.

DEPENDENCY, STRATEGIC COALITIONS AND STRUCTURATION THEORY

To illustrate Structuration theory's departure from some of the more prominent power politics approaches we review the operating assumptions of the two mentioned approaches operating in this vein, dependency theory and strategic coalition theory. Both approaches are well known and have been applied to the El Chamizal dispute, facilitating comparison from the case study

DEPENDENCY THEORY

Widely utilized in international and transboundary political studies, dependency theory varies by degrees in the emphasis practitioners give to particular variables, though all analysts proceed from a shared set of analytical assumptions. First, dependency theorists emphasize the economic foundations of political power, viewing political power as a practical (or structural) derivative of economic development. Second, they tend to take the nation-state as the key unit of analysis-an exception to this rule found in world systems theory which takes the world system as the basic unit of analysis. Third, dependency theorists tacitly assume rational decision making with the proviso that the decisions of individual, corporate, or state actors serve the economic interests of the hegemonic nation-state.

This approach has certainly dominated conceptualisations of politics and dispute settlement on the U.S.-Mexico border. The work of prominent Mexican scholar Mario Ojeda is instructive. Ojeda, borrowing on dependency theory writ large, considers Mexico to be strategically and economically dependent on the United States. Ojeda's views have influenced many scholars writing on U.S.-Mexico relations.

STRATEGIC COALITION THEORY

An alternate approach, strategic coalition theory, offers a competing explanation based on realist and strategic choice assumptions. Analysts like Bueno de Mesquita explain foreign policy decision making as the outcome of rational decisions by individuals and groups striving to realize their preferences by fashioning strategic alliances with other players in situated contexts. The key to this approach is understanding the opportunities and constraints actors face as they strive to attain their preferences and the way they enter into alliances with other political actors to attain their goals.

Several analytical elements distinguish this approach from dependency theory and more traditional modes of explanation. First, though taking a state centric approach to conflict resolution, the analysis of state behaviour is predicated on methodological individualism, where individuals or small sets of individuals and their decisions are the primary units of analysis. Second, in the manner of game theory, strategic coalition theory attempts to explicitly identify actors and their goals or preferences as well as relevant contextual elements of the decision-making situation that would affect the realisation of actors' goals. Third, because foreign policy decision making occurs within a complex organisational and political setting within the nation- state, strategic coalition theory assumes that individual actors will normally enter into strategic alliances with other actors to attain their policy goals. Fourth, insofar as the aims and preferences of decision makers are known, the calculus of choice by actors is assumed to proceed logically

The strategic coalition theory approach avoids some of the excesses of the unitary sovereign nation-state model of international relations often associated with traditional power politics and dependency theories. This unitary approach posits fixed configurations of authority within set jurisdictional zones and tends to reify the behaviour of large organisations and decision-making roles within these organisations as they affect subordinate jurisdictions, authorities, and individuals within the nation-state and jurisdictional authorities, organisations, and roles in other nation-states. By avoiding such assumptions, strategic coalition is able to craft more flexible and more rigorous explanations for decision-making outcomes.

STRUCTURATION THEORY

Structuration theory offers an alternate approach with promise for understanding the dynamics of international conflicts.' A fundamental Structuration theory tenet is the centrality of the individual human agent and its capacity for interpretation and meaning making as a vital element in the exercise of social power. In brief, Structuration theory invites the analyst to examine in detail the social construction of power and authority, taking care to be sensitive to all forms of context. Of its various conceptual elements and critical assumptions four are particularly relevant to the analysis of international disputes: Power, defined as "transformative capacity, is seen as a fundamental element in the constitution of society Power is not in itself a resource but expresses the capacity to mobilize and deploy resources in social relations.

Rules and resources are the media through which power functions. All social action expresses power and all relations of domination and control offer some resources to subordinates for shaping the expression of power, what Giddens calls the dialectic of control. Hence, the analyst's focus should center on identifying the ways power is situated and expressed in society and understanding power as a dynamic phenomenon and an essentially contested state of affairs. Institutions, defined as recurrent, reproduced social practices with the greatest extension in space and time within a societal totality, are not socially fixed but represent a certain order of social relations that are inherently contested.

Institutions also store the instruments of administrative power. Governments are institutions whose administrative purview "corresponds exactly to [their] territorial delimitation". Locale is the setting of social interaction in space and time. Locales vary and may overlap depending on the issues and behaviour that are analyzed. Understanding of this "zoning of time-space in relation to routinized social practices" is critical to understanding the exercise of power in society, Giddens argues. The concept of locales enables Giddens to incorporate insights from dependency theory and related approaches that use regional distinctions in explanation.

Structuration theory's relevance for understanding international territorial disputes is evident in several of its theoretical assumptions. First, individual agents are the units of analysis. Second, Structuration theory avoids reifying the nation-state. Third, power is a key variable, inviting the analyst to study the dialectic of control that is central to all social relations. Fourth, Structuration theory views institutions as social constructs that are mutable, alterable, and fundamentally contested in a variety of ways by those actors affected by such institutions. Political jurisdictions are thus socially constructed artifacts that may be understood and acted upon in a variety of ways, the interplay among various actors determining how their boundaries are structured and what their significance is in any given instance. Fifth, Structuration theory incorporates the study of locales as a key to an accounting of where, how, and why individuals behave as they do.

In the process, Structuration theory dispenses with conventional micro-macro distinctions in thinking about localities, regions, and national centers. Sixth, Structuration theory is sensitive to temporality, not just as set of coordinates along a chronologically continuum but as a mode of cognitive orientation actively linked to other contextual elements of human society. To demonstrate the utility of this approach we now apply it to a well known territorial dispute on the U.S.-Mexico border, the Chamizal controversy while in principle, any instance of international territorial conflict should suffice, the Chamizal case has several features that lend it to an illustration of the Structuration theory approach.

First, the primary stakes are fairly narrow, delimiting the scope of the conflict, making this a more manageable case for purposes of analysis. Second, the conflict unfolds over a long period of time, across a range of formal jurisdictions and social settings with multiple actors involved from the local to the national levels such that spatial and temporal aspects can be highlighted in the analysis. Third, a substantial case literature can be drawn upon for purposes of analysis. To facilitate subsequent analysis the case history below is written from an Structuration theory perspective, though all the essential facts utilized by dependency theorists and strategic coalition theorists are included in the narrative. A comparison of rival approaches follows the case narrative.

THE CHAMIZAL DISPUTE

The diplomatic negotiations aimed at a settlement of the Chamizal dispute proceed in six distinct chronological phases. The Chamizal dispute has its origins in the meandering of the Rio Grande River which, after the Treaty of Guadalupe-Hidalgo (1848) which specifies the middle of the river as the international boundary, continued to wander. After 1852 the river shifted course such that as much as 600 acres of Mexican land was deposited on the northern side of the river in the area where the river transected the communities of El Paso, Texas, and Ciudad Juarez, Mexico, due both to accretion (gradual erosion) and avulsion (rapid erosion). The affected territory was to remain under *de facto* U.S. jurisdiction until formal settlement in 1963.

Notwithstanding the fact that the U.S. and Mexico had formalized arrangements for adjusting such territorial disputes, the Chamizal dispute remained a parochial matter until 1895. The historical record suggests this was due to (a) the area's limited population, (b) the relatively low value of the property at stake, and (c) local property owners' limited capacity to influence state and national officials. The dispute is thus a locally situated problem for forty-three years.

In 1895, affected property owners in Ciudad Juarez (Chihuahua), Mexico, successfully persuaded the administration of Porfirio Diaz to press the issue with the U.S. government, demanding restoration of land or compensation in lieu thereof. The issue became something of a test case for a new commission, the International Boundary Commission, a small binational agency comprised of two national sections headed by individual commissioners and designed to resolve such disputes under the 1889 Boundary Convention. Situated in El Paso the IBCs commissioners were reluctant to concede local interests.

The possibility of working out a local solution was impeded by the outcome of the 1906 Water Treaty, where a hard line proprietary position by the United States, the upstream party, diminished Mexico's water allotment for the Ciudad Juarez area. The IBC's failure to reach agreement effectively transferred administrative jurisdiction to the national foreign ministries which respectively upheld the positions of their national commissioners. The issue was thus de-localized. In 1910, in accordance with the emerging institutional approach to international law and dispute settlement, the two foreign ministers agreed to seek arbitration of the dispute.

Arbitration was undertaken by a panel of three members, one representative apiece from the disputants and a neutral panelist from Canada as the third member and chair of the arbitration panel. The arbitral panel, departing from its terms of reference, divided the tract, imparting roughly one-third of the Chamizal to the U.S. and the remainder to Mexico. Arguing that the panel violated its terms of reference the U.S. State Department refused to be bound by the decision. The issue subsequently became a *cause celebre* in Mexico and Latin America -evidence that the U.S. would never accept an adverse arbitral decision and, by implication, abide by the conventions of the emerging international law regime.

At this point, then, the problem is no longer framed in a discourse of local interests or practical considerations related to local development needs, or a discourse of international comity with bilateral or local significance, but is instead framed as an international dispute with global ramifications as it bore on the role of the United States as an emerging hemispheric and world power. Its symbolism and stakes had broadened considerably. Both discourse and effective authority shifted to national and international locales dominated by national statesmen.

The period following the failed arbitration is turbulent, both at the global, binational, national, and local levels relevant to the Chamizal dispute. At the global level, the onset of the World War concentrated diplomatic attention on European affairs, placing various regional questions on the backburner of national priorities. At the binational level, the Mexican revolution heightened tensions in the border area and disrupted normal channels of diplomatic discourse. In Mexico, national administration was disrupted by the Mexican Revolution. At the local level, Ciudad Juarez was a focal point for revolutionary activity and the threat of violence drew attention away from concern with the Chamizal.

With the Revolution's end and the restoration of diplomatic ties discussions on the Chamizal resumed. Still, national policy in both countries remained isolationist and protectionist, limiting diplomatic options. During this phase, while the issue largely remains nationalized, economic development in the Rio Grande region draws attention to the need to better manage the riparian boundary and settle old disputes. The 13C is delegated the task of reaching agreement on channelisation of the Rio Grande river and exploring the prospects of developing reclamation works mutually beneficial to both countries. Thus, by comparison to an earlier era of zero-sum-discourse, a positive sum discourse gets underway that reframes the Chamizal dispute.

While national righteousness and national control remain the architectural elements of diplomacy on the Chamizal, the locus of influence shifts downward to the local level where Rio Grande communities have a stake in transboundary cooperation. The IBC, despite its federal character, is thus drawn into this discourse on local development, as local actors lobby for projects to develop the Rio Grande. In the early 1930 the Rio Grande Rectification Project to channelize the Rio Grande through the El Paso-Juarez region so as to prevent flooding and conserve water resources for agriculture draws new attention to the Chamizal question.

Moreover, the Chamizal, by dent of its location in relation to El Paso-Cd. Juarez urban expansion, becomes valuable property, and its regularisation is deemed vital for municipal development. Concurrently, both local and state interests in Texas join with those of other states and various Mexican states to lobby for a binational treaty to settle permanently the longstanding dispute over the apportionment of the waters of the middle and lower Rio Grande and the Colorado River.

The result of these manifold changes is a new, nearly successful, effort to settle the Chamizal dispute. In this case, the IBC advanced a settlement initiative in 1929 based on swapping the Chamizal for a nearby tract (Cordoba Island) and *de facto* acceptance of the 1911 award without formally accepting the judgment against the United States. When Mexico resisted, State Department negotiators proposed simply to accept the 1911 award to pave the way for channelisation of the Rio Grande. Local interests were unwilling to go that far, however. The eventual U.S. proposal in 1932 was rejected by Mexico. Offsetting this shift in the locus of interest and control away from the foreign ministries, however, is renewed bilateral friction after 1934 with the Mexican administration of Lazaro Cardenas nationalizing various industries, including petroleum.

As a result, neither the U.S. nor Mexico pursue further Chamizal talks in the 1930's, indeed the Cardenas administration uses the Chamizal case to argue against arbitration of other claims with the United States. In sum, in Structuration theory terms, issues external to the dominant concerns of the nation-state actors combine to partially redistribute the locus of issue control to regional and local locales, though nation-state institutional practice restricts initiatives at these lower levels. Subsequent international developments make the two nations more amenable to a settlement. World War II draws Mexico and the United States closer together while the recognized need for a post-WWII international political order provides U.S. leaders with incentive to settle old disputes in order to assert global leadership.

Hemispheric allies assume particular importance as building blocks of the new international order - the Organisation of American States is an architectural keystone of U.S. leadership within the emergent United Nations system. At the bilateral level, the two countries successfully negotiate the 1944 U.S.-Mexico Water Treaty, apportioning the water of the middle and lower Rio Grande and the Colorado River. The renewal of Chamizal discussions emerges; in fact, as a Mexican initiative associated with the successful conclusions of negotiations on the 1944 Water Treaty With ratification of the 1944 Water Treaty the two countries join the Chamizal issue again.

In 1947, the Truman administration instructed the State Department to settle the issue, if necessary on Mexico's terms. Unfortunately for a settlement, the 1944 Water Treaty had restructured the IBC into a new International Boundary and Water Commission (IBWC) with line jurisdiction on the issue. The IBWC, particularly its U.S. Section, was politically structured so as to be nearly autonomous of the State Department, functioning as a quasi-independent agency, and highly responsive to its local border constituencies, in this case the state of Texas. Moreover, the Texas state delegation to the U.S. Congress had emerged as a crucial voting bloc with various members dominating key committees - Senator Tom Connally, for instance, ran the Senate Foreign Relations Committee - and Texas was a Democratic state crucial to Truman's reelection chances.

In this capacity the IEWC's U.S. Section was strategically positioned to resist any national initiative that failed to satisfy local concerns. Unwilling to concede the Chamizal to Mexico, local interests, the IBWC, and Texas state representatives in the U.S. Congress successfully resisted Truman's initiative in 1947-48, then again in 1950-51. A near compromise in 1951 based on the U.S.'s formal recognition of the 1911 award and a concession of 420 acres of the tract also fails due to a switch of presidential administrations in Mexico. Thus, institutional changes within the international, bilateral, and nation-state locales favoring a settlement are offset by other nation-state institutional shifts and in the institutional nexus between nation, region, and locality affecting the Chamizal question.

The importance of personality and proximity are important here, as is the fact that certain vital instruments of national administrative power are stored at the IBWC, enabling regional and local interests to check national level initiatives. The failure of the two Truman rounds is followed by further efforts to resolve the problem during the Eisenhower administration. While most of the background conditions remain the same, the retirement of the long-term IBC-IBWC U.S. Commissioner, Lawrence Lawson, and the emergence of new players at the U.S. Embassy in Mexico and the State Department influence the negotiations in this phase.

So too does the continued urbanisation of the Chamizal tract which made it more difficult for U.S. diplomats to offer favourable concessions on the issue to Mexico. Mexico's decision to seek a solution to another "Banco" (detached tract) dispute, the Ojinaga, is the basis for renewed discussions between 1956 and 1959. U.S. diplomats were surprised and concerned with this gambit since they hoped to be able to fashion a comprehensive agreement to adjust boundary disputes for the full reach of the river. Yet under existing boundary conventions Mexico had the right to initiate a separate negotiation on the Ojinana tract.

Archival evidence indicates that Mexico's initiative provided the basis for U.S. State Department diplomats partially to wrest control of the Chamizal issue from officials at the IBWC while successfully holding out for treating the Chamizal as a separate but linked question. Also interesting is evidence that diplomats in both countries utilized the terms nearly agreed to in 1951 as a critical reference for their basic national positions. Here, we see how a key personality shift at the IBWC redistributes administrative control, allowing nationally oriented actors to reassert themselves given the strategic opportunity. Control of the administrative record also shapes the distribution of institutional power.

New administrations in Mexico and the United States are part of the changing backdrop for Chamizal negotiations in the 1960s. These administrative changes certainly brought about an auspicious and strategically situated set of actors. Texan Thomas C. Mann, who negotiated the 1951 Chamizal deal on favourable terms for Mexico, was appointed U.S. Ambassador to Mexico. Texas Senator Lyndon B. Johnson was elected Vice-President, thus tying him more directly to presidential initiative. The Texas congressional delegation, albeit powerful and still influential in this case, no longer controlled the vital Senate Foreign Relations Committee. Moreover, President John F Kennedy's Alliance for Progress initiative put a premium on deepening U.S. ties to Latin America, with Mexico a high priority for improved bilateral ties.

At the IBWC, the death of U.S. Commissioner Leland Hewitt meant that Joseph Friedkin, Principal Engineer for the IBWC's U.S. Section, and a seasoned, pragmatic actor extraordinarily familiar with the local scene and the Chamizal negotiations, took the administrative helm. In Mexico, moreover, Mexico's Ambassador to the U.S. during the Eisenhower administration, Manuel Tello, was appointed Foreign Minister, controlling Mexico's negotiations, and he, in turn, asked Sanchez Gavito, the diplomat who negotiated the 1951 deal, to advise: Mexico's negotiating team. In both countries, then, an experienced set of diplomats with longstanding ties and connections to the Chamizal negotiations and credible connections to the various levels of government in their respective countries were entrusted with the proceedings.

On the occasion of Kennedy's state visit to Mexico in 1962 the two countries announced they would place the Chamizal question on the table based on a full consideration of the historical record. The Joint MOU proposed to "give effect in today's circumstances to the 1911 international arbitration award." By this language the U.S. was able to dodge a formal commitment to accept the award while tacitly acknowledging it might consider such an arrangement. Control of the U.S. negotiating team was placed decisively in the hands of the State Department with the IBWC playing a supporting technical role.

The Kennedy administration carefully labored to build local support for a settlement by promising to commit a substantial amount of federal funds to the development of the Chamizal and the metropolitan El Paso community as the outgrowth of any settlement partitioning the tract. Thus the dispute was settled in 1963, largely on the basis of the formula agreed upon in 1951. In Structuration theory terms, the repositioning of administrative personnel in key roles at the nation-state level, particularly those combining both expertise on the issue and personal interests bridging across the various affected locales, and U.S actors' knowledge that certain local (Texas) concerns had to be met in order to amplify U.S. national influence at the international level, made possible an allocative solution that satisfied influentials across locales.

DEPENDENCY, STRATEGIC COALITION, AND STRUCTURATION THEORY EXPLANATIONS

The Chamizal settlement has been explained in various ways. One explanation, drawing on historical conventions, attributes the settlement to the intervention of wise men that put aside past differences to finally reach an accommodation. Another explanation, based on dependency theory, suggests that Mexico, as the weaker party, while righteously defending its legal-diplomatic perspective on the case, was eventually forced to concede in the face of superior economic and diplomatic power. Yet another interpretation, based on strategic coalition theory, sees the settlement as an outcome of strategically situated behaviour operating primarily at the level of U.S. domestic politics.

All these accounts are committed to an explanation that centers on the nation-state. A brief review of the central elements of two of these explanations, dependency theory and strategic coalition theory, helps illustrate the merits of the alternate, Structuration theory, approach.

A DEPENDENCY THEORY EXPLANATION

A dependency theory explanation of the Chamizal settlement is found in Cesar Sepulveda's (1983) study of the El Chamizal problem. Though not as well crafted as some dependency theory explanations, Sepulveda's study stresses the asymmetrical relationship between the U.S. and Mexico where the U.S. as dominant partner was able successfully to resist Mexican settlement overtures for a protracted length of time at some considerable cost to Mexico.

In this explanation the clear implication, though not carefully specified by the author, is that U.S. diplomats and politicians operating from a hegemonic position, were able to determine the timing and the occasion of arriving at a settlement that conceded only part of Mexico's just claims against the U.S. Across the various phases of the negotiations (the lesser known Truman and Eisenhower rounds are not mentioned) the U.S. bargaining approach reflected a unified and consistent effort to achieve a solution that best defended and advanced U.S. economic interests. In the end, this was arguably accomplished. From this perspective, U.S. concessions are motivated by an effort to promote economic growth in the El Paso area and protect downstream Texas agricultural interests on the Rio Grande.

A STRATEGIC CHOICE EXPLANATION

Strategic choice explanations, as noted, proceed from rational choice or game theoretic principles focusing on individuals or small sets of individuals as units of analysis and stressing the transitivity of social choice. A variation of this approach is seen in strategic coalition theory where dispute settlement is seen as a function of coalition formation in the two interlinked arenas of domestic politics and foreign policy

In the case of the Chamizal, Lamborn and Mumme apply this approach with some success, tracking the evolution of coalition behaviour in the United States across the various negotiating rounds to account for the eventual settlement. Their explanation focuses on individuals and groups at various levels in U.S. government as they are implicated in four :sets of variables: the interstate power structure, the interstate issue structure, actors' judgments concerning the implications of different potential outcomes, and theoretical characteristics of the units of analysis to include the structure of the decision-making unit, the domestic decision-making environment, and risking taking propensities and normative values affecting the calculus of choice.

Lamborn and Mumme's explanation compares the interaction of these key variables as they influenced foreign policy and supporting domestic policy coalitions in the Hoover, Truman, Eisenhower, and Kennedy rounds of negotiations. In brief, they argue that while the interstate power and issue structures insulated the U.S. and reinforced U.S. hegemony on the Chamizal question through the Hoover round, the emergence of the Cold War and the new necessities of alliance formation altered strategic calculations in the direction of accommodating Mexican demands.

Truman's initiative to settle the issue on Mexican terms, however, was not sustainable domestically due to the resistance of an alliance of strategically situated bureaucrats (at the IBWC) and state politicians. The opposition coalition weakened, however, during the Eisenhower years after the retirement of influential IBWC Commissioner Lawrence Lawson, and the interstate incentives amplified due to new Mexican claims on the U.S.A. realignment of the domestic coalition coupled to sustained and favourable support by the foreign policy coalition and its willingness to make side payments to Texas to further broaden foreign policy objectives made possible a settlement on the basis of significant concessions to Mexico.

A STRUCTURATION THEORY EXPLANATION

By comparison to the dependency and strategic coalition theory approaches, an Structuration theory approach broadens the explanatory framework and moves away from a state-centric mode of explanation. It does so in several ways. First, it draws attention to the dialectic of control expressed in this instance as the strategic interplay of actors and authorities at various levels with differential resources for influencing public policy, the problematic of crafting winning political coalitions, and the various ways the local actors resist national ones and shape the agenda of dispute settlement.

While some of these elements are captured by other approaches, particularly those interpreting the dispute from a strategic coalition perspective, Structuration theory explicitly requires the analyst to examine this interplay of elements at and across different social and institutional levels. For example, while formal authority for settling the Chamizal dispute is situated at the national level, and control over the negotiations is from the early stages centered at the national level, the story of the Chamizal is, in fact, a story that turns substantially on how local and state authorities in the United States, from the late 1920s onward, resisted national pressures to resolve the dispute on teams less favourable to national interests.

As seen above, local interests are able to fashion alliances with the IBWC after 1945 to resist the U.S. State Department's impulse to settle the issue on terms approximating those of the 1911 Award. The dialectic of control occurs in the context of shifting national positions on the issue as U.S. policy shifts from a highly protectionist strategy to one defined by the Good Neighbor policy and the necessity to settle local disputes in order to better stake out U.S. influence in the post-WWII international order. Local authorities over time are able strategically to position themselves to exert leverage in the context of this changing foreign policy agenda at the national level.

Structuration theory also directs our attention to discourse politics and the rhetorical possibilities of political action. Much of an explanation of the Chamizal turns on how different groups were able, over time, to frame the discourse on a settlement. What we see in the aftermath of 1911 arbitration is a discourse framed by protectionism articulated within the framework of each nation's national experience and ambitions. Mexico, against the backdrop of territorial losses to the United States, chooses to interpret the result as a fair settlement based on third-party appraisal even if the findings exceeded the arbitrators' mandate. The U.S., confident it had the superior technical argument and accustomed to prevailing in bilateral territorial disputes takes exception to the finds and focuses on the arbitrators' terms of reference, a technical question.

Over time, however, the Chamizal discourse in the United States changes. Committed to its technical perspective, the State Department finds itself weighing that discourse against a new discourse associated with America's global ambitions. While the merits of the Department's technical case were embraced by successive sets of diplomats, the substantive values associated with it diminish in relation to growing ambitions and opportunities for global influence. Accordingly, the discourse within the Department and between it and other agencies shifts after WW II.

At the local level, the discourse on the Chamizal is also shaped by protectionism at the outset. Over time, however, the discourse is modified by an emerging interest in local development and securing agricultural and commercial opportunities in the region. The result is a more pragmatic and strategic discourse, or framing of the issues, and actions deemed necessary to secure local interests. In Mexico, where foreign policy continues to be highly centralized, the equity dimension of the Chamizal is sustained and becomes even more symbolically loaded as national politicians employ the case as evidence of a chronic unwillingness of the United States to deal fairly with Mexico.

The symbolic values are thus reinforced, complicating a settlement on strictly pragmatic or practical grounds. In the Chamizal case we also see the importance of sustaining a "historic memory" of the case over time. From the evidence we have, it seems fair to say that the formal diplomatic records at State and the IBWC play a more critical role in incubating, carrying, and defining the discourse on the Chamizal in the United States where few citizens outside the region are aware of the case, whereas, while important to Mexico, the files are secondary to the symbolic and highly politicized values successive waves of Mexican politicians and journalists place on the Chamizal question.

Simply put, what we see is a more private arena of discourse in the United States and a more public arena at work in Mexico. These differences interact with other properties of the case to influence the process and substance of the settlement. Third, it draws our attention to the role of "locale" in framing and shaping the possibilities for a settlement. While the spatial-geographic context affecting Chamizal discussions is utilized in other explanations, standard approaches tend to stress the rising economic value of the Chamizal due to urbanisation development and the demand for additional reclamation works on the Rio Grande as the key variables shaping a solution (e.g., the more valuable the property, the greater the joint incentive to reach agreement). Structuration theory would accept these elements as explanatory factors, but point as well to several other important aspects of the geographic (locale-region) context.

For example, Structuration theory suggests the additional functions of local urbanisation - for instance, in shaping the political map and the structure of political jurisdictions and power relations in Texas and along the border. El Paso's development as a political jurisdiction carries with it additional influence in state and national politics. Structuration theory also points to the "spatial distanciation," or connectedness, between different parts of the boundary (Rio Grande River) and the relevance of understanding the wider context of river basin development as a set of opportunities for social action. One example is the opportunity to link issues and bargain seen in the Ojinaga tract case and other pending banco disputes.

It further directs our attention to the importance of examining the functions of locale at different levels, or as a set of nested locales as; these come to bear on the negotiating process. In this case, for example, fact that a federal agency (the U.S. IBWC Section) is located on the border provides it with a strong link to local clienteles. The State Department not only has a different organisational imperative, but bureaucratically occupies a different spatial framework, with further regionalisation within it. These differences in spatial (geographic) orientation account for important differences in perspective among offices interior to the State Department in this case. Similarly, the U.S. and Mexico's national are situated such that they establish a certain opportunity set for diplomatic influence.

From the preceding discussion is should be evident that Structuration theory's analytical value is largely as a compliment to established methods of examining the dynamics of international territorial disputes. An Structuration theory perspective directs our attention to relational aspects of the exercise of political power that are often neglected or marginalized by state-centric analysis, emphasizing careful description and keen sensitivity to effects of space and time on the social constructions of human agents. While in principle Structuration theory is applicable to the study of all international territorial disputes, as practical matter, given scholarly constraints, it will be difficult to deploy in the study of conflicts of great complexity, in which numerous governments and other social players are engaged. That said, an Structuration theory approach seems particularly fruitful for the analysis of certain types of international territorial disputes and regional conflicts.

As the Chamizal case shows, it can be usefully applied to the analysis of territorial, transboundary, or regionally situated disputes with delimited stakes and protracted temporal duration in which actors at multiple levels of society and government are involved. It should also be useful for examining the behaviour of local or regional actors in support or subvention of the international norms and practices of and among nation-states. Similarly, it may lend itself to examining situations of contested sovereignty where local or regional enclaves challenge authority in established territorial jurisdictions. In sum, while not inimical to established modes of theorizing about inter national territorial disputes, Structuration theory lends theoretical support to recent scholarship that is reexamining the empirical basis of territorial conflict. It also challenges scholars to consider more integrative and complete explanations or, quasi-explanations, concerning these political dynamics. This is good advice that can only advance our understanding of territorially based disputes.

6

Nationalism and International Relations Theory

This chapter explores the ambiguous relationship between nationalism, which we understand as the desire for the convergence of nation and state, and state-centric discourses of realism and liberalism in the discipline of International Relations. Rule's use of the word careening in the quotation above is characteristic of the way in which many students of International Relations tend to take "nation-states" as given. Careening is a nautical term meaning to lean a boat over on one side so that repairs can be done on those parts which are normally underwater. In mainstream International Relations, nationalism is one such part.

Notwithstanding the widely recognised difficulties of defining nationalism, Jens Bartelson argues that, in International Relations, "nationalism ... is portrayed as a baseline fact of international politics, as an immutable outcome of an irreversible process". Yet despite increasing attention given to the impact of ill defined processes of globalisation, and to questions of identity by post-colonial theorists and critical International Relations' scholars, Yosef Lapid and Friedrich Kratochwil could still make the telling observation in 1996 that "international relations seem(s) to have converged on little else but the sustained exclusion of the national problematic ...

relegating it to a fringe phenomenon". Nationalism appears to be both central to and marginalised in mainstream International Relations.

Rule's metaphor implies that during the 1990s nation states; however they are defined, are like boats in need of repair. They cannot be abandoned, yet they cannot proceed as before. His expectation is that once repairs are done the ship of state will ride out the storms following the end of the Cold War. Such thinking encapsulates much that is representative of International Relations during the 1990s. It assumes that a "bipolar world" existed once and world orders come and go as international change heads inevitably towards new, yet to be determined equilibrium points. According to Rule, all we know is that the world does not "resemble what went before" because nationalism will count for "much more than before".

Though Rule was anticipating the growing significance of nationalism during the 1990s for questions of world order, the clear implication, which students of nationalism may find strange, is that nationalism had not counted for much previously. Yet this is precisely the claim. While attention in International Relations to nationalism "above the water line" is to be welcomed, it also highlights previous difficulties. In the first part of this chapter we argue that previously serious study of nationalism was difficult in International Relations because of what Rob Walker defines succinctly as a sharp distinction between politics inside and relations outside the territorial borders of existing sovereign states. William Connolly describes the distinction thus:

If political theory is the academic field where questions of individuality, loyalty, community, rights, belonging, democracy, justice and freedom are debated inside the contours Of the state, international relations is the field where diplomacy, subversion, order through anarchy, war, low intensity conflict, economic interdependence, and national security are observed through the optics of international relations.

Such a distinction led Martin Wight in 1966 to title his famous article "Why is There no International Theory?" suggesting indirectly why theories of nationalism were of no direct concern to students of international relations. In the second part of this chapter we explore different strategies for coping with nationalism after 1945; in particular, those of containment and dilution. Finally, we conclude with the speculative observation that it no longer makes sense to sustain the idea that the study of international relations is best pursued within an autonomous discipline of academic inquiry. Indeed, only by rejecting claims to autonomy is it possible for International Relations to deal more effectively with the contradiction between supporting the sovereignty of nation states and repressing nationalism for the sake of world order. This contradiction, we argue, plagues both realism and liberalism in International Relations.

NATIONS, STATES AND NATION-STATES IN INTERNATIONAL RELATIONS

Students of international relations, it might be argued, are concerned primarily with relations between political entities called nation-states. It does not follow; however, that world order is sustained automatically simply because the legitimacy of state sovereignty is recognised when members welcome a new state into the club of "nation-states". Nevertheless, this presumption is inherent in an academic discipline which traditionally limits its subject matter to the consequences of a world already divided into nation-states. It is also one reason why many students of international relations often struggle on precisely those occasions when the terms of nation-statehood are violently renegotiated.

As students of nationalism are well aware, whether nations correspond with the territorial borders of juridical sovereign states or not depends a great deal on how the nation is constructed and sustained. Unfortunately, by confining their focus to relations among states, students of international relations are predisposed to the view that nationalism is of no central concern because it normally manes itself felt only in the creation of sovereign states. With few exceptions, International Relations is the study of what happens outside nation-states after they form. As Richard Devetak argues, "the state is taken to be an already settled political entity".

International Relations sustain its identity and intellectual autonomy by relegating nationalism to the realm of domestic politics, which reduces it to a phenomenon on the inside of the nation state. By any number of complex historical processes, individuals in physical occupation of a territory may be transformed into citizens of a state, who bond together in defence of their identity and the boundaries of the nation. The sovereignty of the nation-state is then legitimated in the eyes of an international community of similarly constituted actors. Only at this point does the sovereign nation-state enter the international system or society and become of interest to International Relations; which is why, as James Mayall concludes somewhat forlornly, "in the vast literature on nationalism, so few books are written by students of International relation, and conversely why, in the International relation literature, nationalism receives only scant attention".

The absence of any sustained attention to nationalism is a handicap for a discipline which has always concerned itself with having a special prerogative in the study of global politics. It is not clear how students of international relations can proceed without calling into question the autonomy of their discipline. As Roxanne Doty insists, "[i]f we are to gain a better understanding of the practices which impose the kinds of identities and inside/outside distinctions upon which the discipline of International Relations depends, we must engage in concrete studies of those situations in which just these things are put in doubt". One cannot simply add nationalism to traditional agendas in International Relations. Engagement with the nationalist challenge to world order in the 1990s also requires a prior concern with the scant attention paid previously to nationalism in a discipline whose very name - International Relations - presupposes its importance.

NATIONALISM AND WORLD ORDER

Thus far we have suggested that even though the existence of nation states is central to the concerns of International Relations, nationalism as a powerful force is under-theorised. Nevertheless, it is possible to discern a consensus within the discipline regarding the need' in the interest of world order, to contain or dilute nationalist challenges - the "New Tribalism", as Michael Walzer put it - to the status quo of existing sovereign states since the Cold War. The only rider is that existing states will support the status quo and not be seen to initiate or support revolutionary challenges to it. The problem here is that nationalism, used to justify claims for self-determination, simultaneously perpetuates the sovereign states system and undermines it, international Relations runs the danger of downplaying the importance of the very phenomenon which helps sustains it.

Ever since the French and American Revolutions of the late eighteenth century signalled the nadir of dynastic sovereignty, the society of states has been the site of a fundamental contradiction between diplomatic and legal superstructures rooted in the Westphalian compromise of formal equality and non-intervention on the one band, and ins substantive more] justification in the right to self-determination for all "peoples" on the other. Twentieth century euphemisms such as "nation-state" and "United Nations" either merely disguise contradictions which current territorial divisions are assumed to have solved or push them down "to the depths of history".

What Mayall calls the national idea "holds that the world is (or should be) divided into nations and that the nation is the only proper base for a sovereign state and the ultimate source of governmental authority". According to Gellner, the national ideal is one "which holds that the political and the national unit should be congruent". All that is well and good, but an important practical problem is left unattended if defence of the status quo overrides everything else. Violent, nationalist disruption of world order is simply too difficult to deal with quickly. During the 1990s, the Balkans, Somalia and Rwanda seem to have short circuited the system of international decision making at the first hurdle. Was international intervention justified? Despite the. humanitarian dimensions of these modern tragedies, the answer to this question was not easily found.

What then of the Commonwealth of Independent States, Central Asia and India? What are the lessons, if any, of Chechnia, Kurdistan and Kashmir in the search for world order? Dealing with fragmenting or failed states does not derive easily from International Relation's strict inside/outside frame. It raises many questions, but few answers. The problem posed by nationalism for those concerned with the political organisation of the world is that there are no objective criteria to identify the number of states necessary to achieve the national idea, although some combination, imagined or real, of shared history, common language, and ethnic heritage seems to be the most common in the literature on nationalism.

Nationalism fuses material factors, historical myths and the subjective consciousness of their significance for the political legitimacy of either elites which control the state or those who seek to challenge them. Nationalism also "connotes a group of people who feel that they are ancestrally related". While justifiable on the grounds of the right of all peoples to self-determination, such arguments are a nightmare for International Relations. The breakup of the existing territorial division of the world into many smaller and possibly some larger national units is simply too destructive of the status quo even to contemplate, yet in principle an ideal solution to the problem of world order would be to ensure that all states correspond with all identified nations.

Regardless of how one fits globalisation or other dimensions of identity politics into this equation, we can see here how the principle of equating nation with state, which sustains the international community, also frustrates its attempts to fashion an ordered world. Although nationalism is potentially subversive of any particular territorial status quo, it is the basis of territorial sovereignty per se. In short, for students of international relations nationalism is necessarily ambiguous. Regardless of whether one is a realist or liberal, nationalism is both a threat to and justification of the division of humanity into separate sovereign states.

In light of this ambiguity and the tendency in International Relation to relegate nationalism to an internal political sphere the two sections following explore briefly how realist and liberal traditions of world order coped with nationalism in the historical context of post-1945 international relations. Of course, world order is also a contested concept in International Relations. Although it often refers to the pattern of relations among states which best maintains values and processes essential to the status quo, what these values and processes are is the subject of intense controversy.

As Knutsen observes, the dominant discourses of world order reflect two "major ideological traditions which inform contemporary speculation about politics: liberalism [and] conservatism". Since 1945 these have taken the form of diluting and containing nationalism respectively. World order, then, should not be understood as a description of an existing state of affairs. In International Relations it is a purposive political project, one which seeks to realize whatever goals and values to which one subscribes. The first section deals with containment, seeing it was a dominant ideology of the Cold War. We do not aim to be comprehensive. Indeed only the most general description is possible. We seek simply to highlight those aspects which account for International Relations' ambiguous relationship with nationalism.

CONSERVATIVE CONTAINMENT

A traditional realist approach to the problem of world order seeks to contain nationalism within the existing distribution of territorial borders, so the' it does not upset a stable balance of power among so called "Great Powers". As its name suggests, realism sees little need to defend its ideological conservatism because there are, it is claimed, certain fundamental characteristics of inter-state politics, the rejection of which renders rival discourses "idealistic", regardless of their labels. The familiar story starts with anarchy among states. The absence of an international leviathan or world government, it is claimed, generates security dilemmas for states, the existence of which imposes a certain degree of uniformity on state behaviour in the system.

The allegedly ubiquitous struggle for power and security results in either war or cooperation. Preparedness for war is the natural state of affairs because there is no higher authority than the sovereign state which can deal with the security dilemma. The niceties of international law, according to which all states recognise each other as sovereign equals, are subject to the degree to which the inequality of power among them can be managed through the balance of power. Realism is a discourse of tragedy and partial redemption via a community of the powerful, which upholds the minimum goals of maintaining what, has come to be called a society of states.

The maintenance of international stability, according to this traditional discourse, requires a concert of great powers which is able to maintain the balance of power and reduce incentives for the weak to engage in revolutionary behaviour. During the nineteenth century in Europe, one aspect of the struggle to maintain political order was containing nationalism, as violence erupted against the ancient regime and the Ottoman and Hapsburg empires. For traditional realists, the superpowers of the Cold War era were poor substitutes for the nineteenth century Concert of Europe. The Soviet Union itself was painted as a revolutionary power with scant regard for the norms of international society, whilst US foreign policy was often imperial and dangerously hegemonic.

So called "national liberation struggles" and "counter revolutionary activities" were subsumed under this bipolar contest. The "nationalist" dimensions of such struggles in both spheres of influence were ignored, as international relations were reduced to problems of national security. By the late 1970s, nostalgia for nineteenth century European statecraft was replaced by a more complacent attitude within the framework of "structural realism". The very factors that post-Second World War realists in the United States identified as most inimical to international order - bipolarity and nuclear weapons - were credited by Kenneth Waltz as the structural prerequisites for systemic stability.

The Soviet Union, it was argued, had been contained successfully less by the deliberate efforts of the United States than by the incentives for socialisation generated by a bipolar structure which contributed to the evolution of an "adversary partnership" between the superpowers As for nationalism, structural realism was even less concerned with it as an international phenomenon. Bartelson's observations about Waltz's treatment of sovereignty apply equally to nationalism. Bartelson argues that "In the abstract and void state of the latter

Waltz, the social scope of sovereignty drops out as irrelevant together with all other unit attributes except sovereignty itself".

Nonetheless, if one definition of stability is structural sustainability, as opposed to peace, that source of structural realism's complacency is no longer available. With the end of the Cold War, scholars began to examine the potential for a late-twentieth century version of the Concert system, whereby a loose coalition of great powers cooperate to tackle global problems. One such problem in the 1990s was identified early as nationalism's often violent challenge to world order. As with the nineteenth century, a problem for International Relations is the contradiction between upholding the right of peoples to self-determination and defending the existing system or society of sovereign states.

For any Concert, the problem is bow to manipulate nationalism - when to contain and when to recognise it - so that the interests of the great powers and, by implication, world order are best served. In so far as containing nationalism was a an indirect goal of the Cold War, in that explanations of nationalist struggles were reduced to an over-arching bipolar contest, there were three main ways in which this was attempted. First, the superpowers appealed to the theoretical possibility of nuclear conflict between them to impose internal discipline over their respective spheres of influence. The internal pay-off of external threats, imagined or otherwise, was functional for both the Soviet Union and the United States.

While US foreign policy disciplined Central and Latin America, the eventual collapse of the Soviet Union was facilitated by Gorbachev's bold but ultimately self-defeating attempt to redefine Soviet security needs during the late 1980s. He removed previously functional external threats and the Soviet Union fractured on the basis of contested internal national boundaries whose limits are yet to be determined. Secondly, the Cold War imposed certain limits on decolonisation, which were a product of both revolution from below and the inability of European states to maintain their former empires. Nation-building became the imperative for Third World elites occupying new states which proliferated in the late 1950s and early 1960s.

In turn, they were assisted in maintaining new states along colonial lines, particularly in Africa, by external alliances with the superpowers to ward off internal challenges to their legitimacy. Finally, the danger of nuclear war and the mutual interests of the superpowers in sustaining their global supremacy placed strict limits on the degree to which each sought to promote nationalism in the Third World for its own purposes. Particularly after the Cuban missile crisis, the nuclear stand-off of mutually assured destruction promoted the expansion of the Cold War via support of proxy wars in the periphery, but not to the extent of endangering the central balance itself.

Understood in this light, the end of the Cold War and subsequent breakup of the Soviet Union threatened in real and potential ways the compromise fashioned between world order, which was based on the nationalist ideal of universal self-determination, and the sometimes forced distribution (largely, though not exclusively) of territorial borders into two spheres of influence after the Second World War. In the 1990s, the likelihood of containing the wave of nationalism via the coordinated action of a concert of great powers is diminished by the absence of Cold War constraints. What defines a great power in the 1990s is problematic. Despite the rhetoric of a new world order during the Gulf War, advocates of a new containment do so on the alleged enhanced ability of the United Nations to function as planned in 1945.

Optimism was also bolstered by the nature of the war itself. Iraq's invasion of Kuwait fitted precisely into the category of aggression across state frontiers which collective security was designed to deter and, if necessary, punish. With the hindsight of a mere few years, it is clear, however, that President Bush's new world order had a short shelf-life. More than half a century after the Second World War, the institutions created in its wake are in a state of crisis. In particular, the idea of collective security, even in the modified form represented by the United Nations, is inadequate to meet the challenges of fragmentation and civil war.

Some writers note that the ideological divide between East and West may be replaced by a new division between zones of peace and war. This is identified as one of two key differences between the 1990s and the Concert during the nineteenth century. First, the shifting coalitions between Britain, Austria-Hungary, Prussia and Russia were limited by a shared interest in containing nationalism within Europe, which threatened not only war between states but also the legitimacy of monarchical rule.

Germany, Japan, Russia and China appear reduced by such things as economic interdependence and the growth of cooperative security regimes, though conflict cannot be ruled out entirely. Secondly, of the five "institutions of international [inter-state!] society" identified by Hedley Bull as the mechanisms which uphold inter-state order (the balance of power, war, diplomacy, the great powers and international law), only great powers might be thought of as actors.

Today, it is not clear what common interests or incentives they have in acting together to contain nationalism, unless problems arise in regions of direct strategic significance, such as Central Europe, Central Asia or the Middle East. Even then, differences among the great powers have been significant. It is naive to expect a nascent Concert to agree to coordinated and radical reform of the international laws covering national sovereignty and United Nations' operating procedures which might facilitate and legitimize the containment of nationalism. There is precious little evidence that any of the so called "great powers" have either the capability or will to make the effort collectively during the 1990s.

Nonetheless, it is also important to acknowledge a tacit alliance between realist discourses and nationalism in the search for world order. The central realist axiom that international relations is an autonomous domain of power politics is based on a number of assumptions about the territorial state as the container of political community. What Ashley dubs the "anarchy problematique" is both a rejection of the "domestic analogy" for comprehending relations among states, and an equally insistent affirmation of sovereignty as an exclusionary institution. For Hobbes, the problem of international order is a consequence of the solution to a "domestic" state of nature via the Leviathan.

As Seth argues in his incisive critique of Hobbes' approach to the problem of order, the rhetorical move from universal premises to particularist conclusions provides crucial support for the national idea It fills the logical gaps in Hobbes' argument and provides "compelling justification as to why a particular state had come into being and was the one to which obligation was owed". If the political community is a creation of men escaping the inconveniences attendant upon the state of nature then why should they have covenanted particular commonwealths into being, rather than a universal community, ruled by a world sovereign?

Nationalism is an answer to a peculiarly modern dilemma, how to explain and legitimate the existence of a plurality of political communities and give membership an ethical dimension. Thus, although realism tends to privilege order at the expense of other values, its insistence on the dichotomies between inside and outside, community and anarchy, and progress and survival, serves to support nationalism as a substitute for the absolutist state in the modern era. By systematically screening out questions regarding the domestic basis upon which the Weberian state achieves a legitimate monopoly on the use of force within its territorial jurisdiction, realism is unable either to mount a persuasive critique of nationalism as an ideology, or to prescribe changes in the conduct of international relations that minimize the forces of imperialism, ancient or modern, against which nationalism represents a liberating force of self-determination.

LIBERAL DILUTION

Liberal diagnoses of the problem that nationalism poses for world order are also unpersuasive, albeit for very different reasons. Of course, liberals seek to promote a world order that not only minimizes conflict among the great powers, but also increases the scope of human freedom. In particular, three crucial differences between liberalism and realism explain the former's endorsement of what may be called "dilution from below", as opposed to "containment from above". First, liberals seek to attenuate state power over civil society, and promote the principle of governance by consent mediated through the rule of law. Secondly, liberalism is a progressive discourse based on the power of reason working its way through history to supply a telos of emancipation from the constraints of realism. Finally, the interests of states are not static and cannot be deduced in any straightforward fashion from the condition of anarchy.

Since the end of the Cold War, and especially in light of the benign way in which it ended, all three dimensions of the liberal discourse on world order have been re-examined at length. The resurgence of liberal international theory after its subordination to realism for most of the previous forty years even inspired an international Studies Association (ISA) Presidential Address entitled "The Neo-Idealist Moment". One book in particular has attracted a great deal of critical attention during the 1990s because its author, Francis Fukuyama, attempted an ambitious synthesis of all three ingredients in the liberal recipe.

He argues that the dynamics of commercial and republican liberalism are complementary aspects of historical progress towards the end of History. The secular, capitalist, liberal democratic state satisfies the material and psychosocial requirements of human nature, which the Greeks referred to as the striving for physical comfort. Fukuyama also stresses the importance of thymos, which is the desire for equal recognition guaranteed by the rule of law.

Within liberalism, the solution to the problem of nationalism lies in the spread of the conditions and processes which contribute to what Mueller calls the "obsolescence" of war, particularly among liberal democracies. Recall that Kant's plans for perpetual peace did not require the replacement of the inter-state system with world government, but the gradual evolution of a League or Federation of limited constitutional states. Such a vision tolerates, indeed it presupposes, a plurality of constitutional states whose external freedom of action is constrained, and whose conduct thereby does not conform to the Hobbesian image which dominates International Relations.

Accordingly, "civic nationalism" poses no threat to world order, for it does not require citizens to define their identity in a chauvinistic, exclusionary and potentially aggressive manner. Traditional liberal distinctions are a central motif in Michael Ignatieff's analysis of the resurgence of "ethnic nationalism" in the 1990s:

> Civic nationalism maintains that the nation should be composed of all those- regardless of race, colour, creed, gender, language or ethnicity – who subscribe to the nation's political creed. It envisages the nation as a community of equal rights-bearing citizens; united in patriotic attachment to a shared set of political practices and values ... [W]hat holds a society together is not common roots but law. This in turn assumes that national belonging can be a form of rational attachment.

Ignatieff's praise of civic nationalism is a reminder that in the eighteenth century, liberalism and nationalism were allies against the absolutist state, which resisted both. By the late nineteenth century, however, their paths had diverged. In Central and Eastern Europe, nationalist movements drew inspiration from the German Romantic and expressivist reaction to the Enlightenment. According to Gellner, this was due in part to the need to create the societal and structural prerequisites for industrialisation and modernisation in predominantly peasant societies, where elites embraced a cosmopolitan lifestyle whilst retaining the economic privileges of political centralism and the ancient regime.

For Gellner, tensions between liberalism and nationalism emerged and increased as one moved from West to East. In the light of important differences between their respective diagnoses of and prescriptions for dealing with the problem of nationalism in the 1990s, does Liberalism, like realism, promote what it seeks to repress? The answer to this question is yes, albeit by different routes. First, as a number of critics have observed, there is some danger that the policy implications of one influential Liberal recipe for world order - democratic states do not go to war with each other - may focus less on the long-term challenge of replicating Western democratic values in the world at large, and more on ins inverse logic. This is the argument that non-democratic states are inherently prone to war.

If the positive correlation between democracy and peace comes as close to an "iron law" as we are likely to find in International Relations, it is certainly not the case that the opposite holds between democracies and non-democratic states. The potential problems with pursing toe "democratic peace" thesis are two-fold. Either democratic states prudently prepare for war because it is deemed inevitable in a world of non-democratic states, or democratic states set out on a democratic mission to extend the zone of peace by destroying the "other".

There is some validity in toe classical realist charge that the militarisation of US containment policy after the Korean

War stemmed in part from the conflation of an apparent Soviet geopolitical threat with an undifferentiated, ideological obsession with Communism's illiberalism per se. In short, the seemingly benign liberal vision which helps to explain the emergence and consolidation of "pluralistic security communities" in some parts of the world also provides a rationale for the creation of an "other" whose very existence is identified as constituting a threat to the achievement of a liberal world order.

The second danger in embracing the "neo-idealist moment" too eagerly stems from the contradiction between the political and economic components of liberal discourse. Much of International Relations' search for a substantive term to describe "the post-Cold War" era is concerned with the contradictory dynamics of "globalisation" and "fragmentation". Globalisation is, as we have suggested, an ill-defined, blanket term which conveys the limits of state power and autonomy arising from the myriad dynamics of a global economy and culture in which the state- in the absence of any sustained coordination with other states- seems increasingly restricted in its ability to manage its domestic affairs.

It is argued that the integration of global capital, much of it speculative, tends to subordinate politics to demands for flexibility, efficiency and competition on a global playing field which is anything but level. Thus, its ability to outflank the state tends also to blur any sharp inside/outside distinction. Governments become less accountable to those they claim to represent over a shrinking range of issues, so the spectrum of democratic choice for citizens' narrows considerably.

To the extent that globalisation and fragmentation are operating at different social, political and economic levels, one might accept much of Fukuyama's argument and reach the opposite conclusion; gamely, that History is far from over. Furthermore, on the reasonable assumption that global capitalism is exacerbating inequality both within as well as between states, whilst simultaneously reducing their redistributive capacities to moderate any negative consequences, one can have little faith in the liberal expectation that rational forms of civic nationalism will prevail over others in such circumstances.

Finally, Ignatieff's concession that "national belonging can be a form of rational attachment" belies a serious debate. At the bears of those forms of liberalism which subordinate communitarian morality to principles of procedural justice is the promotion of a public discourse of rights and duties which is consistent with and limited by the rational self-interest of individuals. It could be argued that attempts to derive liberal principles from assumptions of rational self-interest have not been conspicuous by their success. Moreover, it is not clear whether principles of justice can be derived from a deontological logic of instrumental rationality without smuggling in some notion of "the good".

If they cannot, then moral principles derived in such a fashion could be criticised for a limited capacity to modify human conduct. Consequently, Ignatieff's distinction between rational (civic) and irrational (ethnic) forms of nationalism (the former is consistent with liberal discourse, the later systematically undermines it) is something of a false dichotomy. As Ross Poole points out:

In assuming the existence of a social world which is devoid of values, liberalism has assigned the task of creating them to the vagaries of individual choice. It then discovers that it has no strong argument against the individual who chooses values antithetical to liberalism. The nation on the other hand, presents itself as a social world which does provide values by which an individual might live.

As with realism, the relationship between the liberal discourse of world order and nationalism is extremely ambiguous. The cosmopolitan appeal of liberalism suggests that the problem of nationalism stems from the weakness and uneven spread of plural civil societies which dilute the source, resulting in the disruptive tendencies of ethno-nationalist conflict If it is thought that world order will be achieved via the internationalisation of the liberal, capitalist, secular state, there are good reasons to believe that liberal solutions may well exacerbate the problem of nationalism.

The ambiguous relationship between the dominant realist and liberal discourses of world order and nationalism raises questions about whether "world order" debates are fruitful. The problem gains greater significance in the 1990s when the supposed solid boundaries between inside and outside are seen to be increasingly porous, and historically contingent connections between nations and states unravel. We conclude this chapter by suggesting that students of International Relations who take their subject-matter literally should therefore be encouraged to reflect critically on the tendency either to limit their field of inquiry to relations among states, or make the sovereign nation-state a rational agent for the promotion of universal ideals.

They need also to confront, rather than perpetuate, an artificial and mutually debilitating academic division of labour between the disciplines of International Relations, historical sociology, international political economy, comparative politics and political theory. Lest this be (mis)interpreted as a belittlement of the field and an attempt to relegate it to the margins of political science, nothing could be further from our intentions. On the contrary, it is precisely our belief in the pertinence of International Relations which makes us suspicious of cordoning off the discipline from "outsiders".

Such proposals mirror the efforts of the sovereign state to guarantee its monopoly over the use of force within a given territory. It would be very odd to insist on the sovereignty of the discipline when nationalism demonstrates that the historically contingent nature of state sovereignty should be a central issue in International Relations. As a twentieth century invention, the distinct discipline of International Relations began on the margins of political science. As Armstrong notes, it developed as a distinct discipline both as a response to events like the two world wars and the cold war and because there were certain phenomena - war, diplomacy, strategy, international law, the balance of power, the numerous ramifications of Sovereignty - that were inadequately, or not at all, treated elsewhere in the social sciences.

Why were the social sciences inadequate for those who believe that such phenomena are eminently suitable for academic study, and require an autonomous, professional niche within the academy if they are to receive "adequate" attention? What of nationalism as one such phenomenon? Unfortunately, the study of international violence became the preserve of a narrow disciplinary focus concerned predominantly with the strategic dimensions of war between states. Mainstream International Relations was interested in other forms of violence and threats to world order, such as revolution, frontier wars, and not only was International Relations handicapped from the start by its peripheral status in political science, it was also, and in large part continues to be, burdened with the enduring problems of "presentism", or what Cox calls the ethos of problem-solving.

This manifests itself in a number of ways, but the combination of marginalisation and problem-solving helps to explain the discipline's state-centrism. Though this is not to suggest that the state can be ignored as an important unit of analysis, as Holsti reminds us, the nation-state cannot be taken for granted either. Similarly, challenges to its power and legitimacy, of which nationalism itself has been historically among the most important should not be discounted. The territorial boundaries of the state need not cohere with disciplinary boundaries, let alone national ones, nor is there any reason why a concern with the problem of war between states should preclude equal attention to other forms of violence.

In this chapter we have argued that the strategies of containing and diluting nationalism during the twentieth century avoid, rather than confront a central paradox of world order, that nationalism will just as likely undermine state sovereignty from within as sustain it. Nationalism subverts the strict delineation between inside and outside sovereign territorial borders. The foundations of world order are not fixed and secure. Neither containment nor dilution has proven effective in dealing with nationalism during the 1990s.

Arguably, then, the increase in intra-state violence emerged during the 1990s as a major source of global disorder. Since this trend is linked inextricably with the decline of state authority and rise of identity politics in many parts of the globe, even those who remain resolutely deaf to calls for new global agendas cannot fail to note that realism and liberalism in International Relations have been challenged in recent years over their reluctance to transcend an inside/outside disciplinary divide which isolates them from a growing number of world order issues. This chapter has argued that nationalism can no longer be studied adequately under the aegis of an autonomous discipline founded on the study of war among states. To continue to do so will simply further restrict mainstream International Relations to foreign policy analysis, national security and strategic studies. We do not deny that conceiving of world order beyond maintaining the stability of already existing state sovereignty is difficult yet this is precisely the challenge posed by taking nationalism seriously.

7

International Development Management in a Globalized World

It is difficult to pick up a newspaper or turn on a television without reading or hearing commentary on the impact of global trends on the fate of nations and the lives of their citizens. Fukuyama tells us that we have entered an unprecedented period where history as we know it is over. Huntington lays out the parameters of an emerging new world order. Commentators on the task of administration and management in the private, public, and non profit sectors catalogue and analyze the ways managers need to change the ways they think and act as a result of the penetration of global economic, political, technological, and social forces. The field of international and comparative public administration (ICA) has not been immune from self-examination and reflection in the context of these global trends.

Three recent articles in Public Administration Review (PAR), part of a symposium in celebration of the 25th anniversary of the founding of the Section on International and Comparative Administration (SICA) of the American Society for Public Administration (ASPA), offer perspectives on where international and comparative public administration has come from and where it needs to go in light of the changes underway around the world. This chapter constitutes a further contribution to the SICA symposium, and adds to the debate regarding ICA in today's world. Our focus is on development management.

This term encompasses the set of ICA theory and practice that concentrates upon organisational and managerial problems, issues, and practices in the developing countries of Africa, Asia, and Latin America, and in the transitional economies of Eastern Europe and the former Soviet Union. For many years mainstream public administration and development management had- with a few exceptions- very little interchange or cross-fertilisation. However, since globalisation has led to closer integration between industrialized countries and those in the developing/transitional world, the lines between these two realms of public management have been blurred, both in terms of analytics and praxis. This integration suggests that development management has applicability to poverty alleviation in the industrialized world. We think that it is an opportune time to take a fresh look at development management.

We consider the current state of development management, and explore the implications of global trends for the subfield's continued applicability to critical administrative problems and its contribution to the broader field of ICA. In the discussion below, we: (1) identify those global trends with the most direct implications for development management, (2) review the evolution and current status of the development management subfield, (3) explore the implications of the global trends for development management, (4) comment on development management theory and practice, and (5) reevaluate what development management has to offer in the global context.

GLOBAL TRENDS

Tracking global trends has evolved into an analytic and prognostic industry in and of itself, and we do not pretend to offer a comprehensive overview of global trends and globalisation. We offer a selective catalog of what we see as the major global trends that impact upon public managers in developing and transitional nations.

ECONOMIC AND FINANCIAL

The triumph of capitalism over socialist ideology has led to a veritable tidal wave of economic and financial reforms in developing and transitional economies. The International Monetary Fund (IMF), the World Bank, as well as other multilateral and bilateral assistance agencies have preached the gospel of the free market, backed up by structural and sectoral adjustment packages with similar contents. Bolstered by these packages, private international capital has flowed into the developing world.

The features of this new economic order are well known: the dominance and independence of transnational corporate investment, interconnected markets, an emphasis on export trade and competitive advantage, unfettered international financial flows, and rapid communication. New contours have superceded the old boundaries. At the supranational level, trading arrangements, such as the GATT (General Agreement on Tariffs and Trade), WTO (World Trade Organization), and NAFTA (North American Free Trade Agreement) reconfigure economic relationships among nations. At the regional and local levels, free trade areas, economic empowerment zones, regional development authorities, direct overseas links, and so on shape new forms of public-private interaction.

A major component of structural adjustment has been the reduction of fiscal deficits and the downsizing of the public sector. Most developing/transitional countries cut back public expenditures drastically, with the effect of radically reducing basic services in public health, education, and social welfare. In some developing countries, communities were left almost entirely without national or state services. Particularly in Eastern Europe and the former Soviet Union, this downsizing was accompanied by government bashing, tax revolt, and distrust in public officials and public problem-solving.

TECHNOLOGICAL

The pace of technological innovation has accelerated. Coupled with the increased financial power of transnational corporations has been an increase in the search for new products, new production methods, and new markets. The East Asian miracle, now tarnished by the financial meltdown of Indonesia and other Asian tigers, was based in part on the combination of global capital and reengineered technologies that combined cheap labor with "high tech" production methodologies in global commodity chains. Particularly in agricultural and natural resource based products, developing countries have become, ready or not, integrated into the global technological marketplace.

Another global technological force is the ever accelerating development of information technology. The ability to transmit and access information around the globe both easily and cheaply is a profound change. The evolution of the Internet, cellular telephones, fax machines, and increasingly inexpensive personal computers has made possible communications and transactions in quantities and at speeds heretofore unimagined.

ENVIRONMENTAL

A powerful set of global trends that threaten the very basis of livelihoods and well-being around the world relate to the natural environment. Unsustainable resource utilisation rates, increased incidence of resource shortages (e.g., water, arable land), environmental degradation of the natural resource base, decreased levels of food security, pollution and contamination of both urban and rural areas, and global warming are among the litany here. These trends do not respect national borders; witness the disastrous effects of Indonesia's forest fires, deliberately set by timber firms, on its neighbours in the region.

Many of these environmental issues have been tackled at the international level and have led to collaborative efforts to address them: for example, the 1992 Earth Summit (United Nations Conference on Environment and Development), the International Convention on Global Warming, etc. Many developing countries are signatories to such international agreements, and with external assistance have engaged in a variety of planning exercises to address environmental problems (e.g., Tropical Forestry Action Plans, National Environmental Action Plans) yet have extremely limited capacity to implement them in any serious way. Further, their economic development policies often exacerbate environmental problems, as trans-national corporations seek to invest where they are the least hampered by regulation.

SOCIO-POLITICAL

Three trends are especially important in this category. First is the emerging primacy of democratic forms of politics and government. The dominance of market liberalisation has been accompanied by democratisation and political liberalisation. This trend has been fueled both by the triumph of global capitalism and by citizen expectations. One of the effects of the information revolution has been that citizens can discover what goes on around the world as well as in their own countries, and there is little the state can do to prevent this. The second socio-political trend is the rise of civil society.

Citizens are increasingly coming together and organizing to represent their interests, express their views, and undertake actions to assist themselves, either independent of, or in partnership with, government. Civil society groups are at the forefront of increased demands on the state in developing/ transitional countries, and take an active role in monitoring state actions and performance. The third trend is the intensification of ethnic, religious, and tribal conflict, which at times has exploded into mass slaughter in places like Bosnia, Rwanda, and ex-Zaire. Among the consequences have been unprecedented refugee flows, complex humanitarian emergencies, and strain and occasional collapse of existing state security and basic service delivery functions.

In thinking about the impact of global trends on developing/ transitional countries, we also need to bear in mind the things that have not changed. These too shape the landscape for development managers and development management. The poor are still poor, and there are a lot of them. In most countries, economic gains have not been evenly distributed, and income disparities have worsened. In many countries for those at the bottom of society gains have been wiped out by population growth. For example, India has an economically powerful middle class, a vibrant software industry, and nuclear capability, but huge numbers of India's citizens continue to eke out a living under conditions of extreme poverty.

Developing country government capacity is still weak, for the most part. Civil servants are underpaid and under skilled. Government agencies operate inefficiently; infrastructure and operations are neglected and crumbling. Outreach is limited; in some areas little effective public sector presence can be detected. Coupled with weak capacity, resources available for public investment and development are still scarce; tax systems are inadequate and/or nonfunctional. Local jurisdictions are particularly starved.

Many countries are weighed down under a crushing burden of international debt that must be serviced, leaving little room for discretionary social investment. As a result, in many countries, critical basic needs in education, health, welfare, and infrastructure still go unmet. A short trip off the beaten path reveals that villages in rural China, India, or the Sahel, or urban slums in Rio or Djakarta look much the same today as they did back 10 or 25 years. Many of the poor are in fact worse off now than they were a decade or so ago.

DEVELOPMENT MANAGEMENT

Before turning to the question of what development management has to offer in today's globalizing world, we need a clearer understanding of what development management is. We start with some thoughts on development itself, because it is hard to separate discussion of development management from notions of development. Both have evolved in tandem. Our rapid and, of necessity, highly compressed look backwards begins in the 1950s where the early post-World War II view of development saw a set of stages imitative of the growth path of Western industrialized societies. If countries could mobilize for take-off or the big push, then they would launch themselves on the road to economic growth.

Development theory and practice was mainly concerned with economics. Experience soon revealed that economics and a focus on industrialisation was insufficient, and analysts and practitioners in developing countries and in international development agencies expanded their focus beyond production to distribution, politics, basic human needs, and cultural values. Although variations in emphasis can be found, today there is relatively broad consensus that besides economic growth, development includes: equity, capacity, empowerment, self-determination, and sustainability.

Along with the evolution of the concept of development have been changes in thinking regarding how to achieve it. The primary trajectory here has been along a path that began with centrally planned, state-dominated strategies to market-led polycentric approaches with the state as coordinator and regulator rather than as the sole or predominant actor. The evolution of development management, as an applied discipline like its parent field, public administration, has shifted along with changes in development strategies. The trend has been away from a techno rational, universalist, public-sector administrative model toward a context-specific, politically infused, multi-sectoral, multi-organisational model.

From its initial focus on institution-building for central-level public bureaucracies and capacity-building for economic and project planning, development management has gradually expanded to encompass bureaucratic reorientation and restructuring, the integration of politics and culture into management improvement, participatory and performance-based service delivery and program management, community and NGO capacity-building, and policy reform and implementation. Currently, development management is a broadly eclectic applied discipline whose analytic and practical contents reflect four related facets, depending upon which perspective is emphasized.

Development management has an explicitly interventionist orientation that derives from its instrumental affiliation with international assistance agencies and programmes whose objectives address socioeconomic development. So first, and most commonly understood, development management is a means to improving the efficiency and effectiveness of foreign assistance programmes and to furthering international agencies' policy agendas. Second, development management is a toolkit; it promotes the application of a range of management and analytical tools adapted from a variety of social science disciplines, including strategic management, organisation development, psychology, and political science.

Third, development management incorporates a Value dimension that emphasizes self-determination, empowerment, and an equitable distribution of development benefits. Fourth, development management is process intervention, where the application of tools in pursuit of objectives is undertaken in ways that self-consciously address political and values issues. Each of these facets represents one essential aspect of development management as a field of theory and practice, and taken together they constitute a whole. However, there can be inherent tensions among them and they can be contradictory.

For example, while it is fairly straightforward to understand how its tools can promote foreign assistance agendas, less clear is whether or not their application in this context will promote espoused values of empowerment and self-determination, and whether or not the donor agency and its procedures can adequately support a genuine process approach. Such contradictions imply that development management means different things to different actors. The choice of balance among its four facets varies, contributing to what some might perceive as development management's ambiguity.

An examination of each of the facets of development management illustrates their interdependencies and helps to answer the question of development management's continued relevance in the globalized world of today. Development Management as Means to Foreign Assistance Agendas: Development management is most often sponsored by international aid agencies, all of which have their own priorities and corresponding agendas. Typically, development management professionals enter the scene upon request from a donor agency for a predetermined task.

It is not always clear if the need for and the design of this task represents priorities of the ultimate client, a developing country actor. In this sense, development management is a means to enhancing the effectiveness and efficiency of projects and programmes determined and designed by donor agencies. This facet of development management is perhaps the most problematic to reconcile with its other facets. First and most obviously, foreign assistance agendas at a minimum compromise some degree of self-determination in pursuit of socio-economic reforms; and sometimes these externally-derived reform agendas strongly limit the ability of countries to modify the reform package in ways that would support local empowerment.

Second, donor programming requirements and incentives- such as loan disbursement schedules, project timetables, and compliance with predetermined indicators- can further inhibit the ability of groups in the recipient country, whether inside or outside of government, to play an active role in tailoring the assistance provided to their needs and their pace of change. These limitations can make it difficult to allow room to accommodate political realities, or to take a process approach. What if, for example, the process leads to identified priorities and targets that significantly modify or contradict the foreign assistance package funding the effort? Third, these same pressures and incentives can also lead to superficial commitment to reform and pro forma meeting of targets.

For example, development clients may go through the motions of complying with requirements and making changes without internalizing them. In recent years, development management specialists have had an impact on how international donor programmes are designed and implemented to take more account of process considerations.

DEVELOPMENT MANAGEMENT AS TOOLKIT

Development management promotes the application of a range of management and analytical tools adapted from a variety of disciplines, including strategic management, public policy, public administration, organisation development, psychology, anthropology, and political science. These tools assist in mapping the terrain in which policy reforms, programmes, and projects are designed and implemented, that is the political, socio-cultural, and organisational contexts of interventions. For example, strategic policy management might begin with SWOT analysis (identifying internal strengths and weaknesses and external opportunities and threats), which would then be followed by other tools to assess the actors involved. These latter tools include stakeholder analysis and political mapping.

The results of these exercises feed into the elaboration of potential response strategies that incorporate flexibility and adaptation. Development management tools merge policy and program analytics with action. It is precisely the blending of the process and value facets with the tools that accounts for the distinctiveness of development management as toolkit. On the analytic side, this means tools that explore the institutional and organisational incentive aspects of achieving results, and that examine the psychology of change efforts, focusing on individual incentives and motivation. On the operational side this means tools and approaches that focus on data gathering, such as participatory rural appraisal, flexible and adaptive design and planning, and action-learning and experimentation.

DEVELOPMENT MANAGEMENT AS VALUES

This facet of development management recognizes that development-promoting activities of any sort constitute interventions in the status quo, and that any intervention advances some particular set of interests and objectives at the expense of others. Thus, helping to implement a policy reform or program more effectively or building managerial capacity in a particular agency or organisation is a value-laden endeavor. Development management as values is expressed in two ways.

First, development management acknowledges that managing is infused with politics; successful management takes account of this fact and therefore is both contextual and strategic. Second, development management takes a normative stance on empowerment and supporting groups, particularly the poor and marginalized, to take an active role in determining and fulfilling their own needs. Development management should enhance the capacity of development actors to effectively pursue their own development: it should be people-centered.

Development management as values is closely related to development management as process, as the section below clarifies. The values orientation also links to tools and the donor-funded provision of external assistance. Management tools and technologies are meant to combine external expertise with local knowledge and skills in a process that employs outside resources in the service of indigenously directed endeavours. Thus, development management blends indigenous knowledge and norms as it seeks to promote sustainable change, whose contours are developed through a participatory dialogue incorporating multiple perspectives.

DEVELOPMENT MANAGEMENT AS PROCESS

The process facet of development management is most closely related to development management as values, both politics and empowerment. Development management as process operates on several levels. In terms of the individual actors involved, it builds on organisational development and process consultation; that is, starting with the client's priorities, needs, and values, development management specialists help to "initiate and sustain a process of change and continuous learning for systemic improvement". Because the process is client-driven, development management serves as handmaiden to empowering individual actors to assert and maintain control, and building their capacity to sustain the process into the future and in other situations.

At the organisational level - whether an individual agency or multiple organisations- development management as process is concerned with the interplay between policy, program, and project plans and objectives, and the organisational structures and procedures through which plans are implemented and objectives achieved. Here development managers look for a balance among these factors and the broader setting where development intervention takes place. This is the contingency notion; that is, the best managerial solutions are context-specific and emerge from a process of searching for a fit among programmatic, organisational, and environmental factors.

At the sector level- public, civil society, and private-development management as process addresses broader governance issues, such as participation, accountability, transparency, responsiveness, and the role of the state. This brings in empowerment in its societal and political dimension, looking at how various sociopolitical groups interact in the policy and program implementation process.

Development management's process facet considers the following types of illustrative questions: Who has a place at the policy table? What process mechanisms allow which groups to play a role, and exclude others? What managerial practices and capacities are required for effective democratic governance and socio-economic development? How can public sector agencies and NGOs best cooperate to achieve joint objectives? As these questions imply, the process facet of development management links with the tool and foreign assistance agenda facets. An important place in the toolkit is accorded to process tools, those that facilitate consultation, joint problem and solution identification, ownership and commitment building, participatory strategy development, and so on. Further, many of these questions arise in the context of evolving international assistance agendas.

IMPLICATIONS FOR DEVELOPMENT MANAGEMENT

We now turn to the globalisation trends overviewed earlier and examine their implications for this subfield of ICA. These implications are presented in relation to the four facets of development management.

DEVELOPMENT MANAGEMENT AS MEANS TO FOREIGN ASSISTANCE AGENDAS

Today there is much questioning regarding development strategies and the role of donors. The head of the United Nations Development Program, for example, has called for a "new architecture for development cooperation." At the World Bank, senior staff is questioning its effectiveness as a poverty-focused lending institution; at the IMF, economists are reflecting upon the effectiveness of its policy prescriptions; and at the U.S. Agency for International Development (USAID), staff and implementing partners are reviewing its comparative advantage in light of funding cutbacks. Further, the constituencies of these agencies have raised their voices in criticism.

For example, the NGO community faults the World Bank for being insufficiently participatory and failing to respect the views and desires of local people. The U.S. Congress faults USAID for being insufficiently concrete about the results it seeks to achieve, managing poorly, and failing to demonstrate impact and value.

What does this mean for development management? As long as international agencies, governments, and, increasingly, NGOs and corporations, continue to engage in efforts to enhance the management, services, enabling environments for economic growth, and quality of life in developing and transitioning nations, there will be a demand for methods by which these efforts can be made more efficient and effective. That said, international development agendas and assistance modalities are in flux- indeed we have seen this already throughout the evolution of development. This is revealed in a closer examination of the four areas of global trends noted above.

ECONOMIC AND FINANCIAL TRENDS

The globalisation of economic activity has perforated the jurisdictional boundaries along which public administration has been organized. National, regional, and local governments have seen their traditional functions, powers, and authority leak away as the new international economic order has become established as the dominant factor in the public as well as the private sector. Governments in developing and transitional countries, along with those in the industrialized world, are searching for efficient, effective, and equitable structures and processes to reconcile the core provision of public services in the new boundary less era.

Development management's focus on process and values, along with its toolkit, can help governments in this search, and holds the potential for a more situationally sensitive application of the so-called new public management, the one-size-fits-all managerial solution that has evolved out of the triumph of the free market and the drive to downsize the public sector. In addition, development management can contribute to capacity-building for the new partners engaged in development.

The global economic and financial trends have brought new actors and new agendas onto the development scene. Predominant among them have been NGOs and civil society groups. As governments have been compelled to try to do more with less, and to cut back on state-supplied goods and services, NGOs have increasingly stepped in to fill the resulting gaps, both on their own and in partnership with the state. One frequent observation is that NGO's managerial capacity is weak, thus development management has an important role in NGO capacity-building.

This new set of actors generally has an agenda that stresses empowerment and people-centered development, which means that the value facet of development management emerges more strongly at the forefront. The private sector constitutes a second set of new actors that has emerged as governments downsize and privatize, becoming more prevalent with the rise of corporate philanthropy. Multinational corporations are sponsoring and/or directly engaging in development activities, both independently and in partnership with donor agencies and national governments; for example, supporting infrastructure projects that benefit the operation of their factories, or providing infrastructure and/or health and education services in those communities that are sources of local labor.

While the more limited agendas represented by corporate interests raise questions for development management's value facet, to the extent that development management can inject community empowerment and local control into those agendas as a function of assisting to implement them, the door is opened to broadening corporate philanthropy and deepening the commitment of multinational corporations to socially responsible actions in developing/transitional countries.

TECHNOLOGICAL TRENDS

New agendas also include the introduction of new technologies, specifically information technology. International assistance agencies are increasingly designing programmes that transfer information and communications technology both in the service of sectoral objectives and broader democratisation goals. For example, USAID's Leland Initiative supports Internet connectivity throughout Africa. Development management professionals can assist in a number of ways; for example, addressing the organisational and process aspects of implementing new communications and technology policies, helping decision makers focus on the equity and distributional issues, and so on.

ENVIRONMENTAL TENDS

The agendas of foreign assistance agencies, international environmental NGOs, and national governments seek to tackle the environmental trends sketched above. Donors, NGOs, and their partner governments have moved from an initial focus on the technical dimensions of environmental problems, to increasingly recognizing their social, organisational, and managerial dimensions.

Development management has been, and will remain, instrumental to designing and implementing sustainable environmental and natural resources policies and programmes in support of these agendas. New challenges for development management will be in the areas of conflict resolution, and advocacy support within the highly politicized arenas that characterize environmental concerns. Development management can usefully contribute at all levels, from the local to the transnational, the latter being particularly important in dealing with environmental trends.

SOCIO-POLITICAL TRENDS

One implication of these trends for development management is that as the programmatic mix of foreign assistance agencies' objectives shifts to respond to more numerous and more serious complex humanitarian emergencies, development management specialists may be called upon for assistance. Despite the potential relevance of development management's process approach and toolkit, this has not yet taken place because of the politics of international relief and the disconnection between short-term emergency assistance and long-term development support.

Another implication of these trends relates to the continuing importance of international NGOs, the growing importance of civil societies worldwide, and the promotion of democratisation agendas. International NGOs have long been important actors in development. While their role has generally shifted from one of providing primarily humanitarian aid to supporting development, and from working independently to contracting and partnering with donors, the activities of NGOs continue to represent an important proportion of development assistance. Like corporations, as private institutions NGOs are empowered to be selective in the services they choose to provide and the clients they work with.

The range of NGO actors and their roles are evolving fast with the growth of civil society globally. New, creative partnerships are also emerging, including those between corporations and NGOs, and corporations and local governments. Reconciling the interests of multi-party sponsorship will be a key challenge for development managers into the future. NGOs and other civil society actors are also increasingly important advocates for or against particular agendas. In fact, some argue that advocacy is the most appropriate role for international NGOs.

Accordingly, as the capacity of local NGOs and civil society grows, tensions emerge between international NGOs and their local counterparts or partners. Development management will be increasingly challenged to integrate the participation of a diverse body of implementers and advocates. More and more, development management is expected to contribute to foreign assistance agendas that promote values, particularly democratisation.

While at first glance such an application would appear to be entirely consistent with the values development management espouses, sometimes foreign assistance agendas, especially the bilaterals, have a more limited definition of democracy and/or choose to limit participation for political reasons, as for example, limiting support for and participation of potentially disruptive elements of civil society such as fundamentalist Islamic groups. These decisions are by nature subjective and can conflict with the other facets of development management. In addition, limited foreign assistance agendas, if pursued in isolation, can generate negative consequences. For example, Coston highlights the potential danger of addressing the demand side of democratic governance promotion, without considering the ability of states to respond to that demand.

DEVELOPMENT MANAGEMENT AS TOOLKIT

Are development management's tools still relevant given the trends identified? Projects and programmes still exist. Policy implementation still poses thorny managerial problems. Attention to participation and empowerment has increased, not diminished. Governments are still wrestling with capacity limitations. Thus it can be argued that a core administrative problem set remains for which the development management toolkit, with its combination of process and technical tools, continues to be useful and applicable. Process tools in particular are relevant- increasingly managers operate in settings where, as Bryson and Crosby say, no one is in charge.

The overarching implication of the global trends for development management as toolkit will be the need to take into account far greater complexity and uncertainty in the administrative environment of development managers. This suggests the need for more attention to theoretical and conceptual integration with practice, so that the key variables affecting administrative capacity and performance are identified and targeted for intervention.

ECONOMIC AND FINANCIAL TRENDS

These trends are perhaps the major source of the uncertainty and complexity that development managers face. The challenge for development management will be to sharpen and refine its analytic toolkit so as to usefully contribute to the debate on the appropriate role of the state, the trade-offs between economic and social development goals that have arisen more starkly in the wake of the current financial crisis in Asia, and the drive for ever more efficient public governance. Because development management's four facets explicitly address politics, values, and process in the context of development goals, and administrative tools and techniques to achieve them, the subfield has the potential to counter the tendency to look for quick solutions based on narrow economic criteria.

TECHNOLOGICAL TRENDS

Information technology advances represent an important opportunity for development managers to enhance existing tools and create new tools. Many of the standard project planning tools already exist in computer form, and several tools specific to international projects, programmes, and policies have been developed. Tools that do more than computerize analysis and store the information, but that use information technology to facilitate participation and empower people are an innovative avenue for development management to explore.

For example, the World Bank has been experimenting with "groupware" as a means to a more participatory process of designing its Country Assistance Strategies. This experimentation is in its infancy. Another area ripe for exploration is how information technology can contribute to organisational redesign for performance in developing country public agencies.

ENVIRONMENTAL TRENDS

Environmental trends pose two particular challenges to development management's toolkit. First, existing and new tools will need to incorporate broader and increasingly diverse constituencies in environmental projects, especially those that cross national borders. This implies a stronger focus on reconciling opposing interests; thus the tools of conflict resolution, negotiation, and consultation will become more important. Further, refined analytic tools are needed for institutional design of feasible policy and program solutions. Second, environmental trends imply severe future consequences of current resource utilisation practices that are difficult to envision.

Again, new tools could be advanced, for instance, with the help of information technology, to more clearly demonstrate the salience of the issues to decision makers. For example, computer games and simulations are being developed in which the players can input and assess various policy alternatives and their impact on the environment. Negative consequences can be shown visually and quite dramatically and alternative policy solutions can be graphically demonstrated using a simulated computer world.

SOCIO-POLITICAL TRENDS

Similar to the environmental trends, among the most important implications of socio-political trends will be the need for crisis management, conflict resolution, and negotiation tools. Development management's experience with such tools in situations of complex emergencies is relatively new and untested. Similarly, with the expansion of democratic governance around the world, and the attendant growth and diversity of civil society, new tools and approaches will be needed to build effective state-civil society partnerships, both national and international. The trends also suggest a need for new tools and approaches to address building constituencies and motivation for sustained reforms to deal with citizen demands for transparency, accountability, and responsiveness.

Also related to reforms, is the need for methodologies that allow policymakers to better assess the political implications and trade-offs of policy alternatives in a democratic and/or politically unstable environment. With respect to the growing importance of civil society, development management may need to borrow more from psychology and anthropology when considering the increasing diversity of development players. For example, how can the participation of the formerly voiceless be promoted in a newly democratic regime when there is no tradition or culture of democracy? How can the deeply internalized ethnic and religious conflicts be addressed?

DEVELOPMENT MANAGEMENT AS VALUES

Development management's self-consciousness about politics and values, plus its focus on empowerment, increases the sub field's relevance to managers coping with the impacts of global trends. Development management involves tools and approaches that: (1) illuminate goal trade-offs and conflicts, (2) clarify who participates in decisions and who does not, and (3) build capacity for empowering managerial and decision processes. Hence, it can contribute to incorporating equity and sustainability into socio-economic development when the thrust of many of the trends may push toward a narrower focus on efficiency and the preservation of vested interests.

An important implication for development management specialists in regard to values is how, given global trends, to deal with the ethics of development intervention. These surfaces most starkly as a potential conflict between development management as an instrument of international assistance agendas versus the agendas of groups within developing/transitional countries and in the conflicts among developing country groups. One response, related to development management's process facet, is to be very explicit about who the client is for any change intervention. In this regard, some development management professionals have shifted their efforts away from the public sector to focus on NGOs and civil society, and to opt for challenging existing power structures.

ECONOMIC AND FINANCIAL TRENDS

These trends have essentially imported private business values into the public sector. Market principles applied to public management transform citizens into customers and emphasize the "bottom line" as a paramount objective. Mainstream public administration is questioning the politics and ethics that support this perspective, and in developing and transitional countries, such questioning is taking place as well. Just as development management's process approach assists in reconciling diverse interests, so too it may contribute to identifying the appropriate balance between private-sector values of least-cost efficiency and public-sector values such as responsiveness, accountability, and equity.

With development management's emphasis on capacity-building, and its recognition that politics and administration are inextricably linked, development management can assist both governments and non-state actors to engage with each other on these issues. Development management has traditionally acknowledged the importance of community self-determination and locally-driven development. The interdependence inherent in a global economy suggests that the challenge for the future will be addressing how to manage an appropriate degree of integration and linkage such that local, regional, national, and international priorities and interests can be balanced. If its empowerment emphasis is directed only locally, development management will likely be sidelined and considered less relevant.

TECHNOLOGICAL TRENDS

These trends raise a number of implications for development management as values. Technology can open up people's horizons and possibilities, but there are always trade-offs. Information technology, for example, can be empowering if it provides information and linkages to societal groups that previously were excluded; but it will favor those groups who have the potential to take advantage of it. For those without the necessary resources and capacities, the gaps between technology haves and have-nots can widen. Knowledge flows and intellectual property rights are other important technological issues. Development management could play a role in helping countries establish and implement equitable and politically feasible trade and technology transfer policies.

ENVIRONMENTAL TRENDS

Given the increasing diversity of environmental actors, noted above, development management's greatest challenge and contribution will be to grapple with the question of whose rights take precedence and how to address the political dimensions of the environmental trends, locally, nationally, and internationally.

For example, in natural resource management, whose interests should receive priority, those of local resources users, corporations whose investments bring in necessary foreign exchange, or national governments, who may or may not effectively pursue the public interest in regard to resource conservation? Development management can also help with designing and making operational the institutional structures and mechanisms that can be used to effectively implement policy priorities in the environment and natural resources sector.

SOCIO-POLITICAL TRENDS

As democratic forms of government spread, development management will be increasingly important in helping governments build the capacity to respond to citizen expectations and to put in place the institutional structures that allow democracy to function effectively. The promotion of democratisation and its associated values is among the agendas of a number of foreign assistance agencies, but those values are frequently translated into a relatively narrow view of what constitutes democracy.

Traditional village governance structures in Africa, for example, are not considered "democratic" due to perceived limits in representation in their consensual model. The notion of traditional benevolent leaders runs counter to Western ideals of democracy. Development management, as Riggs points out, needs to be at the forefront of exploring various institutional options for democratisation that fit with particular country circumstances recognizing that the U.S. model is one path among many.

Concerning the rise of civil society and sub national conflicts based on ethnicity or religion, development management's value facet will need to address critical questions. Whose self-determination and empowerment should take precedence and who can legitimately speak for the constituencies involved? What organisational and procedural mechanisms can be used to develop sustainable solutions to problems of representation, participation, and conflict resolution among competing interests? In the search for answers, it will be important to confront the *naiveti* and mythologizing around civil society's homogeneity, harmoniousness, and civic-mindedness, and develop a realistic understanding of how societal interest groups actually behave.

DEVELOPMENT MANAGEMENT AS PROCESS

In each of the categories of trends we have summarized, the importance of process, as a crucial adjunct to good technical solutions, stands out. To paraphrase the popular aphorism, the trends may be examined globally, but acting to address them means intervening locally. Someone, located in a particular place with particular constraints, capacities, history and so on, needs to determine what to do and then mobilize and organize to do it. Development management's process facet holds important lessons to help move from analysis to action, beginning at the individual level with its emphasis on client-driven change efforts, and extending to the organisational and sectoral levels with its concentration on understanding and building linkages and system-wide capacity.

All of the trends, as previously noted, heighten uncertainty, complexity, unpredictability, and interconnectedness. Development management's focus on iterative solution design, testing and learning, and adaptation is highly salient to coping with these trends. As mentioned, an important set of development management tools and approaches are, in fact, process-focused. These trends highlight and reinforce the relevance of development management as process to helping developing/transitional countries to successfully cope with global trends.

An important implication for development management will be the increasing use of cross-sectoral partnerships, multi-organisational networks, etc. When no one is in charge, the importance of process is heightened for several reasons: to bring to bear everyone's energies and ideas for solving problems, for generating widespread support for solutions adopted, for negotiating agreements on implementation, and for resolving conflicts and disputes throughout. Process changes can also result in shifts in power distributions and dynamics, important variables in shaping the politico-administrative environment.

ECONOMIC AND FINANCIAL TRENDS

As already mentioned, these trends have increased the pressures on governments at all levels to increase efficiency and output, while at the same time pushing them to rethink their core functions. While evidence is accumulating that development management's process approaches can save money in the longer term, through contributing to the design of more feasible policies and programmes and building commitment among stakeholders for their implementation, in the short term these approaches can prove costly and time-consuming. An important area for future development management attention is the cost-benefit analysis- broadly construed- of participatory process approaches. Development management needs to pursue questions that explore and clarify the connection between process inputs and policy and service delivery outputs.

TECHNOLOGICAL TRENDS

These trends affect development management as process in a number of ways. First, advances in information technology hold the potential for vastly expanding the possibilities for stakeholder consultation by government, for citizen participation, and for coordination and integration across organisations engaged in service delivery, as the tools discussion outlined. Information technology can facilitate the identification and mobilisation of contributors to policy issues and solutions. The utilisation of information technology for improving the organisational processes of public agencies is a burgeoning area of application, and relates to the worldwide drive for efficiency and decentralisation.

To remain relevant, development management's process facet will need to keep pace and contribute to learning and adaptation related to information technology and its links to process innovations, organisational effectiveness, and outcomes. Beyond the public sector, information technology has served as an important vehicle through which civil society groups have developed processes of constituency mobilisation, advocacy, and demand-making. In this sense, information technology can multiply the challenge to the state's capacity for, or commitment to, responsiveness, openness, and accountability.

On the other side, as we mentioned previously, technology can create gaps between haves and have nots; there is the potential to create exclusionary processes as well. In developing/transitional countries to a greater extent than in industrialized ones, this gap can be a factor in keeping the poor both from advancing economically and/or participating in democratic governance. Development management's process facet, when combined with values and tools, can help address this issue.

ENVIRONMENTAL TRENDS

As previously noted, the trends here suggest that countries need processes and consultative mechanisms that can deal with priority-setting, clarification of public-private-NGO sector roles, participation of resource users groups, regulatory development and enforcement, and sustainable resource utilisation. Besides the need for such processes nationally, because of the transnational nature of environmental problems, they are required at the international level as well. This is a burgeoning area of application and refinement of development management's process component with much potential for theoretical and practical advances.

SOCIO-POLITICAL TRENDS

Democratisation and the rise of civil society have made citizens hyper-attuned to issues of responsiveness, transparency, and accountability. George Orwell got it partially right: someone out there is watching. But in today's world it is not some government monolith that has its lens turned on its citizens, rather the lens is reversed- citizens are watching their governments. Being responsive, transparent, and accountable are basically procedural and process issues; developing/transitional country governance structures need process capacity in order to institutionalize democratic governance. Development management has an ongoing role to play in building this process capacity from the central to the local level.

Development management's process perspective is also applicable to the other sociopolitical trends. It is clear that civil society groups need the same kind of process tools and approaches as public managers if they are to fulfill their potential. Regarding ethnic conflicts and complex emergencies, process interventions can be important for conflict resolution and negotiation, and as Bryant points out, for seeking to begin as soon as possible to institute processes that help former combatants build a basis for, at a minimum, peaceful co-existence, if not cooperation. Development management's process approaches also have the potential to build upon and mobilize local capacity in the context of emergency situations, thus speeding the transition from relief to development.

BRIDGING PRACTICE AND THEORY

In the preceding discussion we have sought to map, albeit roughly and rapidly, the implications of several categories of global trends for development management. The discussion has revealed that some of these implications lead to applications of existing development management knowledge and practice to areas where they have yet to be brought to bear some suggest the continued relevance of their applicability for areas that are their traditional bailiwick, and still others suggest areas where further analytic work is called for.

Bryant characterizes development management as largely an inductive field, where what is known "has often been learned experientially, and usually from the bottom up, with a focus on a project or a program". Thus, we can anticipate that as development management gains experience with the impacts of global trends on developing/transitional country public managers and their private and NGO sector partners, new knowledge will emerge. However, we think that it is critical to structure such learning so that it moves beyond the anecdotal and gains increased relevance across a range of settings and circumstances.

As globalisation unifies the pressures facing public managers around the world, public administration scholars and practitioners are calling for more explicitly comparative investigation. Riggs advocates such investigation to combat what he sees as the ethnocentrism of American public administration. Heady argues for an integration of the analytic efforts of internationalists and comparativists to address the increasingly universal nature of administrative problems resulting from globalisation, suggesting along the way that development management has been more international than comparative. How can the development management subfield move in this direction?

An important step is to build more robust bridges between theory and practice. This does not mean seeking to develop an all-encompassing and integrative theoretical and explanatory framework. We believe that such a search is ultimately counterproductive and can divert attention from what really counts in the applied field of development management: developing usable knowledge. Esman suggests that usable knowledge will emerge from interactively drawing upon three sources: (1) formal analytics from the professional and academic literature, (2) learning from concrete situations and interventions- that is, the experiential database referred to by Bryant, and (3) experience and judgment of "front-line" development managers and the members of "client" publics. Combining these three sources, while not requiring an overarching theoretical framework, does call for some sort of midrange analytic framework so as to allow for sufficient abstraction to reach generalizable lessons.

Development management, along with its parent discipline of public administration, has been criticized for lacking a unifying "grand theory." It is interesting to note that recent efforts in this direction have been undertaken by scholars under the disciplinary umbrella of the new institutional economics (NIE), which has evolved constructs and vocabulary to describe and analyze many of the same concepts and issues that the development management subfield has focused on for years. However, across the diverse theoretical and analytic lenses that development managers have used, there are more common building blocks for mid-range frameworks than are usually perceived.

For example, concepts such as nested and interactive systems, organisational learning and adaptation, and political economy provide the elements for constructing the kind of frameworks that can usefully bridge theory and practice. Bridging theory and practice will continue to be a key challenge for the development management subfield- a challenge exacerbated by development management's instrumental orientation to serving the needs of international assistance agencies and their developing/transitional country partners/clients.

In the past, international agencies have provided the resources and the opportunities for development management applied research and analysis; with rare exceptions, they are now less willing or able to support such investigation. In today's increasingly complex world, it is unfortunate that there is shrinking patience for understanding and learning, but this in itself is an outgrowth of the impact of the global trends on the realm of foreign assistance, where the constituencies of international aid expect quick results, efficiency, and immediate impacts.

Development specialists have a history of disillusionment and self-criticism; and, like public administration more generally but perhaps more acutely, development management has suffered a chronic identity crisis. While painful and potentially demoralizing, the self-questioning of relevance and effectiveness among development management scholars and practitioners has yielded important advances in the field. Through iterative cycles of analysis and practice, development management has, for example, evolved past the blueprint to elaborate process approaches; and has come to better appreciate and incorporate cultural, institutional, and political factors into the organisational and managerial arena in developing/ transitional countries.

These innovations emerged from a process of trial and error, reflection, and learning. This openness to embracing error and willingness to draw upon' diverse experience bases and analytic perspectives are among the strengths of the subfield, even as they make its boundaries hard to pinpoint or describe. What, then, are the prospects for development management's contribution now and in the future? As our above discussion indicates, we argue that development management remains applicable to current management and governance issues in developing/transitional countries, and as global trends continue to exert their impacts development management may be increasingly important.

Capacity-building is an ongoing and crosscutting need. Process approaches will be necessary to identify, mobilize and incorporate diverse stakeholders and their viewpoints to develop policy solutions that can be successfully implemented and sustained. Around the world, attention to participation and empowerment has increased, not diminished, as core process elements of making democratic governance work. Development management's value facet is critical to reminding policymakers that development involves choices that advantage some societal groups and disadvantage others, and that how those choices are made affects the balance of winners and losers.

At the same time, our analysis points to several avenues to be pursued as the subfield of development management evolve. We single out just a few for mention here. As suggested above, development management needs to explore a closer integration between theory and practice through the development of midrange analytic frameworks. This path involves, for example, bringing institutional analysis and design perspectives to bear more directly on development management's tool and process facets.

Another avenue includes a continuation of development management's interdisciplinary approach, but with a different balance in the mix, giving more emphasis to the fields of comparative politics, anthropology, and psychology. Along this avenue are questions, for example, of path dependence and how the past shapes the present, of the interplay between culture and management, and of the complex interaction of politics and values in shaping discourse both about socio-economic development and its management. A third avenue, also previously touched upon, concerns the implications of information technology for new organisational forms and processes, state-society interactions, and knowledge management.

We see the boundaries between the subfield of development management, ICA, and mainstream public administration becoming fuzzier. As Mittelman observes, "globalisation is about opportunities arising from reorganizing governance, the economy, and culture throughout the world". In informing developing/transitional countries' search world-wide for best practices and lessons to deal with these opportunities- and challenges, development management needs to extend the sub field's scope. This means looking not simply at what has worked in other developing/transitional countries, but at industrialized nations as well.

Conversely, industrialized nations have much to learn from developing/transitional nations' efforts. However, beyond these responses, more is required to ensure development management's continued relevance. An important component to thinking about this question involves Schon's notion of "ideas in good currency". Those of us who see ourselves as development management professionals continue to see relevance in what we do and study, but often make assumptions about the perceptions of relevance of our discipline on the part of decision makers and policymakers, both in international donor agencies and in developing/transitional countries. Yet the extent to which management and administration are in good currency varies. The Reagan/Thatcher era in the 1980s of public-sector bashing is a case in point.

Development management specialists need to hone in on the critical managerial features of the problems that are preoccupying decision makers and demonstrate how the discipline is relevant and useful. It is these decision makers who must be convinced of the fit between development management and current global issues. Development management has made a difference in the lives of citizens in the developing world, but continuing to contribute means remaining "in good currency." This is as much a challenge to the subfield as renewing and advancing development management's practical and applied research agendas.

8

Critical Theory and Global Political Change

Globalisation implies global social and political change. Irrespective of whether one identifies globalisation as primarily driven by economics or as a cultural phenomenon occurring in the context of technological change and a transformation of lifestyles, it is now clear that the social sciences face the challenge of somehow 'making sense of it." The study of international relations, it could be argued, has been complicated by this challenge, and as a result it begins to reach out in a more interdisciplinary manner, including an opening to more sociologically informed research agendas.

Approaches in international relations associated with various forms of critical theory have especially put forward theoretical work, sometimes accompanied by empirical findings, with which to assess and substantiate the nature, quality, and scope of social change in the era of globalisation (whether this is understood as an ideology, masking trends that have essentially always accompanied the expansion of modern capitalism, or whether it is seen as something qualitatively new).

In the International relation discipline, the term critical theory has become a shorthand reference for a variety of attempts to break with the molds of theorizing presented by the dominant strands of realism/neo-realism, or liberalism/neo-liberalism. Thus, it has come to represent the commentary from the margins of the discipline in manifestations as diverse as neo-Gramscian readings, reformulations of Marxist theory, the spectrum of feminist challenges, poststructuralist inquiries, and the theoretical work originating with the Frankfurt school.

Although the affinities among these strands of theorizing from the margins have frequently been stressed, there remain serious disagreements over core issues of "theorizing with a critical motive," which typically revolve around the claims that critical theorists make for their projects. From among the plurality of critical interventions, Andrew Linklater's appropriation of the reformulated approach of Frankfurt school critical theory- mainly as developed in the work of Jurgen Habermas- has made the most consistent bid for integrating the widest possible range of critical concerns into a more unified version of critical theory for international relations.

Perhaps unsurprisingly, this gesture of embrace- still evident in Linklater's Transformation of Political Community - has invited the "embraced" themselves to reassert their positions with reference to the theoretical suggestions of the "embracer." More often than not, the response to Linklater's inclusiveness has been to question the validity of core elements of his theory.

These misconstruals arise in part from the way in which Linklater himself integrates discourse ethics into his theory with emancipatory intent. Following this reconstruction of the potential of the discourse-ethical conception of norm validation for international-relations theory, I focus on what I perceive to be at the core of Habermas's critical project, the dialectic of life world and systems, with a focus on its applicability in international-relations theory. Here, I take into account recent trends toward developing functionalist accounts of integration for the further study of globalisation.

The purpose of this investigation is to underline the relevance of critical theory for attempts to make sense of the globalisation challenge. If political community and social bonds are undergoing significant changes, the self-conscious approach to theorizing social life and political authority from a critical perspective that avoids classification in either classical liberal or republican terms promises a more thorough understanding than approaches that remain couched in a conceptual language that is today challenged by actual change.

INTERNATIONAL/GLOBAL POLITICAL THEORY

As theory with an emancipatory intent, Linklater's version of critical theory has been put on the defensive from a rather wide spectrum of differing positions. These criticisms issue broadly from three camps. First, a Hegelian-inspired neo-Aristotelian retrieval of the normative primacy of the "ethical life" of bounded communities, which, it is argued, debunks the myth of universal principles by unmasking their substantial commitment to the dissolution of cultural particularity. Here, a focus is on the ethical practices of social life, which, it is argued, become devalued in the light of the critical gaze of deontological reasoning.

Second, from the poststructuralist background inspired by Nietzsche, Foucault, Derrida, and Levinas in which the *joie de soi*, or the irreducibly ephemeral nature of the encounter of alterity, is conceived to engender an ethics of resistance to "subjectivication." Third, challenges are voiced from reformulations of historical materialism, where the issue of a transformation led by cultural factors such as the moral learning of humanity is seen to be structurally inhibited until such time as the material circumstances of the systematically disadvantaged masses have been transformed so as to make a transition to a moral society possible.

CRITICAL INJUNCTIONS

The third group disputes the cogency of the Habermasian reconstruction of historical materialism that Habermas advances from the point of view of the "linguistic turn." On such a reading, the new Frankfurt school abandons Marx's insights into the necessity of change in the relations of production en route to the just society. This stance, in turn, however, is plausible only within a conception of a philosophy of history already abandoned by the early Frankfurt school in their engagement with the intellectual heritage of Hegel. The classical Marxist notion of humankind as a "species-subject" that generates itself practically out of the instrumentalisation of the natural environment has become problematic, not the least due to its naturalistic conception of emancipation.

This mode of theorizing, which, in Habermas's view, still reverberates in the theoretical work of the early Frankfurt school, resulted in the latter's identification of reason with instrumental reason and, thus, to the aporia of a critical theory without any prospect for social emancipation. Habermas identifies communicative reason as a distinct form of interaction that circumscribes significant non strategic practices of intersubjectivity. In refocusing critical theory in this way, Habermas presents an account of emancipatory social action as an alternative to the classical Marxist conception of the coincidence of theory and practice in the generation of revolutionary consciousness coming out of the experience of exploitation under capitalism.

The insights of historical materialist analysis, however, continue to form an important component of critical interventions into the dynamics and contradictions of current transformations of social, political, and economic life. Despite Habermas's self-conscious conception of the discourse-ethical foundation of the legitimacy of norms as open and purely procedural, his account of the democratic conditions of legitimacy includes, albeit in a relative conception, the dimension of "basic rights to the provision of living conditions that are socially, technologically and ecologically safeguarded, insofar as the current circumstances make this necessary if citizens are to have equal opportunities to utilize civil rights."

This attests to a revised conception of the Marxist ideal of social justice in Habermas s work, although he approaches this ideal from a far more circumspect angle with regards to its normative implications. More problematic than the (classical) Marxist deferential treatment of the significance of normative issues in social and political change are the charges leveled at the discourse-ethical model from positions that dispute the possibility of its universalist moral intent. Both neo-Aristotelian and poststructuralist criticisms of discourse ethics incorporate such claims, albeit from within different frames of reference.

The genealogical approach of post-structuralism focuses on the power relations that pervade both individuation- the formation of the self- and socialisation constitutively. In keeping with the life-force ethics already known from Nietzsche, and in distinction from its grand theory adaptation in Sartre's existentialism, the Foucauldian conception of "human freedom" requires a radical departure from the fallacies of subjectivism of modern liberal political philosophy.

The anti metaphysical intent of structuralism and its embrace of the "political" as the practice of human freedom. in constant transgression of identity as fixed, grounded, or in other "objectifying" ways circumscribed is seen to engender a mode of political engagement in the encounter with alterity that defies the universalist attempts to essentialize in any way what commands moral respect (natural rights, human equality, the transcendental subject). Thus, a concern with the legislative stance of modern political philosophy and the perils of essentializing once and for all what is to engender duties among human beings is clear in poststructuralist conceptions of human freedom.

LINKLATER'S CRITICAL INTERNATIONAL RELATION THEORY

Linklater engages with these critical injunctions against a critical theory with emancipatory intent and a cosmopolitan outlook in his recent work by restating the distinct way in which the second generation Frankfurt school justifies and commends normative theory. He takes as a guiding argument Richard Rorty's assertion about the radical groundlessness of the human condition that binds the normative background of political society firmly to the value systems of communities.

In Rorty's opinion, the attempt to think reflexivity, the pulse of social learning by critically engaging with the social and political order one lives in, as bearing the mark of a universal potential is to misapprehend the factual contextuality and contingency of the respective universalist aspirations of particular collectively shared conceptions of such goods. From the neo-Kantian position that Linklater advocates, Rorty's diagnosis of the transcultural hubris of cosmopolitanism can be read along parallel lines to the critique of Kant by Hegel. Stressing the importance of the emergence of the entrenched notion of individual freedom in contrast to the limited Aristotelian doctrine of freedom as self-realisation in the polis, Hegel regards the "outbreak of morality" that fueled the liberation of the subject as capable of being sublated in the substantial "ethical life" of the modern Prussian state, for instance.

If such a stance is taken to comprise the Hegelian position-pace the misreading of Hegel it involves- then the framework for normative theory generated out of the choice of an epistemological relativism as the point of departure for this purpose remains conventionalist. This means that scope, manner, and justification for moral action in the community remain within the confines of the interpretive means provided by its shared cultural traditions. As Linklater notes, such an account is inadequate with reference to the critical reflection of the moral practices of the community, which always already arises where the disciplining force of the conventionalized ethical life is confronted with the critical inquest of morality.

To be sure, Rorty's response would be that it is precisely something like the commitment to a universalist discourse of justice that is so particular of the Western liberal world. But this, in addition to almost certainly being empirically false, in turn fails to grasp what possible motive there could be- and how to evaluate it- for a conventionalist ethics to problematize itself to such a degree as to open itself up for critical self-reflection through abstract inquiry. The governability of entrenched power structures that are experienced as naturalized by those governed in a society is obviously much higher in cases where an administrative apparatus must respond to the continuous scrutiny of its members- even if such responses are mainly strategically motivated.

The tension that is thus opened between conventionalist accounts of social integration and the social-justice-driven post-conventional critique in the spirit of Kant is at the heart of what is at issue between critical theory and its discontents. The conventionalist mode of integration sustains the regulation of social and political affairs through the traditionally secured codes and practices that are both constitutive of the emancipatory horizon and the unquestioned standards of conduct in situations of practical action.

As habituated rules and codes of conduct, they become problematised only in situations in which new and previously unanticipated problems occur, according to which new claims can be made intelligible as addressed toward the entrenched conceptions of the ethical life. Classically, this can occur in the form of conflicts that entail either the development of the merging of conventional horizons19 or the appropriation and transformation by one set of conventional ethics of the other (as in classical conquest). The other way in which the problematisation of the ethical life can be realized is through the critique of the entrenched according to the universal, as is the approach of deontic inquests into morality.

This latter mode, however, produces a split between the day-to-day requirements of the ethical life of the life world and the realm of reasoned and argumentatively secured norms as universally valid basis for just laws, as the background of the philosophical proof of validity. This juncture, on which the distinction between values and norms turns, refers to the complementarity of the respective prerogatives of morality and the substantive ethical life. Norms qua the status of the validity claims that they command as norms require that they be affirmed in a noncircular fashion that is argumentatively retrievable and thus intelligible to all for whose affairs they are deemed in any way valid.

It is easy to see how such an account of normative frameworks that focuses in the manner of neo-Kantian political philosophy on the generalized other, rather than concrete others, raises the criticisms of its undue force toward universal homogenisation. Such criticism is widespread in political theory, usually with reference to struggles for recognition within avowedly liberal states and to issues of multiculturalism and patterns of exclusion. It is, to be sure, even more relevant in the area of international relations, where patterns of hierarchisation, exclusion, and cultural incompatibility provide evidence of tangible struggles in which difference often plays a key role.

Thus, the approach of the poststructuralist critics of late Frankfurt school critical theory is frequently to charge its universalist outlook with a coercive disregard for difference. Linklater's interpretation of Habermas's discourse ethics from the perspective of International relation theory has to some extent helped to reproduce this image of the discourse ethics as insensitive to difference in an oppressive manner, which would denigrate its emancipatory pretences.

SOME ISSUES BETWEEN LINKLATER AND HABERMAS

The transmission link from theory to praxis that Linklater constructs in his Transformation too easily lets the discourse-ethical conception of valid norms translate to the realm of the day-to-day practices of substantial ethical life- what Apel calls the "application oriented" context- in order to demonstrate the crucial role of an ethics of responsibility that mediates between the demands of the discourse ethics and the practical discourses of day-to-day life (the latter incorporating strategic and instrumental action). The relationship between the discourse ethics and the realm of substantial problems in the ethical life is thus understood in terms of the relationship of morality and ethical life as laid out and criticized by Hegel.

At the same time, however, the defense of critical theory must incorporate a post-Kantian stance on the relationship between the two, and dismiss Hegel's privileging of the actual over the abstract as results from his critique of Kantian formalism. Insofar as Linklater seems to assume, to some extent with Kant, that universally valid norms can be translated back into substantive virtue ethics, the intent of Habermas's discourse ethics and conception of radical democracy becomes misrepresented.

The ethics of substantive interests (as opposed to interests in the truth and validity of universally applicable norms in the context of problems of justice) needs to be conceived of as a problem of a different order- one in its own right, with, however, grounding linkages to the discourse-ethically-secured background. Habermas's concern is with the practices necessary for the grounding of norms that can ensure the legitimacy of a legal order, of which citizens are both authors and subjects. The task of the discourse-ethical conception of morality must thus be understood to provide constraints in the sense of a constitutional order for both the generation of legitimate law as expression of self-governance and the situated practical requirements of the ethical life.

Linklater pays insufficient attention to this distinction between the discourse-ethically-secured constitutional constraints and dialogic practices where the generalized other is simply not the topos. As a result, Linklater's dialogic community appears in his account frequently as equally concerned with questions of the good life, on the one hand, and questions of justice, on the other. Although he concludes that the task is to "strike an appropriate balance between universality and difference," it remains unclear precisely how this balance is to be achieved if it is to be advanced in the medium of the discourse ethics that requires the orientation to generalizable interest in the first place.

If critical theory in international relations constructed along the lines of discourse ethics is to remain sensitive to difference- as it should- then the self-imposed limitations of normative critique in terms of justice that Habermas and Apel present need to be heeded more carefully. This would complicate assessments of critical theory such as that forwarded by Beate Jahn. In what is perhaps one of the most thorough inquiries into critical theory in international relations, Jahn suggests that one could have learned from Horkheimer that "the holistic" and "historical" analysis that makes theory critical can be had only if one prevents "the interference of values in theoretical analysis."

But her injunctions against the ethical universalism of critical theory, which she criticizes with reference to its thick indebtedness to liberal idealism and to the injuries that the Western tradition of political thought and practice has inflicted upon particularity, remain at root committed to the conventionalist approach at which Habermasian discourse ethics is addressed and against which it raises much stronger points than Jahn permits herself to discuss. In the context of these observations, it is now less clear whether the concerns raised by poststructuralist critics are, in fact, cogent with reference to the discourse-ethical principle that Habermas employs in his theory construction.

The charge that the discourse-ethical approach to grounding critical discourse is indebted to the "metaphysics of the philosophy of the subject," for one, misses the point of the pervasive departure from just this framework in Habermas's turn to intersubjectivity, as well as a carefully crafted account of autonomy that does not rely on a Kantian account of "unencumbered selves." In fact, much of Habermas's attentiveness to the pitfalls of the metaphysic of the subject can be found in his critical engagement with his predecessors (particularly Adorno), whose indictment of the "reason" of modernity as the totalisation of instrumental rationality lead to aesthetico-political stances not dissimilar to some of Foucault's.

Equally misleading is the charge that discourse ethicists are necessarily committed to a substantial "particular framework," a charge that poststructuralists share with neo-Aristotelians. The discourse-ethical conception of morality advanced by Habermas and Apel is grounded only in the presuppositions that are present whenever and wherever "communication" is possible. The lesson learned from the pragmatists- especially C. S. Peirce- is that the conditions for mutual understanding (Verstaendingung) are always already anticipated by both speaker and listener, in an ideal fashion.

But in Habermas's and Apel's discourse ethics, this communication-immanent constraint is seen to generate only procedural constraints for argumentative practice, and only in the realm of discourse directed at the argumentative derivation of norms- that is "theoretical," not "practical," discourses. The only substantive standard in play is the imperative to avoid performative contradictions in the form, for instance, of an argument that rejects the validity of argumentation. Questions for which we should expect discourse-ethically derived answers would be, for instance, those of what kinds of laws we would regard as just, which constitutional arrangements in emerging global governance are biased or discriminatory, or what forms of exclusion/inclusion shape the scope and outcomes of agreements.

The injunction that discourse ethics operates with a utopian content by relying on the notion of non coerced consensus in an ideal communication community is not problematic, once it is realized that this serves only as a regulative ideal in the same way as only generally shared assumptions about truth-telling make the lie a possibly successful inter-subjective strategy. Where the discourse-ethical approach does rely on a more salient modern conception of reason based on argumentative validation- and where neo-Aristotelian critics sense its subversive potential- is in its insistence on a "post-conventional" conception of morality, for reasons alluded to above.

CRITICAL THEORY AND GLOBALISATION

Equipped with the discourse-ethical conception of morality, the following question: How can the universally expected counterfactual ideal discourse community of humanity be seen to institute itself in the context of other more practical integration trends? We get a theoretical construct that allows us to talk, for instance, of the principles underpinning the practices of international law in a universalist sense and that provides the justification of immanent critique, but that needs to be connected with problems created outside its remit.

Because the radical democratic principle of substantive participation according to Quod Omnes Tangit remains an ideal, the possible critical commentary on systems-integrative aspects of globalisation (formalisation of traditional economies, reification, alienation, and compartmentalisation, particularly observable in development contexts) remains of limited impact.

From the position sketched as the foundation of critical theory, with its minimal and non substantive normative principle as grounded in the ever-present ideal discourse community the task is thus to grasp the integrationist trajectories at a transnational level by critically reconstructing the forms of social and political integration through which they become constitutive of world society, or global society.

So far, the globalisation discourse has generally argued for something like a world society to come about in the context of the global extension of relations of trade in the goods and services and the increasingly globally constituted division of labor. This view is sustained by the analogy with social integration at the level of the nation-State- an analogy that draws, for its normative implications, on either Durkheim or Weber. Alternatively, the focus has been on the politically problematic constellation of the expansion of economic activity at the expense of forms of political control (loss of sovereignty, but also loss of state capacity in offsetting consequences of market failure or providing adaptive space for restructuring in the light of shifting targets in economic development).

Habermasian critical theory provides an outlook on these phenomena insofar as it raises to theoretical attention the discreet constitutive contributions to social integration of communicative reason and its mode of furnishing the life world of the practitioners and participants of the discourse of society. The groundedness of the array of social practices conceptualized as the life world, in which the ethical dimension is inextricably linked to the development of ontogenesis and phylogenesis, affirms its significance as provider of the conditions of a normative framework against which social practice is legitimized. The aspects of the ethical life of the life world thus play a crucial role in providing the framework of moral-practical learning through which questions of morality can arise in the first place.

Equally, however, and in its most basic form reminiscent of Hegel's treatment of the social importance of habituated social action, critical theory provides a critical angle on what is otherwise characterized as the practices of depoliticisation. However, insofar as Habermas concedes to the functionalist account of systems integration the fact that social action can be seen to display the characteristics of autopoetic systems, in that within these limits "resistance is futile," Jahn's point that critical theory relinquishes politics seems justified.

Yet this is only a point against a totalisation of the systems-theoretical model, since the concern that Habermas has with functionalism is precisely to show that the pragmatic delimitation of spheres of social action relies on the meaning-constitutive and legitimacy conferring communicative practices of the life world. Identifying two crucial steering media in social integration (money and power), Habermas develops this dialectic of the base provisions of social integration in the life world and the operationalisation via steering media of systems-integration that "insulate" the areas of social action in accordance with the requirements of stabilizing system-immanent modes of action.

These functionally determined social-action complexes are characterized by the hermetic operative closure that regulates and predetermines the range of permissible and operationally benign action-interventions. Thus, in this context, agents appear no longer as persons or autonomous individuals but as functionally defined roles in that their position and function within the web of the system prescribes scope, direction, and possible effects of their action within it. Organisation requires the total independence of its Members from the "binding background" of the old world and from their own roles.

Where such bonds persist, they now occur us corruption. Autopoetic organisation systems are able to compensate for the losses in authority which inevitably accompany the transition of society from stratification to functional differentiation, when the population becomes more widely literate and provided with printed materials, and when the old "economic" order of the households becomes transformed into the modern intimate nuclear family.

For the institutionalisation and organisation of global economic integration, this means that what is termed as a new constitutionalism can be deciphered as a convergence of organisational system-imperatives oriented toward growth in steering capacity through capital accumulation that is set forth from the context of nation-states to the domain of the global. The result of this approach to integration is that it dispenses completely with the traditional notion of society (and thus of world society as a bounded community), because it treats the conventional conceptualisation of society as nothing more than an evolutionary precondition of the form of systemic differentiation that occurs through the setting forth of operative structures of organisation.

THE SYSTEMS OF SYSTEMS THEORY

Crucially, the notion of social systems implied here originates from the adaptation of general systems theory to the study of sociology, in the first instance by Parsons, following from his reevaluation of Durkheim's insights and critique of Weber's conception of social integration as secured only through the institution of legitimized violence. This adaptation of systems theory undergoes a further transformation with its integration with the linguistic turn in philosophy and social studies. Luhmann's appropriation of the systems-theoretic approach under the conceptually unifying angle of intra- and intersystemic communications notably pursues this line and gives it a radical twist.

To Luhmann, systems theory in its language-philosophical transformation can, on the one hand, overcome the philosophical embarrassments left by the paradigmatic status of subject-identity for modern conceptions of the self, as well as, on the other hand, provide the most adequate depiction of social integration under conditions of fragmentation and the transformation of social and political space. By focusing on communication as the mode of interaction in systems integration, Luhmann also avoids materialistic reductions in the explanation of the capacity of systems to organize them in a way that guarantees the parameters of their continuous integrity.

In his parlance, systems become autopoetic, self-maintaining, with reference to their borders as well as the exchanges that they permit with the general systems environment and other subsystems. In Luhmann's analysis, and here he becomes interesting for International relation theory, the conditions of society are no longer tied up with territorial notions of boundedness, privileged essentialisations of cultural values, as in humanist conceptions of social integration. Nor can they be seen to be observable from the point of view of the individual, as in the classical formulations of liberal political theory.

Any notion of transcendence, which since Kant has been tied to the subject's capacity for apperception, migrates into the sphere of the social system, which will henceforth be understood as differentiating out of it increasingly complex sets of subsystems. Unlike Wallerstein's world-systems theory, which still analyzes the conceptual hegemony of expanding capitalism as a pervasive systems-integrative force and thus remains within the framework of reformulated Marxist theories of the critique of political economy, Luhmann's account refuses causal-teleological arguments- motivated perhaps by emancipatory aspirations- and focuses, instead, on a non teleological evolutionary account of the differentiation of social action into media-steered communicatively constituted systems that regulate themselves in accordance with the demands for stabilisation guaranteeing interaction.

This conception of social systems reaches through the core architecture of classical international-relations theory in that it problematizes both the persistent notion of territorially defined sovereignty as the autonomy of states in an international system as well as attempts to conceptualize emerging global governance by extending the institutions of the nation-state to the global level. Because functionally differentiated systems reproduce the mode and scope of their integrity-maintaining communications within themselves, their integrative potential does not rely on any provisions that have to be brought from outside. In terms of the analysis of global governance, systemic imperatives would thus be seen to command the establishment of system-environment distinctions at the global level.

According to this distinction, domains of social action- such as in the economic system- are then operationally integrated and regulated in accordance with the system's maintenance needs. This depiction of social systems and their integrity-maintaining autopoiesis provides an explanatory framework for the immunisation of action spheres from the reach of, for instance, political interventions- at least those types of interventions that may endanger the core integrity of the system in question (from the systems-theoretical standpoint these are of course not interventions at all). To put it practically, the systems-theoretical approach thus conceived provides explanations and analytical tools for understanding the "absence of alternatives" problem in political thought.

Spheres of social action that are communicatively constituted operate in a self-contained manner according to rules that reduce complexity. Economic activity, for instance, has to be seen as comprised by a system of social actions that reduces the complexities entailed to questions of distribution, motivation, and myriad others by means of the steering medium of money. This outlook on integration reflects themes known to neo-Gramscian forms of International relation theory, and particularly to those who have concerned themselves with the problems of "trasformismo." But the systems-theoretic intent deprives the account of integration and exclusion of its critical sting. Modern systems theory permits no privileged position from which and on behalf of which such criticism could be directed at systems from their "outside."

Instead, systems relate to their- over complex- environment by observation and by the system-immanent communicative appropriation of information gained through observation. This insures that systems can learn, in the sense that they can adapt through variation and internal differentiation to possible threats to their integrity from outside. This adaptive stance toward disturbances carried over from the environment does not involve, as in constructivism, a conception of agents in the classical sense, who interact with structure. Rather, structure emerges contingently from the coordinations of integrated systems and their differentiation in the context of systems of organisation.

Equally, any account of human development that may rest on emancipatory premises is blocked. Because the systemic imperative is self-maintenance, the communications permitted and structured by the systems' observation of their environment and the environment that they constitute for each other among themselves are necessarily conservative. Behind the attempt to justify the reduction of world complexity as the ultimate point of reference for social-scientific functionalism is concealed an un-admitted obligation of theory to pose problems in a way that conforms to domination, to serve as an apologetic for what exists in order to maintain its existence.

Applied to political thought, such an understanding of social reality immediately frustrates the bulk of political theory that is concerned with attempting to make social action more responsive to the politics of active citizenship. Instead, the political system itself is seen to reduce the complexities of making decisions about society- which republicans would place with the citizens in an invigorated public sphere - to sets of functional elements that guarantee that decision-making occurs and is recognized in its legality. This functionalist view of the political system is reflected, for instance, in the democratic theories of Schumpeter and Dahl.

Crucially, from the decentered perspective that Luhmann ascribes to the systems-theoretic approach as the only one that can adequately represent the reality of modern social life, the question of legitimacy cannot arise as such any more. Because the functional efficiency of social systems governs their communication and their observation of their environment with reference to their adaptive modifications, the scope of normative inquiry is exhausted with noticing the imperatives that are integral to systems maintenance.

From such a perspective, it is clear that the practice of interventions, such as critique or "antisystemic" actions and communications cannot affect systemic integrity. Either they remain insignificant because they cannot affect the communications that constitute the social-action context within the system (anti capitalist protest fails to impact on the function that wage labor fulfils in the maintenance of the capitalist economic system), or they become part of the process of structural coupling, the systems-reflexive appropriation of the environment (which an agent-centered approach would decipher as co-optation).

SYSTEMS THEORY AND GLOBALISATION

Transposed onto conceptions of globalisation, the picture of systemic integration that emerges from the Luhmannian account would suggest that the story needs to be told in terms that differ from those generally offered in theories of international relations. Social systems can obviously no longer be contained within the conceptual shell of the sovereign nation. Neither can society, for that matter, as Albert has argued. Thus, globalisation could be studied as the global extension of the reach of already differentiated social systems, whose differentiation is a product of the need to reduce complexities for the purpose of enabling social action within the delimited domains.

This shifts the focus from hierarchical accounts of world power and the entailed arguments about the dominance of sets of actors in world politics over others toward the way in which systems integration creates globally extended communicative domains that are operatively closed and functionally defined. Hypotheses about convergence in economic practice, for example, become testable in terms of the actions that are possible in a globally extended social system. Neither differences in language nor systems-extrinsic factors such as the religious beliefs of those who fulfill their roles within the global economic system- or its subsystems- are significant for the functioning of the system.

Regardless of tangible differences, the social sphere of practice i s constituted for the system in terms of its "basal code," according to which exclusion/inclusion is regulated from the system's perspective. In this sense, the global economic system is an operationally closed social system whose evolution is expressed solely in terms of its increasing reach. This also provides a perspective on the agendas for social change of which this system is often seen to be the addressee. For instance, the attempts to renegotiate on "core parameters" of the economic system by exposing it to the critique inspired by the limits to growth hypothesis has thus led to translations of some of the issues raised into system-conforming action patterns, as with emissions trading regimes, internalisation of environmental costs, and the creation of a risk-management industry.

All this suggests that one of the great insights provided by the systems-theoretic approach lies in explaining how systems organize inclusion/exclusion, maintain their boundaries, and thus how they immunize themselves against attempts to "recall" the differentiation process that called them forth. The story that thus emerges tells about the drawing of social boundaries in ways that render those of nation-state borders just one among various important others (one may think about the dependence of entitlements on inclusion). But the crucial question is of whether these insights can be developed critically- that is, with reference to providing an account that affects the story of increasing differentiation and systemic integration from the point of view of an emancipatory interest. Is "solidarity" possible under conditions of increasing complexity in the functional differentiation of social systems?

The answer from the systems theorist's point of view is of course negative. Luhmann's purpose was explicitly to abandon a framework of inquiry in sociology that he perceived to be prejudiced by normative assumptions about social integration. He finds these expressed in, for instance, Durkheim's conception of "organic solidarity" or even Parsons's model of integration based on the "societal community." Consequently, the critical focus maintained by those who reassert conceptions of community or society framed in normative terms appears as a romanticizing attempt to renege on the already manifested differentiation of the modern social world and, therefore, as out of kilter with the actual possibility of steering collective action from a center, be that at whatever level.

This mode of theorizing abandons the normative framework with which the fragmentation of the social could be criticized and instead interprets norms functionally with regard to the role they play in regulating the system/environment exchange and their boundary maintaining functions. In this form, systems theory provides a constructivist account of social action in opposition to the theoretical concerns of critical theory. It also stipulates in a revised fashion the value-freedom of social science that resolves to treat the social in terms of surfaces. The communications between the occupants of the functional roles in the system are the data for the social scientist in the same way as they are the data for the system's continuous reproduction out of communicative practice.

NEW SYSTEMS THEORY, CRITICAL THEORY, AND INTERNATIONAL RELATION THEORY

For a critical theory that is to engage with the systems-theoretical approach precisely because it in some ways offers a convincing account of the self-immunizing and boundary-maintaining properties of functionally integrated social systems, everything, of course, depends on whether the mesh of closed systems can be opened from a critical perspective in a way that leads toward a transformation.

The emancipatory interest of critical theory demands an addressee for whom critical engagement leads to practical change in social relations and enhanced human security- whether this be at the level of the individual, whose emancipation from the pervasive grasp of instrumental reason can be had only in aesthetic withdrawal; the masses of those for whom the global economic order means the structural domination by small minorities; or a humanity involved in exploring transfomationist conjectures about ideal communities.

In all these themes, the approach of critical theory is counterfactual- in the sense that it neither accepts the methodologically entrenched descriptions of the world of social relations as value-free, intransigent, or natural nor that the "facticity of the world of things as well as the human condition" necessarily confers normative impute on how things should be. Critical theory therefore reaffirms the significance of structural factors in understanding the world of the social, and cannot, as systems theory does, theorize structure as a second-order problem that occurs on the back of the "coupling" of purely functionally differentiated systems.

Whereas the systems-theoretical approach permits only of a systems-immanent perspective- the observation and self-observation of the system/environment distinction- the genesis of functionally differentiated systems is viewed by the critical approach as anchored in constitutive arrangements, sustained by discourses in the medium of "ordinary language." As spheres of social action, the social systems are "operatively closed off" on the basis of arrangements that cannot be comprehended from the systems-theoretical standpoint. In order to theorize this, and make it fruitful for an analysis of the problems of late-capitalist modernity, Habermas elaborates on mainly hermeneutically oriented accounts of the life world as the prime source of socialisation in order to demonstrate and explore the dialectical tensions between functionally differentiated systems of social action and the intersubjectively constituted domain of the reproduction of meaning.

Broadly speaking, Habermas regards systems integration as a second-order phenomenon that relies on the communicative structure of the life world. The life world enables and permits the setting forth of functionally defined systems of social action in order to stabilize and regulate certain social tasks, such as the material reproduction in the economic subsystem. It does this by providing, for instance, the normative framework, both in the sense of the necessary arrangements in the institutionalisation through positive law and in the social practical-legitimisation process that needs to underpin it if stability is to be sustained.

Whereas the systems-theoretical approach "requires the withdrawal of normative validity claims from problematisation and critique," Habermas claims that its aspiration to provide totalized conception of the social world based on functionalist analysis downplays the distinct ion between different kinds of communications that are implicit in social life. Contrary to Luhmann's consistently functional characterisation of normative problems as functional problems in the wider context of system stabilisation and maintenance, Habermas points to the necessity for justification as built into the very practice of communication. Since the imperatives of system self-maintenance depend on the latency of motivations and reasons for action- that is, they rely on certain types of information to be precluded from influencing actors- it requires that communication must: be restricted in such a way as not to let these issues arise.

Habermas can criticize this from the angle of his theory of communicative reason because it constitutes precisely the kind of distortion of communicative reason that his approach identifies. From this perspective, ordinary language appears as a resource that can secure society wide social integration, but that is under pressure by its progressive replacement with the integrative force of the abstract languages of power and money. Habermas theorizes this as the colonisation of the life world, where codes that are essentially different to its integrative communicative structure rule into its domain of intersubjectively constituted interaction.

This reformulated theory of the reification of social relations explicates for Habermas at the same time the distinctiveness of communicative reason from modes of strategic or purposive rationality and establishes the normative directedness of all social action as constitutive. But Habermas's life world concept is equally critical of competing conceptions of reading the life world as the "ordinary life" of bounded community. Such a conception not only carries with it the claims of the conventionalist mode of communitarian ethics, which looks to tradition as the source of value, and therefore precludes the possibility of cosmopolitanism; it also overextends the notion of society as community in the light of those forms of social integration that systems theory demonstrates to be abstracted from traditional backgrounds by virtue of their integration through formal language codes (power, money).

In the light of the insights of systems-theoretical insights into the functionalist force of social integration, Habermas advances his thesis of the "rationalisation" of the life world- in accordance with Lawrence Kohlberg's theory of the stages of moral development in individuals- and contends that social integration under conditions of increasing systemic complexity and functional differentiation requires a post-conventional account of morality to ground both critique and justification of the norms in which these processes are anchored.

OUTLOOK

Even on the assumption that the Habermasian conception of the systems-life world dialectic is cogent and provides an interesting as well as critical outlook on practices of globalisation (such as legal harmonisation and problems of legitimacy), and if the normative project of critical theory with emancipatory intent is seen as valid, there remain a number of issues. From the perspective of normative theory, the complementary reconstruction of notions of the ethical life under conditions of post-conventional social integration needs far more attention than it receives in Habermas's work.

From within the framework of late-Frankfurt-school critical theory, Axel Honneth's work is perhaps most geared to the need for a complementary account of the practical moral experiences in the life world. The problem of mediating between the demands of generalized others in the practice of legitimating norms and the world of practical discourses where ethical concerns mix with strategic, instrumental, and practical issues remains difficult and in need of attention. Equally, at the level of the prospects for criticizing globalisation from a normative perspective, there remain doubts as to whether the systems-life world dialectic is too roughly hewn.

Yet, in applying- if at this stage only tentatively- Habermas's conceptual apparatus to issues in emerging global society, it is possible to detect crucial fault lines denoting issues of legitimacy and legitimisation, as well as transformation under the pressure to respond to crisis potentials entailed by forms of social integration that are apparently blind to destructive consequences that make themselves felt in the life world, whether as patterns of exclusion/inclusion, disenfranchisement, ecological degradation, practices of disciplining and silencing, or plain material deprivation.

9

The Study of International Relations: The Missing Link

An elaborate intellectual and policy framework has been constructed in order to preserve and protect "peace." The concept of peace is often used to refer to what Plato would have described as an "ideal form," or to depict a minimalist, realist-liberal version in which there is an absence of overt violence particularly between or within states. These common and differing usages illustrate that the concept of peace has generally been overlooked, and is often deployed in an ill-specified manner, while at the same time implying extraordinary levels of legitimacy.

This chapter explores the consequences of not engaging with the concept of peace and outlines the possibilities inherent in opening up multiple conceptualisations of peace as a critical research agenda central to International Relations.

Peace, and its conditions, is commonly assumed to be well understood by all who make up what is often referred to the "international community" of liberal states. An elaborate intellectual and policy framework has been constructed in order to preserve and protect that peace, which is often depicted as an "ideal form" or conversely merely the absence of overt violence, particularly between or within states. Such ambiguity is reflected in the fact that war and peace have generally been studied together, but as separate concepts, with the emphasis on war and its management.

The establishment of the discipline of international relations (International relation) was intended to help elucidate the causes of war and the prerequisites for the attainment of peace, but IR's orthodoxy has been that peace is an unobtainable ideal form at worst and a limited balance of power at best. The firm differentiation between even a limited peace and war is indicative of this orthodoxy, which increasingly appears to be anachronistic given the claims that many engaged in acts of violence make about peace in the contemporary world. Oppenheim's classic study of international law, dating from the nineteenth century, divided international law into two main bodies associated separately with peace and with war.

This classic distinction has generally been maintained as a pivotal difference representing significantly different discourses and conditions. It reaches back perhaps as far as the work of Gentili and Grotius and is aimed at representing peace and war, conflict, and violence, as distinctly different conditions, which need to be regulated. This focus on peace as simply the antonym of war is perhaps the reason why the concept of peace is rarely disaggregated or represented in plural forms in mainstream International relation.

This has for example, allowed for the contemporary concept of the "liberal peace" to be represented as an objective and universal peace, rather than a product of a long evolution of both the concept and the methods used in its construction stemming from a particular set of experiences, interests, and perspectives. More recent contributions from critically inclined International relation theorists have begun to open up a more nuanced understanding of peace and its many possible conceptualisations and issue areas, which offers potential for returning its consideration to a central position in International relation.

This chapter attempts to open up the question of the different conceptualisations of peace- the problem of peace- as a central research agenda for International relation. It argues that this represents an important "missing link" in International relation theory (and not of the "Piltdown Man" variety). Within the discipline there are various contributions that engage directly and indirectly with the problem of peace. In one way or another, these contributions can be brought together in order to advance our understanding of the problem of peace.

CONCEPTUALIZING PEACE

Peace is rarely conceptualized, even by those who often allude to it. Not only has it rarely been addressed in detail, but also the theorisation of peace in International relation is often hidden away in debates about war and conflict. This is so even in the states, institutions, organisations, and agencies whose officials and representatives often present peace as an ideal form worth striving to achieve, and which dominate the discourses of International relation in policy and in intellectual terms. Making peace in the international system has mainly been conceptualized as Western activity derived from war, from grand peace conferences, and more recently, the sophisticated contemporary institutionalisation of key norms and governance processes associated with the liberal peace.

Where theorists do attempt to engage with peace as a concept, they often focus upon units such as states or empires, thus broadly discounting the role and agency of individuals and societies in its construction and sustainability. For many individuals and actors within the international community, peace is reasonably well described by its Christian interpreters: "Peace is the tranquility of order" according to Saint Augustine. These interpretations, like many, do not exclude lawful self-defense, meaning just war, once all peace efforts have failed. War and peace are, of course, closely connected. This can be traced back throughout history, but specifically relevant to contemporary International relation are two main waves of intervention by European states.

The first was in the name of Christianity during the Crusades of the eleventh to the thirteenth centuries, and during the conquest of the Americas in the fifteenth and sixteenth centuries. The second was a result of nineteenth- and twentieth-century imperialism, which was, of course, conducted in the name of "European civilisation." This tension continues to be reflected in contemporary debates about humanitarian intervention. One only has to examine the ideological formulations of the twentieth century to see how violent peace and its attainment might be.

War has always been used to establish, expand, and objectify a specific version or conceptualisation of peace, a peace that is just in the eyes of defenders or aggressors, as the 1990 Gulf War over Kuwait's sovereignty, or the Crusades over the possession of the Holy Land might illustrate. Defining and constructing peace has therefore always been a self-interested endeavor, even for idealists, though it may also be the case that violence deployed to attain a specific version of peace may be relatively less than the violence that would occur if an intervention did not take place (as with the argument commonly made over the US use of atomic weapons against Japan at the end of World War II).

Many would agree with the assertion that "the logic of strategy pervades the upkeep of peace as much as the making of war." Indeed, according to this view, war has the virtue that it prevents its own continuation by exhausting participants and resources, thus being the "origin of peace." From this somewhat tautological perspective, war has a "natural course" which is impeded by the practices of the "international community" relating to peace.

Though there are many different terms for war in the English language, peace remains a sole denominator. Though it may be subject to multiple interpretations, these are rarely made explicit even beyond orthodox approaches to International relation. Though critical versions of peace research, conflict studies, development studies, and cultural studies, other related areas, and International relation are now implicitly converging on a disparate notion of emancipation as a prerequisite for peace, only peace research really entails an explicit conception of peace as being either negative or positive in character as a focus for its research and normative agendas.

One of the problems that soon become apparent in any discussion of peace is the concept's tendency to slip into either a universal and/or idealistic form, or to collapse under the weight of its own ontological subjectivity. For this reason, a historical narrative of peace is fraught with difficulty and orthodox approaches to International relation are forced to retreat behind rational problem-solving approaches to order, albeit self-interested and unashamedly rooted in a specific context, which are then projected globally on the basis of a claimed universalism.

As a consequence what has emerged has been an orthodox assumption that first the management of war must be achieved before the institutions of peace can operate, at a global, regional, state, and local level. Peace has, in Western political thought in particular, been enshrined first in the belief that only a limited peace is possible, even despite more utopian leanings, and recently that peace can now be built according to a certain epistemology. Militarisation, force, or coercion have normally been the key mechanisms for its attainment, and it has been imbued with a hegemonic understanding of universal norms, now increasingly instilled through institutions of governance.

It is generally assumed by most theorists, most policymakers, and practitioners, that peace has an ontological stability enabling it to be understood, defined, and thus created. Indeed, the implication of the void of debate about peace indicates that it is generally thought that peace as a concept is so ontologically solid that no debate is required. There is clearly a resistance to examining the concept of peace as a subjective ontology, as well as a subjective political and ideological framework. Indeed, this might be said to be indicative of "orientalism," in impeding a discussion of a positive peace or of alternative concepts and contexts of peace.

Indeed, Said's humanism indicates the dangers of assuming that peace is universal, a Platonic ideal form, or extremely limited. An emerging critical conceptualisation of peace rests upon a genealogy that illustrates its contested discourses and multiple concepts. This allows for an understanding of the many actors, contexts, and dynamics of peace, and enables a reprioritisation of what, for whom, and why, peace is valued. Peace from this perspective is a rich, varied, and fluid tapestry, which can be contextualized, rather than a sterile, extremely limited, and probably unobtainable product of a secular or non secular imagination.

It represents a discursive framework in which the many problems that are replicated by the linear and rational project of a universal peace (effectively camouflaged by a lack of attention within International relation) can be properly interrogated in order to prevent the discursive replication of violence. This allows for an understanding of how the multiple and competing versions of peace may even give rise to conflict, and also how this might be overcome. One area of consensus from within this more radical literature appears to be that peace is discussed, interpreted, and referred to in a way that nearly always disguises the fact that it is essentially contested.

This is often an act of hegemony thinly disguised as benevolence, assertiveness, or wisdom. Indeed, many assertions about peace depend upon actors who know peace then creating it for those that do not, either through their acts or through the implicit peace discourses that are employed to describe conflict and war in opposition to peace. Where there should be research agendas there are often silences.

Even contemporary approaches in conflict analysis and peace studies rarely stop to imagine the kind of peace they may actually create. International relation has reproduced a science of peace based upon political, social, economic, cultural, and legal governance frameworks, by which conflict in the world is judged. This has led to the liberal peace framework, which masks a hegemonic collusion over the discourses of, and creation of, peace. A critical interrogation of peace indicates it should be qualified as a specific type among many.

Debates about peace tend to revolve around a simplistic-realist-idealist axis. There can be no peace, peace is merely the absence of open violence but not of threat, or there exists a utopian version of peace, perhaps to be arrived at by pacificism. To date the more common disciplinary focus of International relation has been on war or order in which peace lurks in the background as a minimal or liberal assumption or an ideal form. There has been far more published in the sub disciplines of peace and conflict studies, which have taken up the mantle of interrogating the concept and praxis of peace in a way which International relation should perhaps have done at a disciplinary level.

These thinkers have, in their own different temporal and epochal moments, provided a rich discussion of the concept of peace and how it is achieved, and one which when exported more broadly into the discipline of International relation, sets the contemporary liberal peace into sharp, and somewhat unflattering, relief. More recently, the diverse work of Patomaki, Lederach, Jabri, Walker, Bleiker, Nordstrom, and others has continued to develop a critical approach to the problem of peace, often drawing on the work of Marx, Gramsci, Foucault, and Habermas, among others. Problems related to the role of the international political economy, global justice, hegemony and domination, culture and identity, communication, representation, and exchange have been brought up in this context.

Problems associated with the way violence is inbuilt into certain modes of thought, ontologies, and methodologies have been identified. The need for alternative methods such as discourse analysis or ethnography, in order to address problems relating to justice, emancipation, and unprivileged communication have been identified, as has the blurring of orthodox concepts of peace and conflict. The impetus for the study of peace was initially expressed in a huge body of literature technically outside of International relation. This often referred to the social and advocacy movements that emerged to lobby for political enfranchisement, disarmament, or slavery, and touched upon the ideas of peace through human rights, the abolition of war, world federalism, and democracy, or passive resistance.

This literature often shared a common set of goals and assumptions, though it emerged within different issue areas or disciplines. It was published by a broad range of academics, commentators, economists, politicians, and policymakers in official and nonofficial guises. Some of the best known include Angell's The Great Illusion (which was published before World War I and attacked what he argued was a flawed and populist link between war and economic gain), Keynes' The Economic Consequences of the Peace (which severely criticized the financial arrangements that were to underpin the new peace after Versailles, and was very influential for the post-World War II peace), and Nicolson's Peacemaking 1919 (which provided an insider's wry and highly critical account of the machinations at Versailles in 1919).

After World War I the founding of university chairs in International relation and the establishment of a variety of centers and institutions all contributed to an optimism that war represented a problem that could be solved by the study of peace. Yet, very quickly this research project was surpassed by realist-liberal-oriented approaches, which presented a much bleaker view of the tragedy of International relation, and so deferred the study of peace as a mainstream project.

One of the key early studies in the twentieth century was A. C. F. Beales's The History of Peace: A Short Account of the Organised Movements for International Peace. This was an important volume because it foreshadowed the manner in which peace has been written and thought about since. According to Beales, any study of peace entailed a history of international relations requiring the examination of the philosophical roots of peace, the evolution of "schemes" for world peace, the emergence of peace societies and movements from the nineteenth century, and finally the Concert of Europe and World War I and after. Even at this time Beales was aware of the negative connotations to be found in the study of peace, including "cranks," pacificism, and "peace propaganda."

This observation is still germane in the context of its antithesis- the contemporary heroic, macho, and tragic reading of International relation derived from the dominant realist-liberal-theory axis. Beales argued that both "international man" (a precursor of "cosmopolitianism") and world peace depends upon enlightened self-interest and interdependence, perhaps configured into a "world federation" in which checks and balances control the tendencies that disrupt world peace. This is a very familiar path. Quincy Wright's book The Study of War (1942) reworked these ideas with a focus on the problem of war, but also made an important contribution on the question of peace from an internationalist perspective.

He argued that peace lay in equilibrium, and that efforts were commonly made to objectify peace according to religion, law, arbitration, disarmament, or international organisation. He also complained that the positive idea of peace was often regarded as dangerous and warned against isolationism, neutrality, and pacifism as a negative version of peace. An ambitious reading of peace was now emerging, as developed in David Mitrany's *Working Peace System*. This became a seminal text in the discussion of how peace may be achieved by focusing on the creation of functional institutions to develop an assurance of peace between states as well as "social equality through the working of international services."

This strand of thought has become important in an underlying discourse of "peace through prosperity." This was a forerunner of the popular binary framework of a negative/positive peace, but it mainly focused on the methods for achieving this "peace system" rather than the resultant peace. The agendas relating to the prevention of war, mentioned in the preamble to the UN Charter, led Kenneth Boulding and his team to found the Journal of Conflict Resolution, whose pages are now notable for their adoption of the US positivist agenda for research on war, violence, conflict, and related projects such as the democratic peace.

This attempt to create a peace "science" was a reaction to the failure to prevent war in the period until the founding of the UN, and in parallel with the behavioural revolution in social science in the United States. Working with Kelman and Rappaport, and drawing heavily on the statistical work of Richardson, Boulding argued that the failure of the discipline of International relation had meant that the international system recycled a pathologically obsolescent states-system, which needed to be countered by reformed international institutions and an enhanced research and information capacity. Work was still focused on the roots of violence, however (notably Dollard's work on frustration-aggression theory).

The broader implications of the study of peace were now being realized, pertaining not just to an "international system" of states but also to the communities that comprised states. For example, Deutsch examined the development of political community and how to make conflict productive. He argued that social interactions are guided by participants' perceptions of the other's capacity for awareness, and expectations for participants' conduct. This occurs in a social environment, composed of many interacting subsystems. This broadening of the debate on peace is illustrated by Galtung's notable argument that a positive peace existed when structural violence is removed, and until that point a negative peace prevails.

This provided a guide for peace research as area of study, though it has also been heavily criticized for bringing too many "variables" into the equation of making peace. However, his identification of subtle variations of peace, and of the continuing existence of violence in crude versions of peace often deployed by realist and liberal thinkers, is a seminal contribution. In later work, he has pointed to the Eurocentric nature of the peace envisaged in much of International relation. Burton, Azar, and other scholars associated with the concept of conflict resolution developed a conceptualisation of peace that would fulfill Burton's theory of human needs, and thus lead to a resolution of the deep-rooted dynamics of conflict.

This involved providing for the universal drive to satisfy basic needs including security, identity, recognition, and participation. Azar's notion of protracted social conflict recognized the prolonged struggle of communal groups for their basic human needs which tend to be obscured by the state-centric nature of the international system. He identified the repression of human needs as the root of protracted conflicts, and pointed to the role of structural factors such as underdevelopment. Thus, Azar equates development with peace, further expanding the concept of peace. As Galtung has pointed out, human needs theory can be used to build a priority of issues that should be addressed.

Burton developed his initial approach in his quest to create a paradigm shift in thinking about conflict by drawing on systems theory in which social systems develop and learn through the experiences of their constituent parts. Rapoport developed this idea and argued that the underlying assumptions that are inherent to the system are "default values," which members of the system will rely on when problems occur. This is termed "first order learning." However, the transformation of social systems to deal with conflict requires "second order learning," which entails an ability to challenge assumptions.

Burton and Dukes developed this idea so that the problem-solving approach could become the means to overcome obstacles that prevent second order learning. In these terms, conflict resolution becomes conflict "provention," which examines the human and structural dimensions of conflict in order to promote "conditions that create cooperative relationships" leading to a self-sustaining peace. Curle also made an important contribution here, in that he saw peace as equating to human development in an era where it was more normally associated with the balance of power.

Additionally, Elise Boulding added weight to a more humanist reading of peace with her call for indigenous and integrative "peace praxis." Notes of caution were also being sounded, however. Avruch and Black raised the question of culture and the sustainability of peace. As Lebaron pointed out, culturally sensitive processes of conflict resolution have to mediate between difference social and normative systems. Additionally Volkan and Harris found that hidden meanings mark all inter-communal interactions and that in such cases emotional responses need to be examined.

To a far lesser extent, more mainstream thinkers also engaged with the concept of peace. Carr criticized "utopian" approaches to peace and security, and provided a powerful counterweight to idealist conceptualisations. Hinsley examined early contributions to this debate from within political theory and political philosophy. Aron presented a conceptualisation of three types of peace, ranging from equilibrium, hegemony, and empire, and provided a critique of what he described as "peace by terror," which dominated the Cold War environment he was writing in. Ceadal offered a typology of thinking about war and peace associated with militarism, crusading, defensism, pacificism, and pacifism.

Indeed, Ceadal illustrated how these approaches emphasized the close relationship between war and peace:

Militarism is associated with both war and a victor's peace; crusading with the expansion of a specific version of peace through war; defensism maintains that aggression can be met with force; pacificism, that war can be abolished but that military force is potentially necessary to defend against aggression; and pacifism, that war is always unacceptable. There have been many other texts from the field of International relation theory, conflict management and resolution, and peace research (as well as an enormous literature on "democratic peace theory") but they tend also to focus on the problems that cause conflict rather than on developing a sustained conception of how peace might be understood.

After the end of the Cold War, certain optimism did set in, even in mainstream thinking. Holsti argued that peace lay in a process of the stabilisation of state relations, and that an examination of the major peace treaties and the periods that followed them in the West, from Westphalia to San Francisco, indicated eight prerequisites for a peaceful order. These include a responsible system of governance, legitimacy, assimilation, deterrence, conflict resolution procedures, consensus on the problem of war, procedures for peaceful change, and an ability to anticipate future issues.

These represented a classic liberal understanding of peace given new life, though he acknowledged significant failures in promoting peaceful change, anticipation, and prevention of conflict. This optimism was tempered by a growing realisation of a hegemonic form of peace and its unintended consequences. Clark problematized the emerging notion of liberal peace, but tended to focus on its systemic qualities and implications, and mainly as a by-product of war. According to Clark, the liberal peace is multilateral, increasingly propagated by western practices of humanitarian intervention and by globalisation, is both regulative and distribution, and is associated with the use of force, human rights, and democratisation.

This is a result of the "liberal moment" after the end of the Cold War, most lucidly described in Fukuyama's celebratory study (along with hints at neo-liberal invitations for a pyrrhic victory leading to ecological disaster). Similarly, Ikenberry examined the implications of postwar orders and "peace settlements" for states and institutions. Indeed, Ikenberry made a now well-known argument that understanding order benefits from an examination of the peace settlements that emerge directly after the end of wars.

Howard also presented a critique of the contemporary notion of peace in a similar vein, indicating that the contemporary peace is a liberal invention rather than an indigenous quality. Mandelbaum, though critical of a tendency toward a blind faith in the liberal universal project, was generally supportive of its ultimate goals. As a counterweight to liberal triumphalism perhaps one of the most insightful and critical contributions to this genre was made by Williams, who documented how the "lofty ideals" of peace rapidly became distorted under the weight of self-interest, limited resources, and a lack of will, and the close relationship between liberal war and its solution, "reconstruction."

All of these texts follow a similar path, opened up by Beales's earlier contribution, in which peace is a liberal ideal made possible by correct forms of governance and institutionalisation, possibly even by war, and are a product of the practices and discourses of the post-Enlightenment development of an international community. Perhaps in an attempt to redress some of the limitations of this approach, Rasmussen has recently attempted to directly open up the construction of peace as a research agenda. Where he makes his most important contribution is his introduction of positive and negative epistemological and ontological dimensions to this debate. This is lacking in much of what has gone before, and opens up the possibility that peace is experienced and thought about in multiple and fluctuating ways, and therefore should not be subject to a totalizing conceptualisation.

BEYOND AN ORTHODOXY OF PEACE

One of the key responses to the problem of peace in contemporary literature, which builds upon the works noted above and goes some way to dealing with the problems inherent in orthodox International relation theory, can be found within critical security studies. In particular, despite its association with the failed Marxist project, the question of emancipation has become a focus of this approach to security. Indeed, as Booth has argued "emancipation, theoretically, is security." Though this literature does not directly deal with peace, it offers some important insights into the way peace is being thought of.

Whereas traditional security studies has focused on state-centric dynamics of security that subsumes all else, critical security studies focuses upon an ethical requirement for political action to produce emancipation. This is defined as "the freeing of people (as individuals and groups) from the physical and human constraints which stop them carrying out what they would freely choose to do." For Booth, emancipation produces security, and the type of security he envisages is a form of peace, which would be recognizable to idealists, utopian thinkers, and many liberal thinkers. Peace as emancipation does indeed turn the discipline on its head from a theoretical perspective, though it is far less clear whether from an ontological or epistemological perspective it is as important a step as Booth argues.

This is particularly so because it is so clearly associated with universalism, and in practice with various forms of disciplinary liberalism, which are predominantly driven by (neo)liberal governance in conflict zones around the world, valuing external governance, political rights, and in particular the market over the individual's well-being or social justice in the transition from conflict to the liberal peace. But, as Laclau has argued a universalism that recognizes that individuals create their world- or in this case, peace- may well be a sufficient response to this problem, though of course, liberalism, neo or otherwise, constrains this authorship which should entail emancipations rather a singular emancipation.

If an emancipatory peace is grounded in a set of universal values, this means it can be located at the radical end of the liberal spectrum, and though it focuses on the individual and associated issues from the bottom up, it generally still relies on the need for a hierarchical understanding of the international. This necessitates the need for structures, actors, and frameworks that both protect the individual and enable her to operate freely with a universally determined set of values. This of course means that emancipatory notions of peace cannot escape the dangers of hierarchy: that top-level actors will instill in the system their own biases and interests, while arguing that they are constructing a universal system.

Any universal peace system is therefore open to being hijacked by hegemonic actors. This is not to say that the alternative- a critical and pluralist version of peace- is without difficulties, especially given the requirement this raises for interactions between distinct cultural and social units. This implies a drawing and policing of boundaries, whether physical or normative, and also leads to the danger of hegemonic hijack of the necessary structures and institutions, as is apparent in a communitarian-based international system. In fact, from this perspective, this critical version of peace looks very similar to the communitarian state, though its common units are rather more fluid.

Yet critical and pluralist versions of emancipatory peace are rather more sensitive to the changing pattern of grassroots needs and objectives for peace, and in their radical forms might link with anarchism in the sense that they demand complete individual agency untangled from hierarchical order-producing systems, which are perceived to be ponderously slow in responding to these requirements even if they too are focused upon emancipation. This version of peace, however, has the singular flaw that it probably cannot be organized because this would mean institutionalisation and the authorisation of a hierarchy, again raising the problem of hegemony. This raises the question of whether and how a pluralist form of peace can be negotiated while also negotiating a common framework.

Other key contributions indicate that conflict is reinforced at a social level by dominant discourses and institutions that are indicative of peace itself and its potential to regenerate conflict. Jabri argues, on the basis of Habermas's concept of communicative action, for an approach that leads to political participation without the threat of dominance, and for a politics of solidarity as a basis for peace. Linklater likewise argues that dialogue must incorporate an engagement with the other through discourse ethics, which implies that there is a universal basis for such activities.

Though it is not clear whether this in itself might be a totalizing project, it is clear that Linklater has captured a key aspect of contemporary liberal ambitions for peace. These dilemmas are underlined in Duffield's work, which has developed a sustained critique of the liberal conceptualisation of peace, specifically in the context of governance. Such critical contributions offer an agenda for multiple forms of peace that are intersubjective, and are indicative of the mutual construction of a global order by a broad range of official and unofficial actors. This focus on producing a balance between order, justice, and legitimacy is a constant refrain of reflective approaches to International relation.

They show how a reflexive engagement with the concept of peace is constrained by the Westphalian system, which provides only a limited context for the sorts of changes required to facilitate reflexivity, emancipation, non exclusionary forms of community and mutual security as a basis for thinking about peace. This contains the seeds of an internal contradiction in that if peace is not based upon universal norms how can one create it for an "other"? This is the relativist trap, which though it escapes from a sovereign and territorial praxis of peace, finds itself unable to offer a method of the creation of peace for others that is not in some way indicative of an alien hegemony applied and enforced through a panoptical system of governance, monitored by global hegemons.

At the very least, this implies a critical elevation of normative issues within our understanding of peace, and in particular an elevation of the rights of individuals as agents within a framework of peace. This leads to the question of whether a structure of peace can be universal and benefit all individuals within it equally, or results in what Lyotard has called the "differ end"- the presence of injustice despite everyone's best efforts. Such questions indicate that one of the key challenges facing International relation today is to open itself up to a greater variety of approaches, in order to qualitatively improve the nature of peace that it implicitly promotes, while also accepting that any presentation of peace is merely representation.

Yet, orthodox International relation theory is more or less unable to communicate with outside disciplines, is dominated by anachronistic formulas, and seduced by "bombs and bullets" rather than "peace and harmony." It is a "decadent" discipline often resistant to challenges and focused on formulaic rationalism associated with liberal state interests. What is more, it is obsessed with defining and redefining itself, in relation to a narrow understanding of what is important and which actors are significant. It fails to communicate over disciplinary boundaries because of the energy that has been expended within the narrow realist-liberal debates and their associated ontological, methodological, and epistemological traditions.

The endless rehashing of political theory and philosophy through a "great text syndrome," though not in its elf objectionable, means that the context of International relation is often lost, and blurred with historical and ideational contexts that are relatively irrelevant to contemporary praxis in International relation. This means that the orthodoxy is endlessly self-referential yet lacks an understanding of everyday life and its many marginalized actors. Recent developments in constructivist thought, and mainly spurred by the critical and postmodern challenges that emerged in the 1990s, have moved some way to changing this. But International relation is bedeviled by the practice of theory as ideology rather than simply as a reflective method of analysis.

International relation is mainly, as Sylvester has argued a distant, elitist discipline that ignores the experience and lives of most of the world's inhabitants. Because of these characteristics, orthodox International relation theory perpetuates what Walker has described as its key binaries- inside/outside, self/other, universal/particular, and civilized/barbarian- upon which it constructs a hegemonic order in the interests of key liberal states and actors. If International relation is continually theorized, peace often has not properly been contextualized, partly because of the hold historical theoretical conventions have over their disciples.

It is contextualized by the past, as in realism, by a norm of goodness, mutual restrictions, and freedom as in liberalism, as a structure of economic oppression as in structuralism, or as a materially based abstract world, as in constructivism, without much regard for its human, social, emotive, or cultural contexts. This is derived from the attractions or benefits of "speaking truth to power." This entails presenting intersubjective opinion as truth through orthodox International relation theory so power can be exercised rationally through the coercive and bureaucratic administration of human life in return for the benefits derived from contact with the executors of power. This seductiveness promotes unreflective rationalism, where norms and ethics are deemed to be singularly mono-ideational.

This means that much of orthodox International relation theory is actually anti-peace. Its reduction and abstraction of human life within "international relations," instead made up of "actors, anarchy, interdependencies, threats, rationality," power, and interests leads to dangerous rational calculations that ultimately sacrifice human life. International relation represents its knowledge systems as universal, when in fact they are local to the West/North. Such representational habits and knowledge systems are prone to isolating themselves in order to maintain their belief in universality. For example, Sylvester has shown how Waltzian neo-realism led to a form of International relation in which, "parsimonious explanatory power traded off the gender, class, race, language, diversity, and cultural multiplicities of life."

Similarly, Watson has shown how an enormous percentage of the world's population- children- are surprisingly absent from International relation for similar reasons. Such omissions also relate to method and epistemology: Bleiker has called for an aesthetic approach to International relation to critique and complement the Enlightenment - derived logo centrism (and also for us to "forget International relation theory"), to extend the postmodern turn of the 1980s, and to help recognize that the space between the claimed representation and the represented is the "very location of politics" wherein might be found intersubjective versions of peace.

Another important body of work extends such a critique into a development context, which aims to improve living standards and prosperity using Western knowledge and technology rather than indigenous approaches. This has been heavily criticized not just from the point of view of being counterproductive, but also as being inherently violent and a way of monopolizing the "developing" body and mind in order to homogenize polities within the broader liberal community of states.

This neocolonial/imperial critique therefore requires that local knowledge and culture be reconfigured within a democratic, neo-liberal state-building process entirely controlled by liberal peace builders. As Sylvester has argued, this is in danger of creating "bare life" for those who are being "developed," whereby their intersubjective existence is not valued unless it corresponds to the liberal project. Thus bodies are managed and governed, and resistance is not tolerated. It is described as terrorism or corruption, and those who then police the liberal system are counter described as fascists.

Even if a society aspires to the liberal project, however, neo-liberalism means bare life for many subjects. What appears to be developing as a result of the liberal peace building project of the post-Cold War period follows similar lines to the critique that Fanon adopted of the postcolonial state. He argued such states were economically defunct, could not support social relations, and resorted to coercion to control unfulfilled citizens. Similarly, liberal peace builders now create capacity-less, virtually liberal post-conflict states and governments. They identify local politics as deviant and therefore construct democratic processes with almost immediate effect, but though, for example, they mark local economies as corrupt, they fail to provide welfare for local communities.

Local communities are consigned to a bare life of political rights without economic opportunities, and deaths are put down to poverty or innate violence rather than inadequate action by liberal peace builders. This relates to another set of debates emanating from post-colonial theory and other areas that see Western liberalism constantly juxtaposing itself with others who are identified as "barbaric" again the liberal norm. For Said, of course, the cultural implications of this denoted Orientalism through which liberals discursively dominate and dehumanize the non-liberal, non-Western subject.

The liberal modernisation project clashes with the local where identity and cultural concerns defy rational progress toward liberal governance. Indeed, some have argued, following Polyani, that capitalism and its inculcation into multilateral development institutions are indicative of a disciplinary approach in which social relations are dismembered if they impede neo-liberalism. Polyani argued that fascism was the outcome of neo-liberalism's failure, where civil society's resistance would be disciplined by the state. Despite the efforts outlined above, critical conceptualisations of peace remain to be extensively catalogued, conceptualized, and theorized, especially within the context of the evolution of debates in International relation.

Perhaps this omission is telling in a discipline that has only recently turned to rectifying "oversights" relating to gender, the environment, development, poverty, normativity, and so forth. What is also crucial here is the lack of exploration in International relation of alternative methodologies and concepts of peace, and a failure to recognize that International relation must go beyond its traditional orthodoxies and methodologies if it is to obtain a more nuanced understanding of everyday life during peace (perhaps using ethnographic methods as Nordstrom has done).

The most widely recognized conceptualisation of peace, which has now entered into the consciousness of policymakers and academics, rests upon the various formulations of liberal-internationalist and liberal-institutionalist debates about governance. These have emerged at different points of the realist-idealist axis, and describe an evolution of agreed regimes moderating the relationship of states and their populations. These debates on the liberal peace assume that while the nature of war and conflict may be contested, the nature of peace is not. It is clearly understood to rest on democracy, marketisation, human rights and the rule of law, and development. These assumptions that the conceptualisation of peace is uncomplicated and uncontested are rarely challenged.

This is reflected in the role of the UN in various peace-building practices. Such approaches to conflict imply that there is a prior understanding of what constitutes peace that needs to be defended as well as constructed where it is not present. The implicit conceptualisation in these terms of peace is that any event, structure, or dynamic that occurs in the international system that does not conform to this prior notion can therefore be addressed by a reaction of the UN or other liberal organisations and states. The genre of conflict prevention indicates that an anticipated threat to peace both requires and justifies a liberal organisation or state response. The identification of threats, such as terrorism, human rights abuses, threats to human security and development issues, or to the ethnic, therefore become key to the elucidation and creation of a specific version of peace.

This is the terrain in which peace processes have increasingly come to be seen as opportunities to establish new forms of governance. Around this construction of the liberal peace, there has formed an epistemic community focused upon the activities that are required to construct the forms and institutions of governance now viewed as a sustainable basis for the ending of conflict. Here, power and knowledge in terms of resources and expertise has been amassed in order to export the liberal peace. Yet, it has been the very under-theorisation of peace in International relation that has allowed this specific version of peace to receive a broad and unproblematic acceptance by many theorists and policymakers, despite its troubling flaws.

DEFINING PEACE

Peace, liberal or not, is often assumed to be an ideal form-perhaps limited, possibly achievable, but nevertheless to be aspired to. It is assumed to be universal, and so apparent as not to require serious debate. However, not only is it important to understand the roots and conditions of conflict and peace, but it is also important to start with an understanding of the essentially political, and therefore subjective, nature of the act and project of defining peace. The age-old myth that peace exists as an existential condition, neither temporal nor spatial, needs little thought before it is discredited. Peace always has a time and a place, as well as representatives and protagonists in diplomatic, military, or civilian guise, and exists in multiple forms in overlapping spaces of influence.

It should never be assumed to be monolithic and universal in that the ontology and methodology of peace vary according to cultural, social, economic, and political conditions. Nor should it be seen as necessarily totalizing if it does become universal, though one should always be wary of this possibility. Yet, almost inevitably thinking on peace has also followed the Platonic notion of an "ideal form," which is partly why the concept is so often imbued with such mystical legitimacy. This raises important questions, which thus far remain unexplored relating to the ontological, epistemological, and normative aspects of these debates and in particular of the nature of the now dominant concept of peace- the liberal peace. Perhaps what is more important is the attempt to open up a research agenda on the various forms of peace, to negate its constant use as an ideal form, to give room for the voices of dissent about its dominant models to be heard, and to investigate the potential for alternative or coexisting forms.

Peace may have become a form of "biopower" as described by Foucault, which involves interveners in conflicts taking on the role of "administering life." This requires the importation of expert knowledge into conflict zones, both on the many tasks associated with humanitarianism and security, and to establish "governmentality" in which control is taken over most political, social, economic, and identity functions of groups involved in conflict and in the construction of peace. Both the community and the self are governed in order to allow external actors to create peace. These practices and discourses have rapidly become a normalized part of our understanding of the liberal peace.

This is the dominant approach to the construction of peace, through UN peace operations, humanitarian intervention, and more recently initiated by more or less unilateral uses of force. But what does this form of peace entail? It is assumed that UN peace operations contribute to the construction of a liberal international order made up of democratic states. This is conceptualized through a problem-solving model that initially aimed to stabilize existing order, and more recently has endeavored to enhance it within a liberal international society. In practice this has proven to be highly ambitious, often resulting in a "virtual peace" based upon contested attempts to import liberal democratic models via military intervention, and political, social, and economic institution building and reconstruction.

However, political rights are heavily valued over social welfare and justice, meaning that peace through governance reproduces the empty shell of the state with only marginal qualitative impact on the lives of its inhabitants. It is clear that there are a number of common usages of the concept of peace, ranging from spatial and temporal approaches, to peace as an opposition to threats. Peace is also commonly thought of as a victor's peace, an inside-out peace or an outside-in peace, or a peace dependent upon a specific political, social, economic, cultural, or identity logic or framework. Finally, a critical version of peace is also developing, associated with different emancipatory discourses.

These conceptualisations sketch out an important research agenda and point to the virtual qualities of the liberal peace, problems with the peace-building consensus, and the notion of peace as governance. This seems to undermine many assumptions common to the study of war, violence, conflict, and subsequent responses, derived from the separation of peacc and war as distinct conditions and conceptualisations. The focus on war, force, and power, reinforced by rationalism and legal positivism, may actually revive or justify the use of force or violence and obstruct all but a nascent debate on the concepts of peace.

This is a radical position, but one that requires serious and sustained contemplation by drawing on a broad and interdisciplinary literature, and on a wide range of issues in order to examine the claim that liberal peace entails a viable project incorporating the simultaneous pursuit of sovereignty, self-determination, democracy, development, and human rights within a global cartography in which territorial states vie for limited resources.

This is perhaps not very new in its philosophical and normative dimensions, but the processes, mechanisms, and institutions that have grown up around it are without precedent, though they clearly lack a developed capacity for reflexivity, conditioned as they are by reactivity. To paraphrase Cox's famous aphorism, one must take note of who describes peace, and how, as well as who constructs it, and why. If theory can be problem solving or emancipatory, and is always laden with agendas related to actors' interests and objectives, then so can peace.

By placing the concepts of peace at the center of International relation, a research agenda is implied to develop critical conceptions of peace that can be applied to inform theory and so practice, together with a via media between them. Finally, a discussion of whether there is, can be, or ought to be, a universal basis for peace (such as the liberal peace) can then be explored. Recognition of these requirements are crucial to counter the inherent tendency of utopian, liberal, and even emancipatory institutional attempts to create a single and hegemonic universal blue print for peace that experience shows rarely succeeds.

ENCOUNTERING PEACE THROUGH CONFLICT

This chapter has illustrated the development of thinking about peace and the need for a concerted and critical research agenda on different concepts of peace. A stronger connection between research and policy on ending war, violence, and conflict, with these concepts of peace is required. This should focus on opening the way for more reflexive versions of peace and a necessary via media, before validating any universal claims to know peace. This work has already begun, though it is also clear that there is a danger that by uncovering these discourses of peace, the critical researcher may merely open further pathways for the peace-building consensus to manipulate, reeducate, and engineer target populations.

Is it better, for example, not to make the argument that internationals need to become more involved in cultural issues so that they cannot justify and legitimate social engineering projects? The agents of the peace-building consensus are internally divided about this. Those running the top-down peace-building project tend to see NGOs and agencies as attempting to usurp their prerogatives or as open to manipulation, and for them social justice issues are of marginal significance in the short term. Fukuyama, for example, rails against the "motley" collection of actors involved in state building and argues for a return to the strong, sovereign actor. In contrast, those working on the bottom-up peace-building project tend to see their counterparts as obsessed with power and status, and blind to suffering and social justice.

Research into these complex areas constantly creates difficult dilemmas, which theorizing and distant policymakings are often unaware of, or unable to engage with. For example, how does one respond when, on a UN helicopter taking off after a meeting in a rebel-held village in the Democratic Republic of Congo (DRC), a woman tries to put a sick child on board so it can receive desperately needed medical care in a faraway town? Or when a government official in East Timor asks for more resources so that children can receive a proper education with a prospect of a job afterwards? Or when human rights advocate in Sri Lanka documents the abuses occurring at the hands of his own government?

In these instances the actual outcome was often the reverse of what one would expect if anything more than a limited peace were to be fully pursued. The child was taken off the helicopter in the DRC on the grounds that such a precedent could not be set. The government official in East Timor acknowledged that there were other priorities in the political hierarchy, set by the World Bank and other agencies. The Sri Lankan human rights advocate acknowledged that some abuses may not be easily stopped because they are built into institutions, such as the military. Such actors often recognize that pragmatism may not be the best course for a sustainable peace and do try to respond to these apparent paradoxes.

These and other dilemmas have been thrown up in the course of my own research, and neither International relation, peace, nor conflict studies yet equips us with approaches to respond other than through pragmatic silence and even withdrawal- while often feeling utter horror and powerlessness. As shown above, many authors have concerned themselves with developing theoretical strategies to build more ambitious forms of peace, which have not yet filtered through into the peace building world in terms of the acceptance of collective and individual responsibility to respond critically in such instances. They often know they will not be supported by their organisations or academia, and they therefore disengage.

This is the direct result of the epistemological, methodological, and ontological marginalisation of "peace" as a key concern in International relation, resulting in institutional camouflage that provides protection from having to engage with the other, even if they are in the most terrible of circumstances. For some, this is a necessary protection of difference, or from interventionism, or the danger of "mission creep." For others, this is an abrogation of responsibility to others, and in particular the weak and defenseless at the grassroots level who remain hidden from the eye of orthodox International relation theory and yet make up the bulk of the constituency of the discipline.

What can the pragmatic realist, the missionary liberal, the dogged and determined humanitarian or official, or the uncertain poststructuralist, do in these circumstances? How does an ontological assumption of a minimalist peace, a liberal universal peace, or a pluralist assumption of shifting and intersubjective concepts of peace assist or hinder? How can one reconcile the exploration of desperate issues engendered in conflict with responses and activism, with detached analysis, with the surety of objective knowledge or the uncertainty of intersubjectivity? Why study peace if not to reinforce one's belief in a particular approach to peace, or to critique a particular orthodoxy of peace, and to arrive at a consensual agreement between and within societies about what it constitutes? What motivates a researcher, diplomat, official, or citizen to become involved in such murky issues in which surety can either protect or undermine very easily?

"In the field" (an orientalist description if ever there was) there are many actors and agents who assume the liberal peace without question: There are few who assume that there is an unproblematic peace building consensus. There are "distant" officials; career international workers who care for little more than their next posting while going about their sometimes dangerous jobs; many frustrated NGO personnel and activists who think the international organisations (IOs), regional organisations (ROs), and international financials institutions (IFIs) are needlessly wasteful, bureaucratic, and careless, but also have never really thought about the legitimacy they have attained by bypassing officialdom- and its qualifying hurdles- through their incorporation into the governmental or private peace building sector.

Rarely is there a explicit connection between action and the end goal of a specific type of peace, or a consideration of alternative discourses of p eace and via media between them. The whole apparatus of peace building is sometimes colonial (and, perhaps, racist) in that it implies the transference of enlightened knowledge to those who lack the capacity or morality to attain such knowledge themselves. Yet, the alternative of complete non engagement is far less palatable. This is the most difficult dilemma inherent in the research of conflict and peace: Researchers, NGO staff, policymakers, the military, and officials put themselves in this same position. Often after only a few days in a country, or in archives or a library, blueprint models, solutions, and suggestions are offered about situations not lived through by these interveners.

In Dili in East Timor and Bukavu in the DRC, among many other locations, the many internationals live and work behind barricades and fortresses. Since 9/11 it has become the norm for international premises to be fortified, and to endorse a clear division between international and local actors. In Bukavu, the internationals live in beautiful colonial-era bungalows around Lake Kivu, displacing and replacing the former colonial occupants themselves, while the general populace live in general poverty, the "lucky" few grateful for menial jobs serving the internationals in their homes and offices.

In East Timor, human rights and liberal governance are readily accepted by most, as is the need for development and a market economy. But the inhabitants do not have the necessary physical resources, and therefore face a lonely struggle to achieve these aims because of the approach of internationals that set security and the creation of institutions above their daily experience of life. Well before the events of May 2006 in East Timor, it was clear that poverty and unemployment might undermine the new state. In the DRC, many rebel groups want social justice and welfare but feel themselves to be excluded by the "big man," neo-patrimonial politics of the country, which are also replicated in, and by, the peace building process.

The agencies, IOs, IFIs, and NGOs involved are themselves merely the vanguard of the liberal peace, but they are under resourced, understaffed, and subject to massive pressure from the expectations of the international community. They have great difficulty communicating with local actors in a meaningful way and responding to indigenous attempts to renegotiate the liberal peace, because they have to concur with their own mandates and write reports that chart their progress to its accountable finale. They operate according to distant blueprints, upon which their careers depend. Thus, recognition of the subtle or significant alternatives to the liberal peace in each context is impeded, as is mediation between them.

In many such contexts peace is a often little more than a chimera, a superficial implant, camouflaging illiberalism, transplanted into a soil without water, dependent upon foreign resources, and subject to uncertainty about the longevity of external commitment. It suffers from both a cultural disconnection with its local hosts and offers little in the way of direct and immediate socioeconomic support for individuals during that all important transition period while the liberal peace is taking root. These flaws have arisen in the context of a discipline of International relation that has paid little attention to peace. This dynamic disguises a virtual peace, masking deeper cultural, social, and economic patterns of violence.

It is an expression of relative domination or hegemony by outsiders involved at its most basic level, reflecting the progressive and rational ontology of market forces, institutionalism, and constitutionalism in which individuals are simply represented by statistics and trends. Internationals often believe in their work, and in the liberal peace, but they too are touched by its contradictions. To reach an agreement between officials, or to win a war, is one thing, but to change a social, political, and economic landscape is another, especially through the deployment of techniques that have not been developed in such contexts.

This project is telling of the international community's desire to pass on what it has learned peace; the minimal resources provided by them for this project is also telling. This is often peace on the cheap, a moral succor, flimsy and transient, dependent upon the capacity of its agents and the will and interests of its donors. Those working in conflict and post-conflict zones know this; most importantly, those living and enduring in them are fully aware of it too. Simple comparisons between the financial costs of the peace being constructed in a post-conflict environment compared to the cost of conflict make this explicit. Bare life is the lot of the individual while elites and officials wrestle over the relatively more abundant resources of the reformed or new state in post-conflict situations.

Yet, as the intellectual debates outlined in this chapter show, there are diverse opportunities to rethink the contemporary peace project, to go beyond the deficiencies of the liberal peace, and to recognize that an interdisciplinary renegotiation of multiple concepts of peace is necessary. The study of peace needs to be placed at the center of International relation to allow for a sensitive mapping of the versions of peace that arise out of different theoretical, ontological, and methodological approaches in its many different contexts. This ambitious move opens up a "missing link" in International relation and might facilitate an escape from the incessant spirals of conflict, and failed peace projects, that international relations has so far been subject to.

10

Redress, Rights and Politics

Human rights- as a universal ideology and redress as a specific measure- have been the subjects of increased attention from activists around the globe. Seemingly, the two are in tension with each other: How could rights applicable to a particular people because of wrongs committed against them be held universal? More generally, how are universal rights integrated with group identity, diversity and cultural plurality? In particular, how do local conditions and the agency of the individuals (or the groups) involved, influence the dynamics of rights? This tension is increasingly evident in the way historical injustices and wrongs are addressed in contemporary society, primarily in relation to rights and democracy.

A good illustration of the tension is Northern Uganda, where a dispute is brewing between the International Criminal Court (ICC)- which at the behest of the Ugandan government, indicted the leaders of the Lord's Resistance Army (LRA)- and local groups of the Acholi who prefer to utilize local, traditional reconciliation rituals of their people as a form of conflict resolution. The claim is that the indictment of the LRA leadership, without bringing the perpetrators to justice, only aggravates the conflict and hinders efforts at conflict resolution.

The universal considerations conflict with the local conditions, and even norms. The disagreement stems from the claim by the Acholis that the western law as employed by the ICC is not equipped to address the devastation of the conflict or to offer a resolution that will heal old wounds. This claim has two facets: first, the opposing principles of conflicting worldviews; and second, the practical disillusionment at the failure to deliver justice, by whatever standards. Contrary to the Acholi leaders, the Ugandan government is concerned that traditional reconciliation methods to the exclusion of retributive justice will encourage impunity.

Can there be a via media? There are efforts underway in Uganda by civil society to engage traditional leaders and the government to find a way to bring both sides closer together using indirect methods. These include discussions and studies on historical memory and reconciliation to focus not emir on the LRA crimes, but also to the responsibility of the government, to engage a larger number of stakeholders in the process, and to encourage a people-to-people process. The appeal of the tradition stems largely from the breakdown of security and the judicial system on the one hand and from the complex invention of the local tradition on the other.

Much has been written about the Mato Oput process of reconciliation- both a process and ritual ceremony to restore relationships between clans in the case of intentional murder or an accidental killing- in an effort to find a solution in line with the traditional process. But as is clear to local leaders as well as the international community, the scope of the crisis is not traditional in any conventional meaning of the term and the system which meant initially to handle property disputes cannot accommodate gross violations of human rights and war crimes- at least not in a traditional manner. Perhaps if adapted to the needs of the stakeholders- primarily the various Acholi representatives, but also the Ugandan government- it might prove more beneficial, but it would not be traditional in the sense of the old days.

Instead, it becomes a contemporary traditional- a tradition like never before. The real dilemma is how to imagine a solution that would offer security, reconciliation or justice, let alone all three together. National reconciliation and reinstating justice are obviously desired goals. In Uganda- like in too many other places, because reconciliation and justice seem beyond reach, the call on tradition has stretched its meaning. Yet, it is the sense of continuity of the community which may facilitate new political opportunities. In these, the historical record could provide a bonding space. A second example comes from Poland. In April 2006, Poland announced that it would charge its last communist leader, General Jaruzelski, over his imposition of martial law in 1981.

The charges were brought by the Institute of National Remembrance- Commission for the Prosecution of Crimes against the Polish Nation (IPN), which wits established in 1998 to investigate Nazi and Communist crimes. The IPN is charged with mundane tasks such as preserving documents, providing access and public education. But it also tasked with prosecuting perpetrators of "Crimes Against the Polish Nation." The institute had its most marked impact in its report on Jedwabne- the destruction of a Jewish Community in July 1941, where half of the population of this small eastern European town "murdered the other half- some 1,600 men, women and children." The shock to Poland's public discourse was that this was not done by German troops but by their "neighbours."

The IPN's contribution was to turn it from what Polish nationalists and anti-Semites viewed as a partisan history into an official and formal Polish recognition and acknowledgement of the Polish, as distinct from the Nazi, responsibility for the massacre. The IPN report on Jedwabne points to two approaches to redress: one criminal, the other historical. The historical findings, published in 2002, led to an apology by the Polish president, and marked the official incorporation of the crimes as Polish crimes. The IPN systematically studies the darker chapters of the Polish past. Its work is mostly domestic, but it also collaborates (and struggles) internationally with Russia, the Ukraine and Israel, among others, in constructing a historical narrative that acknowledges the past and provides for reconciliation.

The IPN has other programmes, the most important of which focus on the Holocaust and its effects on Polish-Jewish relations both past and present, the Stalinist repressions and the martial law after 1981 and Solidarity. It was in this context, that the 82-year old Jaruzelski was indicted. The examples of Poland and Uganda demonstrate some of the confounding dilemmas of how wrongs and injustices define our notion of the morally right, how universal human rights are integrated with local conditions and agency, and how redress plays a role in society. As the rhetoric of human rights replaces earlier political rhetoric, such as of socialism and anti-colonialism, the focus on redress- which by its very nature is specific and localized- replaces the abstract and universal claims of the earlier ideologies. It thus becomes a tangible goal for social struggles which had earlier been described in universal terms.

FORMS OF REDRESS

Broadly speaking, there are two types of redress: restorative and retributive. Restorative redress is ultimately voluntary, where the parties pursue reconciliation through negotiation. Over the past two decades, South African Archbishop Desmond Tutu has been the most forceful advocate of restorative redress. It includes reparation, restitution of property, and restitution of cultural property, historical commissions and apologies as a form of atonement. The second type of redress is retributive. In contrast to restorative redress, retributive measures are actively enforced, oftentimes by an external party.

Some examples of the retributive redress include trials for gross violations of human rights (from Nuremberg to Saddam), international tribunals, and the establishment of the International Criminal Court. Truth commissions, in the sense that they include enforcement and voluntary action, fall somewhere between restorative and retributive redress. In addition, vengeance is an extreme form of redress. The possibility that one party will resort to vengeance raises the stakes of redress dramatically and makes it clear that reconciliation is more than an intellectual exercise.

It is important to note that redress is wider than the rapidly growing field of transitional justice. Its goal is broader than the identification of past perpetrators or the discussion of reparation and restitution for immediate victims. Redress also aims to address older historical issues that inform contemporary crises and political tension, including in democracies. For example, it addresses historical injustices towards indigenous peoples who suffer from colonialism and its legacies and those who live in long-standing democracies.

A second distinction between transitional justice and redress is that redress explicitly engages the victimisation of groups as groups and addresses structural dislocation and suffering as opposed to individual victims and individual repair. The inclusion of redress in established democracies exemplifies the centrality of the process to contemporary life. Notably, redress is not limited to a small window of opportunity it is therefore becoming a central component of human rights.

REDRESS AND HUMAN RIGHTS

Human Rights are universal, but can only be implemented locally within a political system that is dependent upon the identity of the groups and individuals involved. Therefore, the seeming inconsistency between universal and local conditions, between the general and the particular is not a contradiction. Rather, redress ought to be viewed as the implementation of universal standards in a local setting. The increasing centrality of redress stems from this process of localisation of rights. In other words, redress brings human rights and conflict resolution together by replacing a universal standard of justice with a standard of justice that is negotiated among opposing parties. This negotiated justice is characterized by attention to the history of the conflict and attention to gross violations of human rights.

Further, it is implemented in a way consistent with the present needs of society. It avoids the clean-slate hypothesis- by which the announcement of principles stands for a sociopolitical-economic analysis- and instead utilizes those principles toward a particular end. By doing so, redress aims to unite the often unfulfilled promises of rights with the aspirations of conflict resolution, ultimately strengthening both human rights and human well-being. By synthesizing human rights and conflict resolution, redress strengthens established democracies and is itself often a testimony to the strength of a democracy in a transitional regime.

The view expressed in this chapter is based on an understanding of human rights as a foundational political theory and a central component of contemporary international relations. The articulation of the "Age of Rights" and the description of human rights today as a "robust regime," are both appropriate. By presenting a challenge to sovereignty and subjecting every government to the critique of a global network of activists and NGOs, human rights presents a set of standards that in a piece-meal fashion turns it into law. As such, the importance and novelty of human rights make morality a central component of international relations. Yet, skeptics abound. Despite the seeming ascendancy of human rights, the skepticism of so-called realists about the value of human rights persists and ought to be addressed.

The UN reform of human rights, especially the replacement of the commission with a council, was meant to address-according to the Secretary-General- the "credibility deficit," which "casts a shadow on the reputation of the United Nations system as a whole." This credibility gap remains alive and well. Almost half of the new council's members come from undemocratic countries, and an even larger percentage fail to support key UN human rights resolutions. The only ray of light, if one could call it such, is the decline in percentage of "Not Free" and "Partially Free" countries in the new council (slightly less than half) as compared with the old commission (which had more than half).

Although the rhetoric of human rights is freely used, the realists remain in a pivotal position. In its first full session, the forty-seven members' states debated many issues, faced forty-four resolutions, and agreed on none. Human Rights Watch concluded that the Council was a "huge disappointment." With this reservation, the need for international legitimacy on various policies using the human rights terminology should not be underestimated. Human rights inject moral considerations in the most explicit manner to Machtpolitik and as such present a serious challenge to the pure-realist school of international relations.

This suggests that in both domestic politics and international relations, holding the moral high ground is important for real reasons. Today, the lack of a moral foundation for any policy ensures its failure. The lack of legitimacy, most notably these days in the U.S.-led war in Iraq, shows how even the strongest democracies and seemingly invincible leaders like British Prime Minister Tony Blair lose much of their credibility due to a lack of legitimacy. This is less so in authoritarian regimes, where morality has a relatively weak claim and geopolitical issues continue to dominate politics; Belarus and Sudan ought to disabuse us of any unfounded idealism. But these are the exceptions in a world increasingly built on legitimacy, as opposed to brute force.

In this context, ethical considerations and human rights ought not to be view as soft politics, but instead, as part of the old-fashioned process of legitimacy that is as real as military force. This of course does not mean that human rights are valuable because of, or merely to the extent that, they are real. Rather, the assumed opposition between realpolitik and morality is unwarranted. Importantly, this perspective suggests that human rights and redress are essential to the process of political transition and the building of democracies. One policy implication is that in pursuing a goal of building robust democracies around the globe, particular attention has to be paid to redress. Since redress is multifaceted, as are democracies, redress has to be explored in a variety of ways.

Expanding truth commissions to include historical commissions such as the Polish IPN, and not limiting them to the South African Truth and Reconciliation Commission (TRC) model, are a relatively straightforward step governments and civil society can take. Extensive reparation programmes could potentially be a good idea but due to serious drawbacks, might be appropriate in only certain cases. A theory of redress for historical injustices has to underscore both morality and democratisation and incorporate the shift in contemporary moral philosophy from classical liberal notions of individual liberty to include sociological insights about the place of the community and the role of specific identity. I have referred to this elsewhere as neo-enlightenment.

It includes a core of liberal rights enveloped by social and cultural values which stem from local traditions and preferences. It is cognizant of the tension between the group and the individual and is committed to address both while refusing to negate either. In amending gross historical immoralities, redress supplements a universal comprehensive standard with a negotiated justice among opposing parties in specific cases.

REDRESS AS A RIGHT

There are various international efforts to institutionalize the right of redress, primarily in terms of a right to compensation. Several key UN instruments that provide a sound foundation for describing redress as a right include:

- The Universal Declaration of Human Rights, Article XIII;
- The Declaration of Basic Principles of Justice for Victims of Crime and Abuse of Power;
- The revised draft Basic Principles and Guidelines on the Right to a Remedy and Reparation for Victims of Gross Violations of International Human Rights Laws and Serious Violations of International Humanitarian Law;
- The Convention against Torture and Other Cruel, Inhumane or Degrading Treatment or Punishment also sets out in detail the right to reparation for survivors of torture, and payments have been made through a United Nations Voluntary Fund for Victims of Torture;
- The difficulty is that their generality makes them aspirational in nature. One aspect in particular of these various instruments is worth mentioning: Since these instruments view human rights as individual rights, they aim at individuals, even though the violations they attempt to redress (crimes against humanity, genocide, slavery) were perpetrated against groups. This dissonance is prevalent in human rights instruments, and as of yet, it has not been successfully addressed.

REDRESS AND THE SHIFT TO DEMOCRACY

Over the last generation, in the process of a global transition toward democratic government, the demands for accountability and redress have become central dogma. The cry "no peace without justice" has become a common refrain in many societies that transition to democracy. It is hard to overstate the centrality of these demands, although it is just as easy to overstate their accomplishments. The words justice and accountability do not have universal meanings. The concepts become concrete only in the local context. In Bosnia, for example, justice today means arresting and putting on trial Ratko Mladic and Radovan Karadzic.

Such a trial would leave tens of thousands of crimes unattended to and in this regard, the effort is symbolic since it is hard to see how this would stand for justice in a ravaged society. But prosecuting Mladic and Karadizic is at the same time concrete and feasible. Achieving it would provide a measure of justice that is subject to criticism, but is nonetheless real. It would allow Bosnians to turn their attention to the great number of other problems. Justice in this sense is a station on a modern Via Dolorosa. Over the past thirty years, redress has become increasingly important to democratisation.

When the transition to democracy began in the early 1970s, in Greece, Portugal and Spain, the process was primarily forward-looking. It avoided dealing with the widespread abuses of deposed authoritarian regimes in order to embrace a new beginning. This decision was a practical one: Democrats feared that if the old regime were held accountable for its crimes, it would be much more resistant to change. It is only recently-thirty years after its transition and seventy years after its civil war- that Spain began to engage its memory of the Franco regime. The next phase of transition to democracy took place in Latin America during the 1980s. It was here that transition began to include- hesitantly and imperfectly- the question of accountability

This included the establishment of partial commissions of inquiry, both by governments and by civil society. There were ten governmental commissions, including Argentina's National Commission on the Disappeared and Chile's National Commission for Truth and Reconciliation, both of which had a measure of success in the rising democracies. Nongovernmental groups such as those in Brazil and Uruguay stepped in when official processes failed. The results were mixed. Despite frustration with both the process and the outcomes, human rights organisations gained power and exposure and grew bolder. An important result was that sovereignty lost legitimacy as an excuse for abusing human rights. This greater scrutiny of human rights abuses contributed to ending the Cold War.

With it, starting in 1989, there was a shift in focus. In addition to demanding an end to abuse, human rights advocates began to demand redress. The demands for accountability in Latin America migrated to and accelerated in Eastern Europe. This reinforced the claim for redress as a new global standard and instigated numerous instances of struggles over accountability including South Africa's Truth and Reconciliation Commission, leading to the birth of a new norm and the formulation of a new right. The last few years have seen a second round of redress in various countries. In Latin America for example, Argentina and Uruguay are revisiting the crimes of the 1970s and 1980s, new trials are taking place and archives are being opened.

In Chile and Colombia, new commissions investigate older human rights abuses. Let me make a generalisation: Since 1989, countries that embraced a process of redress are more likely to have a strong democracy than those which have not. In the first group, I include the expanded EU countries and South Africa. In the second group, we find fragile and partial democracies that did not redress historical injustices like Russia, Ukraine, and even Kyrgyzstan. This is a trend, however, and not a rule. Countries like Haiti, Chad, and Uganda, which have had various commissions, are nonetheless struggling politically.

Obviously, redress is not the end all and be all. Democratisation includes various components: elections, freedom in civil society and of the press, an independent judiciary, etc. Ill addition to these components, I believe that redress is also becoming central to a healthy democracy, although it has not yet been adequately incorporated into the study of democracy. Redress is attractive to perpetrators because its amorphous nature involves more symbolism than action. The lack of major resource redistribution allows perpetrators and beneficiaries of the criminal regime to hold on to the fruits of their crimes.

Moral condemnation and moderate material payments are often a low price for legitimacy in a contested world. So the obvious question is: why do victims find this tepid brew adequate? The answer is that this minimal redress is nonetheless significant for the victims, who are often the poor and disposed. While it allows for only marginal instead of dramatic revolutionary change, this lack of specificity actually allows victims to view the process as consequential. For them, even the small financial compensation matters. Reparations, for example, are usually determined at a level that is meaningful to the victims, but insignificant for the perpetrators.

The paradigmatic case of the moral economy of reparation is of Germany with Israel and Jews over the Holocaust. The total sum- on the order of $70 to 100 billion over five decades- is large, remains meaningful to the victims and was essential for Israel in its early lean years, but was never significant to the German economy. Indeed, since much of it was paid through export of goods, it increased demand in Germany for industrial goods and contributed to economic growth. In a way, it was a win-win situation. The symbolic aspect of redress is manifested most clearly in apologies. The purpose of redress (beyond the immediate relief for the victims or even exoneration for the perpetrators) is to bring about reconciliation in the face of gross violations of human rights. The road to reconciliation begins with acknowledgment.

Apology is one type of acknowledgement. Apologies have become a frequent public performance. From politicians to athletes, the airwaves are filled with trite and at times, even manipulative apologies. Although they may be hard to identify among this cacophony, there are still powerful and moving apologies. Regardless of the criticisms, victims often need this form of recognition. Apology reifies the memory of the conflict and validates the identity of the victims as victims. It pays respect to the victims and, as such, creates a political space for compromise.

The restitution of cultural property provides still another aspect of redress. Cultural property is a particular form of restitution which is of special interest in terms of adjudicating historical wrongs. It is characterized by its central symbolism to the identity of the group or nation. It often includes religious sites and objects. One example is anthropological museums that repatriate human remains to native peoples. In a post-conflict and post-colonial world, a whole industry of repatriation is growing parallel to museums, collectors and auction houses. This includes political movements. Antiquities excavated by looters from every continent as well as numerous other artifacts are being repatriated.

The notorious looting in Iraq was representative rather than exceptional in the aftermath of war. (The opposite is also true. In particular, the destruction of cultural property was a relatively easy way to inflict damage on the enemy and its identity. The Taliban were the most notorious, but these phenomena are actually frequent in war.) One significant aspect of redress that is rarely integrated into discussions about transition to democracy or human rights is the role of historical commissions. Historical commissions that investigate past violence are a valuable way to acknowledge human rights abuses and reconcile conflicts.

There have been numerous historical commissions worldwide. During the 1990s, there were more than forty Holocaust-related commissions. Historical commissions have been sponsored by governments, corporations and various non-governmental organisations. Certain bilateral commissions serve as a form of mediation between governments such as the

Czech-German Commission concerning the Sudeten Germans. Other commissions are domestic and are formed as a result of internal or international pressure. These commissions are often legitimized by international representatives or organisations.

In Switzerland, both the Volker and the Bergier Commissions addressed crimes committed by a democracy as a bystander in the war. In the Baltic States, these commissions investigate Nazi and Communist crimes, thereby establishing both international and domestic legitimacy. At times, there is an urgent need for a historical commission to resolve a contemporary conflict. However, in some cases, the countries are unable to bring themselves to constitute a commission. One example of such an absentee historical commission is in Turkey and Armenia. The urgency has only increased as numerous official calls for the establishment of a commission have failed.

A second example is in East Asia, arguably the most-urgent place in need of a historical commission, since it is one location where conflict over historical memory could lead to a global war. The most volatile issue between Japan, China and Korea is the memory of Japanese colonialism and crimes. In the conflict between China and Japan, much of the national animosity is filtered through historical memories and misrepresentations. This animosity could quickly escalate in the face of all economic downturn or a rise of populism. Another type of historical commission is one which relates to an established democracy.

These commissions often address crimes of colonialism and racism. One prominent example is the Australian Bringing Them Home Commission that investigated the kidnapping of Aborigine children who were placed in adoption in order to allegedly save them- a process which accelerated the decline of the Aborigine as a people. The commission found the government guilty of perpetrating genocide, though no killing was involved. An additional example is the Royal Commission on Aboriginal Peoples in Canada, which brought to light the sorry state of the native residential schools.

Race-riot commissions in the United States, like the Tulsa and the Rosewood Commissions, are additional examples of the potential good provided by historical commissions. Further legitimisation or tins process can actually bring about a greater measure of redress with few downsides. Community engagement with its own memory, including the more troubling aspects, is a relatively straight-forward way of bringing a measure of fairness to public life. One distinction between a historical commission and a truth commission is that the historical commission aims to address structural injustice related to national identity without aiming to punish individuals. It provides explanation and contextualisation while rejecting myths that are often employed by nationalists.

A historical commission aims to describe a historical period and events in a way that acknowledges injustices and thereby brings recognition to victims. This recognition may include a formal apology, reparation or restitution. It also often leads to changes in the self-perception of the nation which may be manifested in museum exhibitions and new textbooks in schools. The commission opens the national historical memory for creative discussion rather than closing off debate, thereby enabling the building of relationships between former enemies or antagonists. An appropriate example of the complexity of historical commissions and human rights is provided by the Czech-German Commission regarding Sudeten Germans.

Following the Second World War, the Sudeten Germans, totaling approximately 2 million, were expelled from Czechoslovakia under the Benes Decrees with the support of the Allies. The international conventional wisdom before the Geneva Convention of 1949 was that separation of ethnic enmity was the preferred way to avoid conflict, even when it included what we call today, ethnic cleansing. Tens of millions have been expelled in various conflicts in the first half of the 20th century in various regions.

In contrast to the ethnic Germans who were expelled from Poland and the East, the Sudetens kept their organisation and became an item on the Cold War agenda. Although the expulsion was not carried out by the communists- Czechoslovakia was a democracy from 1946 to 1948- it became a communist injustice. The animosity of the Sudeten towards the Czech was validated by rightwing Bavarian politicians who supported their claims. Other consequences of the politics of memory include the fact that over the years, the claims have increased regarding the number of people expelled and dead. There has been an attempt by the Expellee organisations to construct a subtle parity with Jewish victimisation, but this is a different, although related, issue.

Following the end of the Cold War, a historical commission was set up by Germany and Czechoslovakia. it eventually issued a report that was supposed to resolve the conflict over historical differences between German and Czech memory, thereby facilitating reconciliation and eventually leading to the accession of the Czech Republic to the European Union. Among the notable conclusions was that the Sudeten Germans' claim of 250,000 dead among the expellees was wrong, and the Czech claim of 30,000 was more accurate. The commission called for education and collaboration rather than reparation by the relatively poor Czechs to the rich Bavarians.

The commission's work raised many human rights issues, perhaps foremost how to contextualize the status of the Sudeten victims. Can there be undeserving victims? Does such a concept make sense? And how does a human rights perspective engage conflict resolution, when the resolution involves recognition of gross violations of human rights? This dilemma is at the heart of the tension between humanitarian work and human rights. Further, may we ask ourselves how to deal with the memory of these atrocities and to contextualize these memories in order to promote reconciliation rather than further conflict?

In the last few years, there has been an increasing interest in Germany of Germans as victims of the Second World War. A major contention point with Poland arose over the establishment of a center for expellees in Berlin. Is it possible to view expellees out of context? Should German and Polish refugees have the same status as victims? The Polish government does not think so. In 2002, on the eve of the accession of the Czech Republic to the European Union, a diplomatic crisis erupted when Czech Prime Minister Milos Zeman, described the Sudeten expellees as Hitler's "fifth column."

German politicians pounced on his comment as part of their domestic agenda and as a last-ditch effort to block the accession of the Czech Republic to the European Union. The members of the German-Czech Commission tried to be proactive and issued a statement that contextualized the expulsion in the general atrocities of the war and lobbied against reducing the relations of the two nations to decrees viewed out of context. Was the context 1946 to 1948? Or was it 1938 to the period between 1949 and 1989? The question remains of how to think of victims as perpetrators.

THE ABUSE OF HISTORICAL RHETORIC

But there are two opinions on this in Europe. One group of scholars or persons, most of them politically motivated, say the Holocaust occurred. Their there is the group of scholars who represent the opposite position and have therefore been imprisoned for the most part. Hence, an impartial group has to come together to investigate and to render an opinion on this very important subject, because the clarification of this issue will contribute to the solution of global problems. Under the pretext of the Holocaust, a very strong polarisation has taken place in the world and fronts have been formed. It would therefore be very good if an international and impartial group looked into the matter in order to clarify it once and for all.

Sometimes words convey their exact opposite meanings. This call by Iranian President Ahmadinejad for a historical commission on the Holocaust uses the rhetoric of historical commission and impartiality, but projects ignorance and ill will. Notwithstanding the few Holocaust deniers, the enormity of the crime has become the global standard for state crime, used by indigenous peoples as well as most other victimized groups, its a point of comparison for their own suffering. Whatever one may think of the uniqueness of the Holocaust, there is clear agreement that it was an extreme case of violence and crime and a near-extermination of a people. President Ahmadinejad presents the concept of polarisation, which is largely a figment of Iris own imagination.

There is clearly no division among German and Jewish historians and when the Historikerstreit debate raged in the 1980s, it did not divide along ethnic or national lines but rather, along political-ideological lines. The debate itself did not question the veracity of the Holocaust; rather it questioned whether other criminals matched its enormity. As Ahmadinejad showed, the commission format of impartiality and non-discrimination can be exploited under the rhetoric of a moral claim.

Similar to the role of authoritarian regimes on the UN Human Rights Council and their attempt to hijack the agenda and utilize the moral cache for their own goals of abuse, the increasing prominence of historical commissions, and of redress as a political and rhetorical tool, has encouraged nationalists to hijack such goals as tools to fit their own ends. While Turkey is not an authoritarian state, even though freedom is constrained, its sincerity in calling for a historical commission regarding Armenians is untested. There is a difference between political grandstanding and serious reconciliation. Human rights are and will be manipulated by politicians, the same goes for historical commissions.

Resolving conflict without following the steps of reckoning and reconciliation can lead to a cold peace or cease fire- metaphorical or real- but not to lasting relationships. In such cases, the resumption of conflict lurks near and affects the protagonist's policies. Consider the peace between Israel and Egypt- it has been a generation of relative quiet and even collaboration on avoiding regional conflict- yet there have been very few policies aimed at building trust and mutual development. In fact, there are no cultural or academic relations between the two countries.

Catholic and Protestant Ireland, Turkey and Armenia, Muslim and Christian Bosnia, India and Pakistan: These are just a few examples of where conflict resolution never graduated into reckoning or redress and thus never achieved true reconciliation. I believe that can be changed. One way of accomplishing this is to devote greater attention and resources to redress. Attending to the memory of a conflict- its victims, crimes, and perpetrators- when done properly, can create a public atmosphere that is open to reconciliation.

One way of attending to this memory is constructing a shared narrative of the history of the conflict, which is the mission of the Institute for Historical Justice and Reconciliation (IHJR). Our goal is to build an identity of the protagonists that recognizes the conflict, yet does away with the lies and propaganda that feed historical conflicts. The IHJR has participated in projects of reconciliation in five areas: Uganda, Palestine-Israel, Jewish-Polish, Turkey-Armenia, and the former Yugoslavia. Each project is different, but in each, the participants are scholars who represent mainstream views within their own communities.

The purpose is to address a particular contentious point in the conflict, aiming to show that reasonable people can agree on much of the empirical evidence, that they can narrow the interpretive confrontation, and that they can recognize a historical reality that facilitates reconciliation. Redress has come to be viewed as a right. Redress and demands for accountability derive from and express a belief in fundamental human dignity and equality. Similar to other human rights, the more inclusive and extensive the description of redress becomes the more aspirational and less feasible it is. In its lack of fulfillment and accountability, redress reflects the general status of human rights.

It is part of a system of socially regulated claims, subject to a debate of whether such claims for justice carry corresponding duties. In a word, redress is the embodiment of the predicament of human rights- it conveys a widening social contract, it claims universality, it is supposedly permanent, although it is historical and changeable. Over the last two decades, new democracies that did not embark on redress tended to be more fragile than countries that had gone through transition and engaged in the process of redress. This is a situation where good scholarship can contribute to reconciliation. By telling the story of the relation of democratisation, conflict resolution, human rights and redress, scholars can contribute to implementing human rights and reconciliation.

This chapter covers three broad topics: the relationship between social theory and social problems, the truth-value of theories, and the importance of theorizing about the role of the state, i.e., national government, in the achievement of social justice. First, much contemporary social theory has interest in ameliorating of social problems, a goal of classical social theorists. Second, many social theorists tend to fall into two camps, those who are more concerned that their theories be correct (have truth value) and those who want their theories to be useful.

Each camp, however, fails to see that truthfulness and utility are important to theoretical developments meant to have any viability in regard to amelioration of social problems and realisation of social justice. Third, without the legitimate, tangible incentives and moral exhortations inherent in policies issued by national governments, these goals cannot be achieved. The contemporary global economy requires national level leadership.

This chapter draws on Mouzelis and Unger, whose "old fashion theory books" apply a set of critical arguments on conceptual themes. It also relies on Popper whose efforts to demarcate scientific theories/knowledge from other bases or claims of theoretical knowledge (e.g., ideology, religion, law, logic) provide a useful criterion by which to judge the capacity of social theories to adjudicate truth claims. Evans, Rueschemeyer, and Skocpol and others provide theoretical insights into the importance of the state in safeguarding against the erosion of the public sphere, promoting protections against the vicissitudes of the market, and providing the institutional structure within which contested aspects of social justice can be settled.

Finally, this chapter illustrates how normative or emancipative social justice theories, types of which Popper would reject on principle because they are not scientific, can nonetheless provide a basis for empirical investigation for purposes of knowledge building in a way that Popper would in all likelihood approve. To do this, the author relies on examples of his own conceptual and empirical works that can be used in support of arguments justifying a positive role for national government in the amelioration of social problems and the achievement of social justice.

It should be clear from the outset that this chapter will be silent in regard to theory development for its own sake, a position advocated by Kiser and Hechter. Somers criticized Kiser and Hechter's "theoretical realism" (the thesis that belief in an explanation depends on belief in the a priori theory from which it is imputed) and posited "relational realism" which places greater emphasis on the pragmatic aspects of explanation. Somers's position is adopted in this chapter. The author contends that amelioration of social problems and the realisation of social justice are better served when theories are developed with problem resolution and social betterment in mind rather than as a byproduct or epiphenomenon of formal theory development.

TYPES AND USES OF THEORY

Any classification of types and uses of theory is inherently arbitrary and suspect, perhaps at best reflecting latent if not overt biases of whoever constructs such a scheme and at worst leading to epistemological paralysis if pressed for logical consistency and coherency. Nonetheless, for analytical purposes classification schemes are necessary to get the present discussion going with some degree of clarity so that contestation when warranted can move forward rather than end in a stalemate. Wagner, albeit "dated" but nonetheless useful as a backdrop to the subsequent discussion of how contemporary social theorists lost their moorings, identifies three main types of social theories that still have relevance: positive, interpretive, and evaluative.

Positive social theories are those whose authors consider themselves and treat their theories within the tradition of the natural sciences. For analytical purposes, these include neo-positivists, human ecologists, structural functionalists, social behaviourists, and bio-psychologists. Interpretive social theories are those whose authors adhere to the general methodological rules of science, but in contradistinction to the natural sciences. These social theorists adhere to the Weberian conception of "value-free" science, while the "value-relevant" nature of the human subject matter nonetheless relies on a methodology of social inquiry that is *sui generis*. Interpretive social theories include cultural understanding, action and interaction, social psychology or symbolic interaction, and social phenomenology.

Evaluative social theories are those whose authors neither consider nor treat their theories within the realms of positive or interpretative science. Rejecting both positive "objectivity" and interpretive "value-neutrality," evaluative social theorists proceed on the basis of their philosophical premises, ideological convictions, and value systems. Systematic philosophical expositions, coherent ideological orientations, sets of social ideals, or systems of moral principles form the basis of such theories. Evaluative social theories include social philosophical, ideological social and humanitarian reform. Given these three strands, whatever convergences in social theory that occurred in earlier times are now gone.

MODERN SOCIAL THEORY

MOUZELIS

To the extent Mouzels is correct, social theorists went wrong when they failed to go beyond Parson's adaptation (A), goal-attainment (G), integration (I), and latency or pattern-maintenance/tension management (L) scheme (AGIL) for the analysis of social systems and instead got bogged down in theories of rational choice, structuration, figuration, and the like. He seeks to preserve objectivity, associated with positivist social theory characteristic of the Durkeimian-Parsonian functionalist tradition, and value-neutrality, associated with Weberian interpretive social theory tradition. Mouzels argues against the over determinism of the former and the neglect of hierarchical, institutional structures in the latter. He also argues against philosophical and ideological approaches to social theory that weaken ties between theory and empirical research. Such theorics collapse the boundaries between and within intellectual disciplines, boundaries that are requisite for theoretical development.

Mouzels argued that Parsonian theory, while providing a conceptual framework for the study of cultural, social, and personality systems, overemphasized "systemness" or determinacy at the expense of agency on both the macro and micro levels of analysis. Micro-level rational choice theorists got it wrong by exclusively focusing on an inadequate if not incorrect conceptualisation of individual decision making and by omitting any consideration of the context within which preferences are formed and decisions made.

Interpretative theorists got it wrong by identifying action/ interaction, or symbolic interaction, with micro-level analysis and institutional structures with macro-level analysis and by systematically neglecting social hierarchies they failed to link the two. Transcendent social theorists, that is, those who attempted to transcend the micro-macro dichotomy nonetheless retained the functionalist logic inherent in Parsonian theory. That logic incorrectly applied AGIL systemic attributes appropriate for collectivities as wholes to subsystems that do not necessarily refer to any specific sub-collectivity with its own clearly defined goals and decision-mechanisms.

As such, Bourdieu's "habitus" for example, downplayed the voluntary, interaction-situational dimension of human agency and thereby retained functionalism's deterministic character. Mouzelis posits that the road ahead for social theory resides with linking micro with macro and action with institutional structure in a way that facilitates empirical research on the constitution, reproduction, and transformation of social systems. The detailed particulars of his nascent scheme for doing so go beyond the scope of this chapter. Briefly, Mouzelis retains the Parsonian AGIL logic of systemic wholes, but recommends viewing all institutional spheres (economic, political, legal, educational / familial / religious) in terms of technologies, modes of appropriation / control, and ways in which such controls are legitimated.

This view would provide the appropriate tools for showing how institutional incompatibilities lead, or fail to lead, to group conflicts on the economic (A), political (G), legal (I), and cultural (L) level. In addition it would allow "who" questions about the constitution, reproduction, and transformation of social wholes.

UNGER

Unger exhorts us to resuscitate and retain the explanatory ambitions and emancipating potentials of classical social theory. "A politicized social theory can coexist with natural science" Unger proclaims, "without either imitating its methods or claiming an unjustified exemption from the responsibilities of causal analysis". Social explanations incorporate causality but they do so in an "anti-necessitarian" fashion, eschewing "false necessity" by encompassing contingency and thereby allowing for possibility. The particulars of Unger's prescriptions for transformative institutional experimentation have been sufficiently criticized elsewhere and they need not concern us here.

More to the point of this chapter is Unger's concern for the place and role of social theory in our efforts to ameliorate social problems and achieve social justice. Unger argues that "deep structure" and "deep logic" theories such as those in the Marxist and neoclassical economic traditions have failed on their own terms because there is no teleological sequence or underlying basic logic of the kind they posited. Positivist science falls short in Unger's view in part because its underlying assumptions about cumulative knowledge building have turned out to be unwarranted.

Positivist science also falls short in part because of its "refusal to take the distinction between the formative context and the formed-routines, or between structure-preserving and structure-transforming conflict, as central to the practice of social and historical explanation". Deconstructionists in the

Foucaultian tradition also fall short. Such theorists fail to construct, that is, as it subjects a current state of affairs to seemingly endless critical inquiry, deconstructionists fail to make a positive case for a desirable alternative that can withstand their own scrutiny.

As an alternative, Unger advances "super theory," that is, a set of social theory practices that informs general explanatory theories with historical particularities. Such a "super-theory" approach to constructing social theories, while empirically grounded in historical particulars, would "explore the interplay between the attractions of empowerment through the invention of less imprisoning social contexts and the countervailing forces that prod us into the prison". The goal of this explanatory super-theory would be to "identify a formative set of institutional arrangements and of enacted beliefs about the possible and desirable forms of human action" to show how these "compulsive routines" are politically constructed and how they limit transformative political action.

Mouzelis would take Unger to task for downplaying the vital role more limited or middle range theories can play in regard to improving the usefulness of social theory for purposes of problem solving. Nonetheless, both theorists retain agency as an essential component in social theory. Retaining agency precludes the over determination characteristic of contemporary social theorists such as Giddens and Bourdieu. Concomitantly, both theorists retain the link between theoretically driven empirically based research and social transformation, while retaining the prospect of emancipation from unjust conditions.

As such, their work is consistent with that of Albert, Cagan, Chomsky, Hahnel, King, Sargern, and Sklar who have also explicitly linked social theory as a component of scientific inquiry to social theory as an instrument of social transformation. Their agendas for the development of social theory are consistent with Popper's criterion for good scientific theory, namely generating hypothetical statements that can be falsified, which, as Kumar acknowledges, many of the post-industrial and post-modernist theories do not satisfy.

POPPER AND THE TRUTH-VALUE OF THEORIES

Karl Popper set out a model of natural science in The Logic of Scientific Discovery and he extended it to the social sciences in The Open Society and Its Enemies and The Poverty of Historicism. Popper maintained that no scientific theory could ever be conclusively proved or declared true. The best we could do is to make predictions repeatedly and attempt to refute or falsify them. Social theories for Popper were regulative ideals or logical fictions constructed for purposes of deducing predictions that could be tested, or shown to be correct or incorrect. Popper saw no fundamental divide between natural or social science in the sense that scientific truth claims were in principle hypothetical and potentially falsifiable.

The test of falsification aided in the adjudication of competing scientific truth claims. Popper drew a divide, however, between science and metaphysics. The latter's truth claims were constructed in such a way they were not amendable to falsification, that is, to testing empirically. The test of falsification would be inappropriate to adjudicate truth claims across the scientific non-scientific divide. Popper's anti-foundational approach to science defied the relativism associated with post-modernist theorists' denial of the validity of making truth claims. Unlike poststructuralists and pragmatists, Popper maintained that we could approach truth from experience.

In this regard, he echoed the views of logical positivists who also believed that the only legitimate knowledge was that derived from experience. Popper objected to the logical positivists' view of science based primarily on verification and posited instead that truth could be approached primarily from errors. In Popper's view scientific methods entailed the creative production of hypotheses that could lead to predictions that in turn could be verified or refuted by experience, with the potential for refutation or falsification as the more significant attribute of the two for scientific advancement.

Hence, Popper regarded any discipline that did not lead to empirically testable predictions, such as Marxism or psychoanalysis, as a pseudoscience. Instead, much like Unger, Popper's contention that truth per se is best stated hypothetically and treated provisionally (that is, subject to testing empirically or to falsification) encourages a readiness to make bold assertions or conjectures in regard to how things are or are likely to be and the honesty to recognize and wherewithal to acknowledge when they are shown to be incorrect. That such conjectures can be shown to be incorrect Popper does not doubt, thereby removing him from the camp of post-modernists for whom truth is better abandoned as an object of inquiry and who view theory less as a pragmatic test shot at empirical targets and more as a vital component of creating the object under study as well as their explanation.

Popper's falsification criterion has been critiqued, correctly in my opinion, for insufficiently specifying what counts as falsifying criteria. The charge failing the test of falsification in which a single counter-observation can falsify a theory is, in my view, an overstatement and it may reflect a misunderstanding of his work. Much depends on what a theory purports to explain and how adequately a crucial test is designed and implemented. A single counter-observation of a hypothesis need not result in rejection of a theory per se, especially in the absence of a competing theory that could be subjected to empirical test or even with the availability of an alternative theory that does not allow for such a test.

Further, as Munro notes, if it is logically possible that an observation statement can be wrong, it is also logically possible that the theory, although apparently falsified by it, might nonetheless be true. Popper's insistence on the importance of empirically-based methods as grounds for scientific truth claims and theoretical development should by no means be construed to imply that such methods were the only valid forms of inquiry for purposes of obtaining important insights into human development. Disciplines such as moral psychology and political philosophy, which benefit from logical argumentation, provide sufficient evidence that such is not the case. Nor should falsification be construed as the only criterion that theories must meet to be considered scientific, as Baert contends.

Coherency, logical consistency, and parsimony are also important. Nor should theory only provide researchers with statements that can be tested. Theoretical progress also consists in generating better researchable questions. The insistence in this chapter is only to place ourselves as social scientists in the position such that our theoretical assertions about causal relationships have the potentiality of being shown to be wrong. In addition, we should admit as much when someone does so. Our ability to act accordingly is crucial in regard to truth claims about the efficacy of intervention strategies, whether designed by government to meet public purposes or by practitioners such as social workers to improve the social functioning of clients.

BRINGING THE STATE BACK IN

The proper role of the state in the society in general and in the economy in particular continues to be one of ambivalence, if not contestation. The increasing influence of international governing bodies and transnational corporations challenges the relevance of national governments and nation-states. Evans notes that international bodies have a dampening effect on the expansion of the state's role in the economy in countries that become major capital exporters, especially centers of international finance capital. These dampening effects should by no means be construed as a cessation of state influence or importance as an actor in global affairs. As Evans also notes, national governments are vitally important to expanding economies and international relations in developing countries.

Caputo contends that the role of the state is vital for purposes of social justice to securing basic human rights for all citizens and, under specified laws, for non-citizens within nations. In addition, the state plays an important role in regard to poverty reduction, particularly in regard to the legitimate or just redistribution of wealth within as well as among countries. No one overarching theory of the state emerges from the plethora of historical and comparative studies of the state in the post-World War II period. The development of middle-range theories about state autonomy and capacity as a society-shaping and global-influencing institutional structure remain an elusive but nonetheless worthy goal.

How to achieve the right balance of prosperity, civility and liberty is no easy matter, but the role of the state remains crucial. The need remains for state-related social theory amendable to falsification. The theoretical tasks at hand are to identify under what circumstances which components of the state can foster conditions for people to create public goods and to specify the causal links between government action and social benefits. Such links in turn can then be subject to empirical scrutiny. The empirical task is to check out whether the causal links do what the theories purport and if not to suggest modifications that can also be subject to empirical scrutiny.

Caputo found that socioeconomic status and race/ ethnicity were robust predictors of physical health and they provided support for expanding Rawls's index of social goods to include social determinants of health. The theoretical issues boiled down to whether it would ever be reasonable and rational to accept a tradeoff in which some health inequality was (1) allowed in order to produce some non-health benefits for those with the worst health prospects or (2) reduced in order to produce health benefits for those with the worst health prospects. Justifiable grounds were examined for absolute gains in overall health even if some were made worse off (but not too seriously) and for relative health statuses in which resources would be redistributed to those worst off either at the expense of those better off (again, not to a serious or life-threatening extent) or with no overall gain in health.

The purpose of the study was to determine under what conditions appeals for social justice might be warranted for absolute gains in health and for relative health statuses. Falsifying conditions that would determine the merits of social justice arguments for government action to reduce health disparities included, for examples whether Blacks were found to be worse off than Whites or whether women fared worse than men in regard to measures of physical and mental health when controlling for a variety of hereditary, background, lifestyle, and other cumulative and structural factors over the life cycle.

The finding that White and Black females fell below White males on the measure of mental health lent support to advocates of social justice who claim that the relative status of groups can form the basis of legitimate governmental and social interventions on their behalf. On the other hand, the finding that Black males were less likely than White males to fall below the typical U.S. person on the measure of physical health used in the study challenged blanket appeals for race-related interventions for redistribution of resources based on appeals to social justice. The implication was that absolute (i.e., aggregate) gains in physical health could be pursued even if Black males were not the beneficiaries or had no net gains.

The intent here is to present, not defend, these findings and their implications. Limitations of the study, such as the participation only of non-institutionalized persons in the NLSY79 sample and the infant/childhood mortality rates of

Black males, can be found in the article. For purposes of this chapter, the merit of the theoretically driven and normative based study is that it was done in such a way that findings are subject to falsification from further scrutiny and policy prescriptions are made with caution in mind since they would need to be modified accordingly if findings were shown to be incorrect.

Caputo examined work-related discrimination. This study pitted two social justice theories against one another: the classical utilitarian tradition of maximizing the greatest good vs. the liberal utilitarian tradition of maximizing good without worsening the situation of the most disadvantaged persons. On-going debates about affirmative action often pit justice claims of Blacks and women for preferential treatment on liberal utilitarian grounds against those of white males for merit-based decisions on classical utilitarian grounds. In the study, young labor force participants reporting discrimination in their efforts to get good jobs were found to obtain more additional education and job training than those who reported no such discrimination over the same time periods.

Findings suggested net aggregate gains as well as gains by historically work-related discriminated groups (namely Blacks and women in this study) and as such challenged blanket social justice appeals for race- and gender-related interventions for redistribution of resources. Findings imply that social justice advocates would be on firmer footing to the extent they advance public policies ensuring access to education and training in the broadest possible sense affirming opportunity for all rather than specific disadvantaged groups.

As with Caputo, the intent here is to present, not defend, these findings and their implications. The peer review process of the manuscript made clear that the findings are controversial. In the final analysis, they were deemed to warrant both further discussion (hence, the decision to publish) and scrutiny. In conclusion, the merits of Caputo and Caputo are that 1) they are theoretically driven; 2) normatively based; 3) done in such a way that findings are subject to falsification; and 4) suggest appropriate state action in light of findings and limitations. These two studies are among several others of mine that to different degrees tie together theory, falsification, and normative aspects of social justice in regard to social problems.

What links much of my empirical work is that the studies are premised on the prospect of using normative criteria as a basis for deciding appropriate calls for state action to remedy social problems. Each is guided by social theory taking the form of moral or social philosophy for purposes of making an evaluation and each met Popper's falsification criterion. Related hypotheses are constructed such that they could be shown to be met or not and the social justice arguments that identified a potential area of state intervention either held firm or fell accordingly. If social theory is not to wither or not to remain primarily an academic exercise which may address social problems in an epiphenomenal way rather than head on, then theoreticians should use Popper's criterion as one of the main considerations when constructing theories, have a specific social problem in mind, and specify normative criteria upon which to judge whether study findings warrant state action to achieve social justice.

BIBLIOGRAPHY

Axelrod, Robert. 1984. *The Evolution of Cooperation.* New York: Basic Books.

Bull, Hedley. 1966. "Society and Anarchy in International Relations" in *Diplomatic Investigations* edited by Herbert Butterfield and Martin Wight. London: George Allen and Unwin. 35-60

Campell, David & George, Jim. 1990. ' Patterns of Dissent and the Celebration of Difference: Critical Social Theory and International Relations', *International Studies Quarterly* Vol 34, 1990: 269-293.

Carr, Edward Hallet. 1962. *The Twenty Years' Crisis, 1919–1939: An Introduction to the Study of International Relations,* 2nd ed. New York: St Martin's.

Cox, Robert W. 2001. 'The Way Ahead: Toward n New Ontology of World Order', in Wyn Jones, Richard, ed, *Critical Theory & World Politics.* Boulder, Colorado: Lyenner Rienner.

Cynthia Weber. 2004. *International Relations Theory. A Critical Introduction,* 2nd ed., Taylor & Francis.

Devetak, Richard. 2005. 'Critical Theory', in Burchill, Scott et al, *Theories of International Relations,* 3rd edition. London: Palgrave MacMillan.

Emin Fuat Keyman. 1997. *Globalization, State, Identity/ Difference: Toward a Critical Social Theory of International Relations,* Prometheus Books.

Forsythe, David. 2000. Human Rights in International Relations. Cambridge: Cambridge University Press.

Gilpin, Robert. 1983. *War and Change in World Politics*. Cambridge, England: Cambridge University Press.

Goldstein, Judith, and Robert O. Keohane, eds. 1993. *Ideas and Foreign Policy: Beliefs, Institutions, and Political Change*. Ithaca, N.Y.: Cornell University Press.

Jim George. 1994. *Discourses of Global Politics: A Critical Introduction to International Relations*, Lynne Rienner Publishers, US.

Keohane, Robert O, and Helen V. Milner, eds. 1996. *Internationalization and Domestic Politics*. New York: Cambridge University Press.

Knorr, Klaus. 1975. *The Power of Nations: The Political Economy of International Relations*. New York: Basic Books.

Krasner, Stephen D., ed. 1983. *International Regimes*. Ithaca, N.Y.: Cornell University Press.

Linklater, Andrew, 1986. 'Realism, Marxism and Critical International Theory', *Review of International Studies* Vol 12, 1986: 301-312.

Onuf, Nicholas G. 1988. *A World of Our Making: Rules and Rule in Social Theory and International Relations*. Columbia, SC: University of South Carolina Press.

Peterson, V. Spike. Editor. 1992. *Gendered States: Feminist (Re) Visions of International Relations Theory*. Boulder: Lynne Reinner Press.

Thompson, William R. 1988. *On Global War: Historical–Structural Approaches to World Politics*. Columbia, SC: University of South Carolina Press.

Tickner, J. Ann. 1988. "Hans Morgenthau's Principles of Political Realism: A Feminist Reformulation", *Millennium: Journal of International Studies*. 17:3, 429-440.

Walter Carlsnaes, Thomas Risse and Beth A. Simmons. ed., 2002. *Handbook of International Relations.* Sage: London.

Waltz, Kenneth N. 1979. Theory of Internati*onal Politics.* Reading, Mass.: Addison-Wesley.

Waltz, Kenneth. 1959. *Man, the State and War: A Theoretical Analysis.* New York: Columbia University Press.

Wendt, Alexander. 1992. *Anarchy is what States Make of It: The Social Construction of Power Politics,"* *International Organization* 46:2 (Spring) 391-425.

Young, Oran R. 1978. "Anarchy and Social Choice: Reflections on the International Polity," *World Politics* 30 (December): 241-263.

INDEX

T

U